D0200329

Living SUPER-NATURALLY in Christ

Bill BRIGHT

NewLife
PUBLICATIONS

Living Supernaturally in Christ

Published by
NewLife Publications
A ministry of Campus Crusade for Christ
P.O. Box 620877
Orlando, FL 32862-0877

Design and production by Genesis Group
Printed in the United States of America

ISBN 1-56399-146-2

For more information, write:

Australia Campus Crusade for Christ—P.O. Box 40, Flemington Markets, NSW 2129, Australia

Campus Crusade for Christ of Canada—Box 529, Sumas, WA 98295

Agape—Fairgate House, King's Road, Tyseley, Birmingham, B11 2AA, United Kingdom

Campus Crusade for Christ—P.O. Box 8786, Auckland, 1035, New Zealand

Campus Crusade for Christ—9 Lock Road #03-03, Paccan Centre, Singapore 108937

Great Commission Movement of Nigeria—P.O. Box 500, Fudaya Village, Bauchi Ring Road, Jos, Plateau State, Nigeria, West Africa

Campus Crusade for Christ International—100 Lake Hart Drive, Orlando, FL 32832-0100, USA

Contents

APPENDICES

Acknowledgments

God has used many people through the years to enhance my understanding of the truths I have tried to communicate in this book. I am grateful for each of them.

My special thanks to Helmut Teichert, creative producer and team leader, for his help developing, organizing, and overseeing this project, and to esteemed members of the team: Nancy Sawyer Schraeder for her contribution in researching, writing, and wordsmithing; Marion Wells for writing video scripts which were a resource for this manuscript; and Joette Whims for technical editing. I am indebted to the *NewLife* Publications staff: Dr. Joe Kilpatrick, publisher and general editor; John Barber, theological editor; Tammy Campbell, editorial assistant; and Michelle Treiber, cover coordinator and print broker. My gratitude also goes to Lynn Copeland of Genesis Group for her design and typesetting.

There is one person more than any other who deserves special recognition: my beloved bride of over fifty years, Vonette. Daily we share the adventure of *Living Supernaturally in Christ*.

Foreword

You have a choice. You can either live a life devoid of power, doing the best you can, gutting it out for God, expending your strength and energy on your efforts, or you can live supernaturally in Christ. The choice is yours.

Too many believers think the Christian life is doing the best they can through their self-effort. They have no dynamic or power other than self-discipline and determination. Change is usually motivated by guilt and is unhappily short-lived. Unfortunately, there is not much difference between these Christians and their unbelieving neighbors.

Many believers are ignorant of the way God originally intended us to live. The consequences of living our lives in our own strength and worldly lifestyles shows up in our marriages, how we raise our families, how we run our careers, and ultimately in our relationship to God.

I would seriously doubt that living "naturally" satisfies any real believer in Christ. Sooner or later, deep frustration will emanate from within. God has supernaturally given us an identity in Christ. When our lifestyle does not match up with our true identity, we become frustrated. A lack of biblical truth will ultimately lead to despair and depression. Eventually, if left uncounseled by the majesty of Scripture, hopelessness will set in, and again, statistics will prove we as believers are no better than the rest of the world.

I have always been troubled on behalf of those who have received Christ, and who then have come to the conclusion that living the Christian life just doesn't work. The lives of many believers are characterized by defeat and discouragement. They are disillusioned souls who are playing religion, typified by going to church, reading their Bibles, saying their prayers, and confessing their sins. It is time that we come to grips with this liberating truth: On our own, the Christian life is not simply difficult. It's impossible. You can't live it. God doesn't expect us to live it on our own.

Christianity is not the problem. The problem is with people who are trying to live the Christian life apart from the help of the Holy Spirit and not appropriating their new life based on their identity in Christ.

Living Supernaturally in Christ is for those who struggle to live a life they don't possess and to those who have a life they do not live. Christ came that man would be enabled by the Holy Spirit to have life, purpose, and real identity. We were engineered to be used for the intelligent purpose for which we were created—to have an infinitely high, intimate relationship with Christ. He is the supernatural source of life for all mankind. We are to be supernatural light in a naturally dark world.

The apostle John writes, "In Him was life, and the life was the Light of men" (John 1:4). Christ came to live His life in and through us. Our life, light, and liberty are found in the Lord Jesus Christ.

I have personally known Bill Bright for more than thirty years. His vision for reaching the world has greatly inspired me and lifted my own vision. He is truly a man of God. You can't lead a worldwide ministry the magnitude of Campus Crusade for Christ while living naturally in your own strength. I am thoroughly convinced that the only way to account for the successful outreach of Campus Crusade, or any ministry for that matter, is due to the truths expressed in this book. Dr. Bright exemplifies the message of this book.

DR. CHARLES STANLEY
Senior Pastor
First Baptist Church, Atlanta, GA

Preface

*Y*ou are about to read some of the most revolutionary truths contained in the Word of God. We have the unspeakable, awesome privilege of knowing the creator God and Savior of the universe, who left His place of glory to become the God-Man, Jesus of Nazareth. He came to die on the cross to pay the penalty for our sins and was raised from the dead. And now—miracle of miracles, marvel of marvels—this holy, incomparable, peerless Son of God has come to dwell within every believer. The most important truth I know is "Christ in you, the hope of glory" (Colossians 1:27, NIV). Since the dawn of history, nothing has ever been written that compares with this truth.

Through the years, it has been my practice to ask Muslims, Hindus, Buddhists, atheists, Communists, people of all religions and cultures: "Who is the most important person who has ever lived? Who has done more good for mankind than anyone who has ever lived?" Every knowledgeable person answers, "Jesus of Nazareth." He is the most wonderful person who has ever walked the face of the earth. His life was peerless; His teachings were revolutionary; His influence is unsurpassed.

This same Jesus lives in you and desires to live out His life and continue His supernatural work through you. What an awesome privilege! Yet many Christians live defeated lives.

Perhaps you are overwhelmed by problems and circumstances, and you doubt that God can use you in any meaningful way. This is a lie of Satan! You are God's dearly loved child—a son or daughter of the Sovereign Ruler of the universe. You have received a marvelous inheritance both now and for eternity. You are a saint set apart for His glory, a member of the body of Christ, and a citizen of His kingdom. As a citizen, you are Christ's ambassador to help take the good news of eternal life to the world.

Christ came for one purpose: to seek and to save the lost. Jesus declared in John 3:16, "God so loved the world that He gave His only Son, so that everyone who believes in Him will not perish but have eternal life."

I have asked millions of people all over the world, "What is the greatest thing that has ever happened to you?" Without hesitation, all believers—rich and poor, old and young, famous and ordinary— answer, "The greatest thing that ever happened to me is knowing Jesus Christ as my personal Savior and inheriting eternal life." Then I ask the second question, "What is the greatest thing you can do to help another person?" The answer is always, "Help them to know Christ, too."

What a blessing and honor to introduce others to our marvelous Lord. When you understand and live out your amazing identity in Christ, you will draw people to Him. The Holy Spirit working in you will empower and mature you in Christ so you can begin to think, speak, and behave like your wonderful Savior.

What a thrilling adventure to live the abundant life Christ offers— a life of power, victory, freedom, peace, and joy both now and in eternity. For Christ living in and through you produces life supernatural!

To help you incorporate into your life the vital truths you will learn, each chapter concludes with several Life Application questions. It is important that you devote time to these exercises so your life will be transformed.

Why not ask a friend or family member to join you in reading this book and discussing the Life Application questions? Together you will discover the amazing new identity and victorious life that is your spiritual heritage in Christ.

PART I

Our Faith
in Christ

CHAPTER 1

Our Supernatural Identity in Christ

eaning. Purpose. Success. Significance. Love.

Each day, millions of people around the world hope, covet, and labor to obtain these profound yet elusive ideals. Those who pursue these desires by grasping for riches, fame, or power, seldom, if ever, obtain true contentment and happiness.

In 1923, an important meeting was held at the Edgewater Beach Hotel in Chicago. In attendance were nine of the world's most successful financiers—men who had found the secret of making money. What became of these powerful men?

The president of the largest independent steel company, Charles Schwab, went bankrupt and lived on borrowed money for five years before his death. The president of the largest utility company, Samuel Insull, was a fugitive from justice and died penniless in a foreign land. The president of the largest gas company, Howard Hopson, became mentally ill. The greatest wheat speculator, Arthur Cotton, died abroad, insolvent.

The president of the New York Stock Exchange, Richard Whitney, served time in Sing Sing Penitentiary. A member of the President's Cabinet, Albert Fall, was pardoned from prison so he could die at home. Three of the men committed suicide: Jesse Livermore, the greatest "bear" on Wall Street; Ivan Krueger, the head of the greatest monopoly; and Leon Fraser, the president of the Bank of International Settlements. All these men lived in luxury, had access to the most powerful and intellectual people of their day, and enjoyed the finest the world could offer—yet they lived unhappy, empty lives. They died disillusioned, despondent, defeated men.[1]

Can we as Christians experience what these multi-millionaires sought but never attained? Is it possible for us to have a consistent sense of purpose? To feel special in this world of more than six billion people? To bask in unconditional love? To experience what is truly meaningful? To live a supernatural life that is beyond our imagination?

The awesome Creator of the universe answers with a resounding *yes!*

A LIFE OF IMMEASURABLE RICHES

The apostle Paul proclaims in Romans that we have been chosen to share God's glory: "Since we have been made right in God's sight by faith, we have peace with God because of what Jesus Christ our Lord has done for us. Because of our faith, Christ has brought us into this place of highest privilege where we now stand, and we confidently and joyfully look forward to sharing God's glory" (Romans 5:1,2).

The Bible promises that we are in a place of highest privilege. When you consider your routine of work, bills, and day-to-day struggles, do you have difficulty feeling privileged? Perhaps you see celebrities smiling from the television screen and magazine covers and think how fortunate they are. Yet, as Christians we have value and significance beyond anything this world can offer. And if we fully understand the riches of God's glory in this life and the next, we will never be the same.

There is a story about a wealthy Englishman, Baron Fitzgerald, who had an only child, a son whom he dearly loved. From the moment the boy was born, he was the center of his father's affection. Often, the baron would sneak off to the nursery to play with his son. After being away on a trip, the baron would hurry home to find his son waiting at the door, ready to jump into his arms.

The family enjoyed many years of happiness. Then one day tragedy struck. The baron's wife passed away leaving the boy, now in his early teens, motherless. Grief-stricken, the baron devoted himself even more to the care of his only child.

A few years later, the son became very ill. After many sleepless nights, the baron buried his beloved son.

Through the years, Baron Fitzgerald had acquired a masterful art collection from around the world. Since he had no heir, the baron left instructions in his will that an auction should be held at the time of his death to sell his entire collection of art.

Shortly after the baron passed away, his exquisite art collection—appraised in the millions of English pounds—was displayed in preparation for the auction. As private collectors and museum curators studied the artwork, one piece received little attention. It was a painting of low quality by an unknown, local artist. No one stopped to admire the humble painting, a portrait of the baron's son.

As the auctioneer pounded his gavel to call the large, expectant crowd to attention, the attorney read from the baron's will. The first painting to be auctioned was the portrait of "my beloved son." The auctioneer asked for a bid and the room fell silent. After many uncomfortable moments, a thin voice broke the stillness. An old servant who had known the son and loved him offered the sole bid—less than one English pound. The portrait of the baron's only son was his. The audience applauded politely, eager to proceed with the bidding on the real works of art.

At that point, the auctioneer rapped his gavel and, turning to the attorney, asked him to read again from the will. The crowd hushed. This was quite unusual. To the astonishment of everyone, the attorney read these words: "'Whoever buys the painting of my son receives my entire art collection.' The auction is over!"[2]

THE CHRISTIAN JOURNEY CAN BE DEFINED AS AN EXCHANGED LIFE: OUR LIFE EXCHANGED FOR CHRIST'S LIFE.

This remarkable story demonstrates a father's deep love for his son, and how, even from beyond the grave, the father wished to reward someone who shared in his love. Because that old servant simply loved his master's son, he received an inheritance worth millions.

God assures us in His Word that we also have received a bountiful inheritance through a beloved Son—Jesus. Many years before Jesus was born, the prophet Isaiah described Him in words similar to that humble portrait: "There was nothing beautiful or majestic about His appearance, nothing to attract us to Him" (Isaiah 53:2). Yet if we love Jesus Christ and give our lives to Him, we, too, obtain the immeasurable riches of an inheritance in heaven and a supernatural life on earth. In 1 John 5:12, we are promised, "Whoever has God's Son has life; whoever does not have His Son does not have life." As Christians, we can have an intimate relationship with our heavenly Father and we can experience meaning, purpose, and a life of supernatural victory— all because of Jesus Christ.

But who is this Jesus in whom we have so much?

THE SOURCE FOR EXTRAORDINARY LIVING

The Bible describes Jesus this way: "Christ is the visible image of the invisible God. He existed before God made anything at all and is supreme over all creation. Christ is the one through whom God created everything in heaven and earth. He made the things we can see and the things we can't see—kings, kingdoms, rulers, and authorities. Everything has been created through Him and for Him. He existed before everything else began, and He holds all creation together" (Colossians 1:15–17). In Jesus, God became flesh so we could see, hear, and touch the invisible God. Through Christ, God intricately created every living thing, and Jesus continues to hold our complex universe together even now.

This is our marvelous Savior.

Jesus is the subject of more than three hundred Old Testament prophecies. He fulfilled specific predictions concerning His birth, His betrayal, His crucifixion, and His resurrection, confirming that He is the promised Messiah.

Jesus performed countless miracles, including feeding thousands of people with a few loaves of bread, healing the sick, casting out demons, and raising the dead. He walked on water and calmed a storm, proving that even the forces of nature obey Him.

During His extraordinary life on earth, Jesus demonstrated unfailing grace, astounding wisdom, amazing understanding, and sacrificial love unequaled throughout human history. His character was pure, selfless, and completely without sin. Only God in the flesh could have embodied all these characteristics.

One anonymous author made this striking comparison between the supernatural life of Jesus and the lives of famous people:

Socrates taught for 40 years, Plato for 50, Aristotle for 40, and

Jesus for only 3. Yet the influence of Christ's 3-year ministry infinitely transcends the impact left by the combined 130 years of teaching from these men who were among the greatest philosophers of all time.

Jesus painted no pictures; yet some of the finest paintings of Raphael, Michelangelo, and Leonardo da Vinci received their inspiration from Him. Jesus wrote no poetry; but Dante, Milton, and scores of the world's greatest poets were inspired by Him. Jesus composed no music; still Haydn, Handel, Beethoven, Bach, and Mendelssohn reached their highest perfection of melody in the hymns, symphonies, and oratorios they composed in His praise. Every sphere of human greatness has been enriched by this humble Carpenter of Nazareth.

His unique contribution to the human race is the salvation of the soul! Philosophy could not accomplish that. Nor art. Nor literature. Nor music. Only Jesus Christ can break the enslaving chains of sin and Satan. He alone can speak peace to the human heart, strengthen the weak, and give life to those who are spiritually dead.[3]

Jesus Christ is the true Messiah, the Son of God, and Savior of the world!

EMBRACING CHRIST'S SUPERNATURAL LIFE

Imagine a condemned prisoner sitting on death row waiting to be taken to the electric chair. He has said goodbye to his family and has tried to prepare himself for the inevitable. He hears footsteps, then keys rattling in the lock. Finally, the door to his cell swings open. But instead of taking the prisoner to his death, the guard tells him that someone has offered to die in his place. He has been pardoned. He can walk out of that prison cell that very moment as a free man. Imagine the relief and joy that prisoner would feel.

But now imagine the guard's reaction if the prisoner stubbornly refused to leave the cell. What if the prisoner told the guard that he was relieved he was not going to die, but that he wanted to stay in prison? The guard would think the prisoner was ungrateful and even crazy.

Sadly, this is the experience of many Christians. Because of Christ's perfect sacrifice on the cross, our sins have been forgiven. And because He rose from the dead and conquered death, we can live at peace with God both now and for eternity. Every knowledgeable Christian is aware of these important truths, and each of us has accepted God's pardon. However, many of us never fully embrace the supernatural freedom and abundant life God has in store for us.

Why is that?

One of the reasons many Christians miss out on the abundant life Christ offers is that they do not really see the prison as a prison. They do not quite believe God has something better for them beyond what they have experienced. *They do not want to let go of the beliefs and values of this world.*

These Christians would rather continue living the life that is familiar to them. They have trusted Jesus as their Savior, but are unwilling to change many aspects of their lifestyle. They cling to habits and priorities that do not please our holy God. Little do they know that the values and pleasures of this world are the bars and chains which keep them from experiencing true freedom.

When Paul first preached the gospel to the Ephesians, many of them eagerly responded. But Ephesus was an extremely pagan city centered around the worship of Diana, a goddess of fertility. Many Ephesians attempted to combine their pagan practices of sorcery with their new life in Christ. It was only after a man with an evil spirit attacked several men who were misusing Jesus' name that the believers in Ephesus turned from their pagan past. Acts 19:17 states, "A solemn fear descended on the city, and the name of the Lord Jesus was greatly honored." As a result, the new believers brought their incantation books and publicly burned them.[4]

To us, it may seem obvious that worship of a goddess of fertility and Christianity do not mix. But what are we clinging to from our past? Often, we do not want to discard the old, comfortable way of living, so we try to blend the old and new together. But this produces heresy and stunts our spiritual growth.

Each time we base our self-worth on accomplishments and appearance rather than on who we are in Christ, we are choosing to follow the value system of this world. Every time we choose our actions and priorities based on what is popular or currently accepted rather than on what matters to God, we are short-circuiting God's power in our lives and sabotaging the amazing plan He has for us.

The supernatural life Christ offers requires that we turn our backs on the old and wholeheartedly embrace the new. God wants to introduce us to a whole new way of thinking, seeing, and living, if we will only surrender completely to Him.

A second reason believers stay in prison is that *they are trying to live the Christian life through self-effort.* They seriously desire to live a productive life for Christ, but they try to do it in their own ability. For a time, they may appear to make progress, but then they encounter an obstacle they cannot overcome. Sometimes others lead them astray. As a result, they become mired in discouragement and defeat.

These Christians mean well, but they have not yet realized that they cannot live a supernatural Christian life through self-effort any more than a caterpillar can fly or a lamp can light up by itself.

Consider the following analogy.

Scientists have learned that each of us has a genetic code, or DNA, within us. This blueprint helps determine our size, appearance, natural talents, and even some of the ailments that may plague us in life. This code contains so much information that if it were put into a book, it would fill 600,000 pages. Yet every single cell in our body carries this code. No two people have the same code. If a person's code is even slightly defective, physical abnormalities or mental retardation may result.

God had a spiritual genetic code for humanity. Adam was made in God's image and perfectly reflected God's character. But when Adam sinned, that spiritual image became distorted. Since then, the image of God has been distorted in all people.

Because of this, following our Lord in our own strength is futile. It is like trying to change our hair color from gray to blond. It might look good for a while, but sooner or later the roots will show. The only way to right this situation would be if someone could change our genetic makeup.

That is exactly what happened, spiritually speaking, when we received Christ. God removed the distorted "gene," and replaced it with Christ. After Paul relates his spiritual conflict, he declares, "Who will free me from this life that is dominated by sin? Thank God! The answer is in Jesus Christ our Lord" (Romans 7:24,25).

It is impossible to live the Christian life through self-effort. God wants us to live supernatural lives by faith as we invite Christ to live His life in and through us.

A third reason many Christians never fully embrace the supernatural freedom and abundant life God has in store for them is because of *the schemes of Satan*. We live on a spiritual battlefield with an enemy dedicated to our destruction. Satan, the great deceiver, hates the things of God and wishes to destroy those who are loyal to Christ. He is committed to preventing us from experiencing the supernatural life God offers. He is bitterly opposed to fulfilling the divine purpose for which God created us. He attacks us through our flesh, the world system, and evil spirits who seek to deceive, afflict, and enslave us.

Satan's schemes include the following:

- *Ignorance*—Satan realizes that if he can prevent us from knowing about our new identity in Christ, we will not live supernaturally.

- *Doubt*—Satan persuaded Eve to doubt God's goodness so she would disobey God in the Garden of Eden. He knows that if our understanding of God is twisted, we will not trust God's character and Word. As a result, we will not live supernaturally.

- *Distractions*—Satan entices us with worldly pleasures, so we miss out on God's infinite blessings. He knows that if we are unwilling to let go of sinful habits, we will not live supernaturally.

- *Guilt*—Satan is the great accuser. He condemns us when we fail, in our self-effort, to live holy lives. Because we feel unworthy to accept what God offers through grace, we will not live supernaturally.

- *Discouragement*—Satan blinds us so we will not see our loving Father at work in our lives. Then, when we become frustrated with our lack of spiritual growth and lose hope, we will not live supernaturally.

Satan will do everything possible to prevent you from inviting Christ to live His life in and through you. In fact, Satan does not want you to read this book. And once you do, he certainly does not want you to apply the biblical truths you learn. Because if you do, you will be fulfilling the purpose for which God created you. But take heart. God is infinitely more powerful than Satan. Scripture asserts this wonderful truth, "The Lord is faithful; He will make you strong and guard you from the evil one" (2 Thessalonians 3:3). We are promised in 1 Corinthians 10:13, "He will keep the temptation from becoming so strong that you can't stand up against it. When you are tempted,

He will show you a way out so that you will not give in to it." With God's help, we can resist every ploy of Satan.

STEP OUT OF YOUR PRISON

Do you want to live a supernatural life in Christ? Then step out of that prison. Do not let the entanglements of the world, self-effort, or the schemes of Satan keep you from experiencing the wonderful freedom God has in store for those who love, trust, and obey Him.

The next two chapters will explain the importance of faith and the five essential steps to living a supernatural life in Christ. With faith as our foundation, we can access all the riches and joy Christ offers. Part II, "Our Identity in Christ," explains who we are in Christ and the spiritual benefits we have because of our new identity. We will learn about the blessings of our spiritual inheritance and how we are a part of a great eternal kingdom. Knowing who we are in Christ will enable us to live like we belong to Him. Part III, "Our Life in Christ," explores how we can live with Jesus as our role model. His power will transform the way we think, speak, and behave—with incredible results.

Living transformed lives in Christ's power will enable us to be victorious. Part IV, "Our Victory in Christ," focuses on the marvelous promise that through Christ's resurrected life, we can overcome the world!

As you explore the wonderful truths of God's Word as explained in this book:

- *Invite* Christ to live His life in and through you.

- *Believe* what God says about your supernatural new identity in Christ so you will gain a correct self-perception.

- *Live* according to God's truth and your new biblical self-image. And as a result,

- *Experience* the supernatural benefits of Christ living in and through you.

If you have placed your trust in Jesus, the risen Son of God, turned from your sins, and accepted by faith the reality of His death and resurrection, you have an amazing new identity. You are God's dearly loved child in whom He delights, an heir of His incredible blessings, a saint with a new nature, a member of the Body of Christ, and a citizen of Christ's kingdom. As Paul explains, "Therefore, if anyone is in Christ, he is a new creation; old things have passed away; behold, all things have become new" (2 Corinthians 5:17, NKJ). You have been given a whole new nature. A sinless nature. Christ's nature. Instead of your old life, you have an abundant and eternal life. His life.

What a privilege and what a gift! Through faith and the power of the Holy Spirit, you can experience an extraordinary life that reflects your new identity in Christ. It is a life beyond your circumstances and limitations. It is a life of love, meaning, and purpose. It is Christ living in and through you. It is life supernatural!

Life Application

Thank Your Heavenly Father—Paul exclaims, "Thank God for His Son—a gift too wonderful for words!" (2 Corinthians 9:15). Express your gratitude to God for saving you and for making you a new creation in Christ.

Renew Your Mind—Memorize and meditate upon this wonderful promise in God's Word:

- "Therefore, if anyone is in Christ, he is a new creation; old things have passed away; behold, all things have become new" (2 Corinthians 5:17, NKJ).

Act by Faith—As you read this book, ask the Holy Spirit to open your spiritual eyes so you can see and understand the new identity, resources, and blessings you now have in Christ. Each day, invite Christ to live His life in and through you. Begin your day with a prayer, surrendering and dedicating your life to the lordship of Christ. Ask Jesus to think with your mind, speak with your lips, and love others through you. Determine to believe what God says about your supernatural new identity in Christ, so you will gain a correct self-perception. As you are bombarded with insecurities and attacks on your self-worth, remember who you are in Christ. Live according to God's truth and your new biblical self-image. Rely upon the timeless truth of God's Word, not your feelings or the viewpoint of others to determine your decisions and actions. As a result, you will experience the supernatural adventure of Christ living in and through you.

CHAPTER 2

Faith: The Key to Supernatural Living

opular ballads, advertisements, celebrity testimonials, and politicians all extol the merits of faith. Some encourage us to "keep the faith." Others to "just believe." But belief in itself is empty. Like little children putting their faith in Santa Claus or the tooth fairy, we can believe with all of our heart that someone will come through for us or that something good will happen—and be gravely disappointed. The results of our faith do not depend as much on how deeply we believe as on the object of our faith.

In whom or what do we believe? Popular opinion polls? Astrology? A romantic interest? All these will fail us. The only One who is infinitely faithful and worthy of our wholehearted trust is our wonderful God—Father, Son, and Holy Spirit. When we place our faith in Him, the result is supernatural.

Several years ago, a farming community found itself in the midst of a drought. The once hearty soil had become as hard as bronze in the unrelenting sun. The parched crops lay wilted, and the anxious farmers grumbled at the incessantly cloudless skies. Finally, the ministers of the community scheduled an hour of prayer in the town square at noon on a Saturday. They encouraged the townspeople to bring objects of faith as inspiration.

On Saturday, the town square was brimming with people. Their faces filled with anticipation, their hearts hopeful, they clutched their "objects of faith"—Bibles, rosaries, crosses.

The hour of prayer ended and, as if on command, clouds appeared and a gentle rain began to fall. The townspeople cheered and held up their treasured objects in praise and thankfulness. In the middle of the joyous crowd, one object of faith stood out from the others. A nine-year-old child had brought an umbrella.[1]

Faith is not merely believing. It requires action. And acting in faith is the only way to live supernaturally in Christ.

WITHOUT FAITH, IT IS IMPOSSIBLE TO PLEASE GOD

Faith is essential to the Christian life. Paul states in Romans 5, "Since we have been made right in God's sight *by faith*, we have peace with God because of what Jesus Christ our Lord has done for us. *Because of our faith*, Christ has brought us into this place of highest privilege where we now stand, and we confidently and joyfully look forward to sharing God's glory" (vv. 1,2). And the writer of Hebrews proclaims, "It is impossible to please God without faith" (11:6).

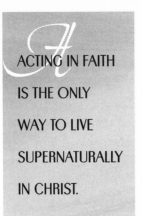

ACTING IN FAITH

IS THE ONLY

WAY TO LIVE

SUPERNATURALLY

IN CHRIST.

But do we really comprehend the faith that God requires?

All of us have natural, everyday faith. This is the faith we exhibit in the ordinary things we do. When we sip a glass of water, we trust that the drink is pure. When we board an airplane, we have faith that the builders of the plane, the air traffic controllers, and the pilot know what they are doing. This type of faith comes from our senses. If the water looks odd or smells funny, we do not drink it. If the pilot reeks of alcohol or the air traffic controllers are on strike, we do not board the plane.

We need our senses and natural faith to live our physical lives, but the Bible explains that spiritual faith is "the confident assurance that what we hope for is going to happen. It is the evidence of things we cannot yet see" (Hebrews 11:1). Spiritual faith does not depend on our senses, but is based on God's consistent and trustworthy character. As George Mueller, 19th century British social reformer and devoted Christian, explained, "Faith does not operate in the realm of the possible. There is no glory for God in that which is humanly possible. Faith begins where man's power ends."[2]

Although our circumstances may appear hopeless and our feelings may tell us to give up, we must not allow ourselves to be limited by the visible, tangible world. Instead, we should place our trust in the amazing promises of our invisible God.

Yet many times our faith extends only as far as we can see. An African impala antelope can jump to a height of more than ten feet and a distance of more than thirty feet. Yet these magnificent creatures can be kept in an enclosure in any zoo behind a three-foot wall. The reason? The antelope will not jump if it cannot see where its feet will fall. The impala's dependency on its senses robs it of its freedom.[3]

We, also, are often limited by our need to see or touch before we will believe. Instead, we must improve our spiritual vision so that the flimsy walls of fear and doubt cannot doom us to a life of spiritual mediocrity.

FAITH IS THE KEY; JESUS IS THE DOOR

Jesus is the object of our faith. As stated in the previous chapter, He is truly worthy of our faith. He is the door to our salvation and the immense blessings God has in store for us. Jesus states in John 10:9, "I am the door. If anyone enters by Me, he will be saved." When we believed in Him and received Him as our Lord and Savior, we did so by faith. Ephesians 2:8,9 declares, "It is by grace you have been saved, through faith—and this not from yourselves, it is the gift of God—not by works, so that no one can boast" (NIV). By placing our faith in Christ, we received not only the blessings He has planned for us, but His very life.

Before coming to Christ, we were dead spiritually. Paul explains in Ephesians 2:1, "Once you were dead, doomed forever because of your many sins." We could not do anything to change our situation any more than a dead body can get up and dance. Yet Paul continues with this amazing declaration: "God is so rich in mercy, and He loved us so very much, that even while we were dead because of our sins, He gave us life when He raised Christ from the dead...For He raised us from the dead along with Christ" (Ephesians 2:4–6).

A Hindu man heard about Jesus, but he could not comprehend how the great Creator God of the universe could stoop to become a human being. He wondered why God would want to humble Himself to that extent. Because of his religious background, this man had a profound reverence for life. One day as he was walking in a field, he came upon an anthill. He stopped in wonder to observe the activity of these amazing creatures.

Suddenly, he heard the noise of a tractor plowing the fields. He looked up and saw that the plow would soon destroy that anthill. The ants' home would be gone and thousands would be killed. He was frantic. He wanted to save them. He thought, *I could write a warning in the dirt, but they would not know how to read it. I could shout to them, but they would not know what I was saying. The only possible way I could communicate with them would be to become an ant myself!*

In that moment he saw why God, the Creator of the universe, had made such an incredible sacrifice to become one of us. The God-Man, our Lord Jesus Christ, died on the cross to save us from being plowed under by sin.

In the midst of our hopeless condition, God intervened to provide a means to life. When we place our faith solely in Jesus to save us, He opens the way to an abundant, fruitful life of faith. Paul tells us, "It is through faith that a righteous person has life" (Galatians 3:11).

FAITH IS THE CONDUIT; THE HOLY SPIRIT IS THE POWER SOURCE

Paul explains to the believers in Galatia, "We Christians receive the promised Holy Spirit through faith" (3:14). To experience true life, we must continue the Christian journey the same way we began it—by faith and the power of the Holy Spirit. Paul warns, "After starting your Christian lives in the Spirit, why are you now trying to become perfect by your own human effort?" (Galatians 3:3). Only God could save us, and only God can empower us to live a victorious Christian life. We are able to move beyond the limitations of our senses and circumstances the same way we were made spiritually alive: not by relying on ourselves, but by putting our faith in Christ and depending on the Holy Spirit's provision, power, guidance, and protection moment by moment.

We cannot live an abundant, effective Christian life without the power of the Holy Spirit. Jesus Christ is our example. The Holy Spirit was intimately involved in every aspect of His life and ministry. The Holy Spirit made possible Christ's coming as a Man with a fleshly body. The Spirit descended upon Jesus at His baptism. He led Christ into the wilderness to be tempted by Satan. The Holy Spirit anointed Christ and inaugurated His ministry.

Jesus declared through the words of the prophet Isaiah, "The Spirit of the Lord is on me, because He has anointed me to preach good news to the poor. He has sent me to proclaim freedom for the prisoners and recovery of sight for the blind, to release the oppressed, to proclaim the year of the Lord's favor" (Luke 4:18,19, NIV).

But the Holy Spirit does not wish to call attention to Himself. He is the enabler, the empowerer, the equipper, the counselor, and the helper. He desires to promote the work of God and glorify Christ (John 16:13,14). He does this in several ways:

- The Holy Spirit bears witness of Christ and reminds us of Christ's teachings (John 14:26).
- The Holy Spirit indwells and empowers every believer (1 Corinthians 6:19).
- The Holy Spirit manifests Christ's nature within us (Romans 8:9).

What an amazing privilege to have the same Holy Spirit who empowered our Savior living inside us. Only through the supernatural presence of the Holy Spirit can we experience a supernatural life because the Holy Spirit works in us to reflect Christ in our lives.

FAITH IS THE VEHICLE; SUPERNATURAL LIVING IS THE JOURNEY

The term "Christian" literally means "little Christ." God wants us to reflect Christ to those around us as we journey through life.

Every morning, I express in various ways this basic desire of my heart, "Lord, I want to be a suit of clothes for You. Walk around in my body. Think with my mind. Love with my heart. Speak with my lips. Seek and save the lost through me." I pray that none of my own failings and fleshly concerns get in the way of what Jesus would like to accomplish through me. I realize that His will, His wisdom, His power are infinitely greater than my own.

Only by trusting and surrendering our lives to God can we accomplish anything of eternal value. Only by daily placing our faith in Christ can we experience supernatural living.

The Christian journey can be defined as an exchanged life: our life exchanged for Christ's life. We must die to our old self and invite Christ to live His resurrection life through us. In Galatians, Paul tells us why: "I have been crucified with Christ and I no longer live, but Christ lives in me. The life I live in the body, I live by faith in the Son of God, who loved me and gave Himself for me" (Galatians 2:20, NIV).

A story is told about Joseph Parker, a former pastor of City Temple in London who was a skilled musician. One evening, he attended a piano concert by the great Paderewski. This magnificent pianist amazed him. Afterward, the minister returned home and stood before his own piano. Suddenly, he called to his wife, "Bring me an ax! Today I heard great music for the first time. By comparison, my music amounts to nothing at all. I feel like chopping my piano to pieces."

Parker realized he could never play like the great Paderewski simply by following his example—even if he practiced eight hours a day. To do so, he would need Paderewski's very hands, yes, the very soul of the great musician.[4]

Our old self is no more able to live the Christian life than that pastor was able to play the piano like Paderewski. But when we receive Christ, we receive the very hands and soul of Jesus. And God wants His soul and hands to minister through us. What an amazing adventure life becomes when we invite Christ to live in and through us!

Are you missing out on God's blessings because you do not have an accurate spiritual self-image? Discover who you are in Christ and the spiritual riches you have inherited. In the next chapter, we will explore what it means to die to self and live in Christ. We will discover five essential elements to living in Christ. But remember—none of these elements is possible without faith.

By faith, you received your salvation.

By faith, you can invite Christ to live in and through you.

By faith, you can live a supernatural, victorious Christian life.

Praise God that our wonderful Savior is exalted above all things, and He is the one who frees us from the prison of Satan's kingdom of sin and self-effort!

Life Application

Thank Your Heavenly Father—Tell God how much you appreciate Him. He was willing to come to this sin-cursed earth from His glorious home in heaven so He could die on a cross for your sins. Express your appreciation for the intimate relationship you can have with Him for the rest of eternity. Meditate on the fact that He has sent the Holy Spirit to indwell and empower you so that He can exalt Christ and enable you to live out His life through you.

Renew Your Mind—Memorize and meditate on the following promises from God's Word:

- "Since we have been made right in God's sight by faith, we have peace with God because of what Jesus Christ our Lord has done for us. Because of our faith, Christ has brought us into this place of highest privilege where we now stand, and we confidently and joyfully look forward to sharing God's glory" (Romans 5:1,2).

- "It is impossible to please God without faith. Anyone who wants to come to Him must believe that there is a God and that He rewards those who sincerely seek Him" (Hebrews 11:6).

Reflect on Your New Life in Christ—In Hebrews 11, read how men and women of faith lived victoriously in difficult circumstances. Now reflect on several trials in your life in which you failed to react in faith. How would faith have made a difference in what you said and did? What steps can you take in the future that will help you respond in faith?

Share the Blessings—Tell others about the amazing truths of supernatural living in Christ.

CHAPTER 3

Christ Living In and Through Us

*Y*ou haven't really lived until..."

We often hear this phrase in ads or from people we know claiming that we have not truly experienced life until we have driven a particular car, vacationed in some exotic locale, or indulged in a certain delicious dessert.

But are these earthly pleasures really what produce true, meaningful life?

Jenny, a happy five-year-old with bouncy, blond curls, was waiting with her mother in the checkout line of a discount store when she saw a string of glistening white faux pearls in a pink foil box. "Oh please, Mommy," she asked, "can I have them? Please, Mommy, please?" After quickly checking the back of the little box for the price, the mother looked into her little girl's pleading blue eyes and shook her head.

When Jenny got home, she dumped the contents of her piggy bank on her bed and counted out seventeen pennies. That night, she did more than her share of chores. The next day, she asked the neighbor if she could pick dandelions for ten cents. Then on her birthday, Grandma gave her a new dollar bill. At last she had enough money to buy the necklace.

Jenny cherished her little fake pearls.

Each night when Jenny was ready for bed, her daddy would come upstairs to read her a story. One night when he finished the story, he asked Jenny, "Do you love me?"

"Oh yes, Daddy. You know I love you."

"Then give me your pearls."

"Oh, Daddy, not my pearls. You can have Princess—the white horse with the pink tail from my collection. Remember, Daddy? The one you gave me. She's my favorite."

"That's okay, honey. Daddy loves you. Good night." And he gently kissed her cheek.

The next week, after the story time, Jenny's daddy asked her again, "Do you love me?"

"Daddy, you know I love you."

"Then give me your pearls."

"Oh, Daddy, not my pearls. But you can have my beautiful baby doll—the brand new one I got for my birthday. And you can have the yellow blanket that matches her sleeper."

"That's okay. Sleep well. God bless you, little one. Daddy loves you." And he tenderly kissed her goodnight.

Several nights later when her daddy came to pray with her, Jenny sat crumpled on her bed with her legs crossed. Her chin trembled and her face was wet with tears.

"What is it, Jenny? What's the matter?"

Jenny slowly lifted her small clenched fist to her daddy. She opened it. Inside was her pearl necklace. Her voice quivered as she said, "Here, Daddy. It's for you."

With tears forming in his own eyes, Jenny's daddy accepted the cherished dime-store necklace. Then he reached into his pocket, pulled out a blue velvet case, and gave it to her. Inside was a strand of genuine pearls. He had them all the time. He was just waiting for her to give up the imitation pearls so he could give her the genuine treasure.[1]

The genuine treasure God wants to give you is a life supernaturally empowered by Christ. What a tremendous adventure that is. Yet if you were to honestly examine your life, what would you discover? Are fake treasures robbing you of an abundant life in Christ? Does your heart desire a comfortable lifestyle carefully wrapped in a fancy box? Are you clutching in your hand a longing for the world's approval or for love at any cost?

Counterfeit riches will keep you from receiving the real treasure

God has for you. God wants to fill your life to overflowing with His love, His grace, and His power. He holds this life "in His pocket" eager to present it to you. How true is the biblically inspired quote from the missionary and martyr Jim Elliot, "He is no fool who gives what he cannot keep to gain what he cannot lose."[2]

Our Lord Jesus declares in Mark 8:34,35, "If any of you wants to be My follower, you must put aside your selfish ambition, shoulder your cross, and follow Me. If you try to keep your life for yourself, you will lose it. But if you give up your life for My sake and for the sake of the Good News, you will find true life." *The Living Bible* states that only those who do the latter "will ever know what it means to really live."

Paul vividly describes true life as Christ supernaturally living His life within us. After Paul's dramatic conversion, he traveled to many countries telling others about Jesus. Beatings, imprisonments, shipwrecks, and even a stoning did not diminish his passion for his Savior. No circumstance could deter him from living victoriously for his Lord. He lived boldly and joyfully for God because he knew that every situation was part of God's amazing plan. While imprisoned in Rome, he did not wallow in self-pity, but witnessed to the soldiers who were chained to him twenty-four hours a day. As a result, the good news of our Lord spread throughout Caesar's palace!

About forty years ago when I visited Rome for the first time, I was very eager to see everything of significance. After visiting the Coliseum, the catacombs, and other important sites, someone took me to the dungeon where Paul lived for several months before he was martyred. As we descended into the dark, dirty hole,[3] I was captivated with the fact that God mightily used a man who spent his last days in the filth of a dungeon. I knelt there in the dirt and surrendered myself anew to the Lord, even as Paul had done, and asked God to work His perfect will in me.

That evening, I went across the road to the Roman Forum where I witnessed a spectacular pageant portraying the drama of ancient Rome. The Forum was where Roman generals received awards and applause for the countries they had conquered. Here the senators met to legislate the laws that governed the entire Roman Empire. Here Julius Caesar, emperor of Rome, was assassinated.

As the presentation continued, I was enthralled by the grandeur, power, and opulence of ancient Rome. Then something occurred to me. Who knows the names of the senators, the generals, or even most of the emperors? Not many people. But billions of people know about Paul, the slave of Jesus, who through the centuries has been used by the Spirit of God to transform the lives of hundreds of millions of people. Then I saw with new depth and appreciation how important it is to be crucified with Christ and be a slave of Jesus. And I realized why people name their dogs Nero after the emperor of Rome and their sons Paul in honor of the great apostle who was a revolutionary for the glory of God.

In Galatians 2:20 Paul explains the secret to living supernaturally, "I have been crucified with Christ: and I myself no longer live, but Christ lives in me. And the *real* life I now have within this body is a result of my trusting in the Son of God, who loved me and gave Himself for me" (TLB).

Paul gave up his life and all the world's false treasures for Jesus. He allowed Christ to live His life in and through him so completely that he could not "speak of anything except what Christ has accomplished through me" (Romans 15:18, NIV). As he let Christ renew his mind, he adopted God's perspective on the world. Everything Paul did, every day he lived, he did through faith by trusting in his living Savior. Paul describes this process in detail in the Book of Romans.

To help you better grasp the important truths of Romans 6 and Galatians 2:20, an acrostic has been developed. You can remember the five essential steps to living supernaturally in Christ by the acrostic CROSS:

C　*Concentrate* on who you are as a new creation in Christ (Romans 6:3–5).

R　*Regard* yourself as dead to sin and alive in Christ (Romans 6:6–11).

O　*Offer* your body to God as an instrument of righteousness (Romans 6:12–15).

S　*Surrender* your will continually to God (Romans 6:12–15).

S　*Stay* dependent on Christ throughout the day (Romans 8:9–14).

CONCENTRATE ON WHO YOU ARE AS A NEW CREATION IN CHRIST

The Word of God promises, "Therefore, if anyone is in Christ, he is a new creation; old things are passed away; behold, all things have become new" (2 Corinthians 5:17, NKJ).

The first step to living in Christ is to simply recognize and accept the truth about who you are in Him. When you became a Christian, you became a new person. The core of who you are is no longer the same. All your sins—past, present, and future—are forgiven, and Christ has clothed you in His righteousness.

Paul says in 2 Corinthians 5:21, "God made Him who had no sin to be sin for us, so that in Him we might become the righteousness of God" (NIV).

We often describe a generous person as someone who will give the shirt off his back. Jesus gave us the righteousness off His back. Isaiah says, "When we proudly display our righteous deeds, we find they are but filthy rags" to God (Isaiah 64:6). But Jesus exchanged our rags for His righteousness—and we will be clothed in His righteous garments for all eternity.

One day a man toured a paper factory in England that makes the finest stationery. He asked, "From what is the delicate paper made?" He was shown a huge pile of old rags. He was told that the rag content is what determines the quality of the paper. The man would not believe that those dirty rags could be used for anything good.

Six weeks later he received a package of paper from the company with his initials embossed on it. On the first page were written the words, "Dirty Rags Transformed."[4]

The same is true of our life in Christ. God has taken our attempts at righteousness, which are filthy rags, and transformed them through the righteousness of Jesus Christ. Because we are now clothed in Christ's righteousness, our sins are forgiven and we are justified— declared righteous! Our old nature no longer has power over us because we have a new identity and a blessed future.

A businessman tells a story that illustrates this point well. He was selling a warehouse property that had been empty for months. Vandals had smashed the windows, damaged the doors, and strewn trash around the inside. As the businessman showed the property to a prospective buyer, he explained that he would replace the broken windows, correct any structural damage, and clean out the garbage.

"Forget about the repairs," the buyer said. "When I buy this place, I'm going to build something completely different. I don't want the building; I want the site."[5]

It is the same with our loving Father. He has purchased us with the blood of His Son, and His plan is to create something beautiful and eternal. God is not simply sweeping a warehouse slated for the wrecking ball. He is building something completely new. All He wants is the site and the permission to build.

Romans 6:4 proclaims, "Therefore we have been buried with Him through baptism into death, so that as Christ was raised from the dead through the glory of the Father, so we too might walk in newness of life" (NASB). And Colossians 3:1,2 declares, "Since you have been raised to new life with Christ, set your sights on the realities of heaven, where Christ sits at God's right hand in the place of honor and power. Let heaven fill your thoughts." Our mighty Savior conquered the power of the old life in you. It has been crucified! Recognize the beauty of your new creation, and set your mind on what pleases God.

REGARD YOURSELF AS DEAD TO SIN AND ALIVE IN CHRIST

Paul declares in Romans 6:11, "You should consider yourselves dead to sin and able to live for the glory of God through Christ Jesus."

Because of Christ's sacrifice, we are as dead to sin as a corpse is dead to this world. It cannot respond to any pleasure the world offers. No appealing aroma, glitzy picture, or sultry music can cause that dead body to get up and indulge. In the same way, we are to consider ourselves dead to the desires and attractions of sin.

Because you are a new creation, sin no longer dictates your behavior. Romans 6:6 explains, "Our old sinful selves were crucified with Christ so that sin might lose its power in our lives. We are no longer slaves to sin." How exciting to be able to choose life and live for God's glory rather than wallow in the despair and guilt that results from sin!

Yet we walk around in flawed, finite bodies that want to do wrong. In God's eyes we are dead to sin, but each day we have to consciously submit ourselves to the power of the Holy Spirit and decide to live according to how God sees us—according to our new nature. Paul writes, "I advise you to live according to your new life in the Holy Spirit. Then you won't be doing what your sinful nature craves. The old sinful nature loves to do evil, which is just opposite from what the Holy Spirit wants. And the Spirit gives us desires that are opposite from what the sinful nature desires. These two forces are constantly fighting each other, and your choices are never free from this conflict" (Galatians 5:16,17).

We are in the midst of conflict because we house Christ in a body of flesh. The Word of God states in 2 Corinthians 4:7, "This precious treasure—this light and power that now shine within us—is held in perishable containers, that is, in our weak bodies. So everyone can see that our glorious power is from God and is not our own." But even this tension can bring glory to God. Paul offers the solution to the dilemma in our passage in Galatians, "The life I live in the body, I live by faith in the Son of God, who loved me and gave Himself for me" (2:20, NIV). We must place our trust in our loving Savior, and, by faith, see ourselves as God does—as dead to sin and alive in Christ.

On a cold March day, a man stood on the edge of Niagara Falls and watched birds swoop down to snatch a drink from the clear water. As the birds dipped down for a drink, tiny droplets of ice formed on their wings. As they returned time after time for additional drinks, more ice weighed down their bodies until, finally, they could not rise above the cascading waters. Flapping their wings, the birds suddenly dropped over the falls.[6]

This is how sin acts in our lives. Some sins may seem small, but they are like those tiny droplets of ice. Each time you choose to follow your old habits of sin, you are saying "no" to the new life Christ has given you, and, like those birds carried over the edge of Niagara Falls, you may pay dearly.

Colossians 3:3 promises, "You died when Christ died, and your real life is hidden with Christ in God." Christ redeemed you and gave you eternal life that begins *now*. You have the power of the Holy Spirit to withstand temptation. Consider yourself a new creature instead of a sinner, for sin has no power over you. Remember, you are dead to sin and alive in Christ!

OFFER YOUR BODY TO GOD AS AN INSTRUMENT OF RIGHTEOUSNESS

Paul urges, "Do not let any part of your body become a tool of wickedness, to be used for sinning. Instead, give yourselves completely to God since you have been given new life. And use your whole body as a tool to do what is right for the glory of God" (Romans 6:13).

Our bodies can be used for great good or terrible evil. Compare Adolph Hitler with Mother Theresa. Or rock singer Jim Morrison of The Doors, who destroyed his body in his pursuit of pleasure, and the martyr Jim Elliot, who offered his body to accomplish a great good.

In Romans 12:1, Paul urges believers, "Dear brothers and sisters, I plead with you to give your bodies to God. Let them be a living and holy sacrifice—the kind He will accept. When you think of what He has done for you, is this too much to ask?"

Instead of living for our own selfish purposes or to fulfill the purposes of this world, we must dedicate all we have and all we are to our wonderful God. Offering ourselves means nailing to the cross our bodies, possessions, and everything we are. This is what Paul meant when he wrote, "I have been crucified with Christ." We must give ourselves completely to our marvelous heavenly Father for Christ to live in and through us.

As I look back on my own experience of walking with the Lord for almost half a century, and as I have studied the Scriptures and observed the lives of thousands of believers around the world, I have concluded that it is absolute folly for a Christian to live one split second out of the perfect will of God. If we realize how wonderful our great, holy, and righteous God is and what He has done for us, we never can be satisfied with living a mediocre Christian life. The privilege of knowing, loving, and serving our Lord is so awesome that to sacrifice this for any pleasure—money, sex, power, fame—is ludicrous. Nothing compares to the abundant life Christ wants to live in and through us.

In 1813, King Frederick William III of Prussia found himself in trouble. Wars had been costly, and he was seriously short of finances. He could not disappoint his people nor capitulate to the enemy. After careful reflection, he decided to ask the women of Prussia to bring their gold and silver jewelry to be melted down for their country. For each ornament received, he exchanged an iron cross as a symbol of his gratitude. On each cross was inscribed, "I gave gold for iron, 1813."

The response was overwhelming. The women of Prussia prized their gifts from the king more highly than their expensive jewelry because the crosses were proof that they had sacrificed for their king. Soon it became unfashionable to wear jewelry, and thus was established the Order of the Iron Cross. Members wore no ornaments except a cross of iron for all to see.[7]

We have an amazing calling! As Christians, we are to proudly display the cross of Christ. When we exchange the "treasures" of our former life for a cross, God will use us to win the greatest war of all—a spiritual one. He has a wonderful and perfect plan and, in His mercy, He allows us to play an integral part if we will only consecrate ourselves as instruments of His righteousness.

> WE ECHO THE REBELLION OF SATAN WHEN WE CHOOSE OUR OWN WAY INSTEAD OF GOD'S WAY.

SURRENDER YOUR WILL CONTINUALLY TO GOD

Paul encourages believers, "As slaves of Christ, do the will of God with all your heart" (Ephesians 6:6).

Before the fall of Satan, there was but one will in the universe—God's will. Dr. Donald Grey Barnhouse explores this idea in his book, *The Invisible War:* "The quality of eternity is the fact that there is but one will—the will of God. Then all was holy, all was righteous: there was no evil whatsoever." But then a second will came into the universe, "rising from the heart of Lucifer...In addition to the voice of God, there was now a second voice saying: 'I will.'"[8]

We echo the rebellion of Satan when we choose our own way instead of God's way, when we exert our will over God's will. Each time we claim our "rights" and fail to submit to the perfect will of our marvelous Creator and Savior, we cause discord, pain, and guilt. The only means to bring peace and joy back into our lives and to this fallen world is to crucify our will by surrendering our fleshly desires and our stubborn pride to the Lord. We must say as Jesus said to His Father, "Your will be done" (Matthew 26:42).

Jesus is the perfect example of one who submitted His will to God. Although He Himself was God, Jesus declared in John 6:38, "I have come down from heaven to do the will of God who sent Me, not to do what I want." How amazing that Jesus surrendered all His rights and His personal ambitions to accomplish the will of His heavenly Father.

In contrast, we often demand our rights from our government, our family, and our church as we pursue our own selfish desires. Instead, we should follow the example of our Savior and commit ourselves to "do the will of God."

When Vonette and I were first married, we each made a list of our hopes for the future. Vonette's list included children, good health, a nice home, and other blessings. As I began to write, I became over-whelmed with the desire to offer everything to my amazing Lord who gave me my wife, my salvation, and my very life. Together, Vonette and I surrendered our belongings, our dreams, ourselves, and every-thing we had and would ever have to God. Following Christ's exam-ple of obedience to His loving Father, we signed that contract and committed ourselves to be slaves of Jesus. As I look back on my life, that act of making a contract with God—of surrendering myself to Him—is the most significant event of my life. It determined every-thing that I have done through the years.

Surrendering ourselves to God will have far-reaching effects on our lives. At the entrance of the RCA Building in New York City stands a gigantic statue of Atlas, who, with all his muscles straining, is holding the world upon his shoulders. This beautifully proportioned and powerfully built man can barely stand up under his burden. On the other side of Fifth Avenue is Saint Patrick's Cathedral. Behind the high altar is a little shrine of the boy Jesus, perhaps eight or nine years old, holding the world in one hand.[9]

How true this is for us. When we hold onto our life and pursue our own desires, we are like Atlas, struggling under the weight of an unpredictable world. "Submission" is not a popular concept today, but our ability to submit to God determines whether we struggle through life like Atlas or enjoy the blessings of entrusting our "world" to the all-powerful Creator of the universe.

Jesus submitted to His Father even to the point of dying on the cross for our sins. We, too, must submit to Christ. We must give all of our life—our desires, needs, personal rights, and even our choices—to Him and ask Him to change our hearts so we will want to do what pleases Him.

STAY DEPENDENT ON CHRIST THROUGHOUT THE DAY

Scripture declares, "You are not controlled by your sinful nature. You are controlled by the Spirit if you have the Spirit of God living in you …For all who are led by the Spirit of God are children of God" (Romans 8:9,14).

Once we realize that we are new creatures and picture ourselves dead to sin, we must offer our bodies, possessions, and will to God each day. But only with Christ's power can we "take up our cross" daily. Only Jesus can give us the power to live the Christian life, so we must remain vitally connected to Him. He is the source of our spiritual nourishment.

Jesus uses the illustration of a grapevine and branches to describe our dependence on Him. In John 15:5, He declares, "Yes, I am the vine; you are the branches. Those who remain in Me, and I in them, will produce much fruit. For apart from Me you can do nothing."

For many years, Campus Crusade was headquartered in California. During that time, Vonette and I decided to take our boys on a summer vacation to Northern California. While we were there, we visited a vineyard. On gently rolling hills, we saw row upon row of grapevines. Some of the oldest vines were as thick as my leg and supported numerous branches loaded down with luscious grapes. We learned that the sturdiest vines could produce a harvest of close to eighty pounds.

But each winter, some of these branches had to be pruned for the vine to produce well the next year. What happens when a branch is cut off? It has no source of nourishment so it withers and dies. But if it remains on the vine, it grows and bears fruit. Notice that the branch does not struggle or work at producing a bountiful harvest. Growth and fruit are the natural result of abiding in the vine which draws up nourishment through its roots.

So, too, we will bear fruit if we draw upon the abundant nourishment of our Lord. But how do we remain in Christ so that we receive a constant flow of spiritual food?

Feed on God's Word. Paul tells Timothy, his son in the faith, "All Scripture is inspired by God and is useful to teach us what is true and to make us realize what is wrong in our lives. It straightens us out and teaches us to do what is right. It is God's way of preparing us in every way, fully equipped for every good thing God wants us to do" (2 Timothy 3:16,17). The Bible is God's love letter to us. The more we read it, the better we get to know Christ. And the better we know Him, the more we will trust Him. To know Him is to love Him and to love Him is to obey Him.

Pray. Prayer is communication with God. The Gospels are filled with accounts of Jesus praying to the Father. Paul tells us to "pray continually" (1 Thessalonians 5:17, NIV). This involves both talking to God and listening to what He has to say to us.

Be sensitive to the leading of the Holy Spirit. Jesus told His disciples, "When the Spirit of truth comes, He will guide you into all truth" (John 16:13). As you read the Bible and pray, listen for the Holy Spirit's gentle prodding through a verse you have just read, a word spoken by a wise Christian, or an impression placed upon your heart.

Confess your sins. Sin will short-circuit your connection to God. Scripture promises, "If we confess our sins to [God], He is faithful and just to forgive us and to cleanse us from every wrong" (1 John 1:9). You can receive God's forgiveness by confessing your sin—agreeing with God that it is sin—and by repenting—changing your attitude and behavior and making things right with those you have wronged. Then, you can enjoy God's wonderful forgiveness and the fullness of the Holy Spirit.

Stay vitally connected to Christ's body. Paul compares believers to a body with Christ as the head. Imagine a finger trying to function apart from its hand. In Hebrews, we are told, "Let us not neglect our meeting together, as some people do, but encourage and warn each other, especially now that the day of His coming back again is drawing near" (Hebrews 10:25).

Our loving Savior provided the sacrifice so we can have a relationship with God. Christ wants to empower us through His Holy Spirit and protect us so we may live an abundant life. A meaningful life. A life only possible if Christ lives through us.

Recognize who you are—a new and holy being, no longer dominated by sin, but consecrated for righteousness! And, by faith, surrender your will to God. Crucify your pride, your love for this world, and your need for other people's approval. And in all these things, draw upon the life-giving sustenance of Christ. Then you will live supernaturally, because your loving Savior will powerfully live in and through you.

Jesus changed Simon's name to Peter and powerfully predicted the beautiful new creation he was to become. Saul was renamed Paul, emphasizing that he had become a new man with a higher calling. Inviting Jesus Christ to live in and through us transforms not just our name, but our very lives.

In Part II, we will explore our new identity in Christ. As a follower of Jesus Christ, each of us is a child of God, an heir of God, a saint, a member of Christ's Body, and a citizen of Christ's kingdom. Knowing the truth about who you are will open the door to a supernatural self-image and a life that is abundant and filled with purpose.

For "you haven't really lived" until you live supernaturally as our loving Savior, Jesus Christ, makes possible.

What an amazing adventure!

Life Application

Renew Your Mind—For each chapter, an acrostic has been developed to help you remember the major points explored in that section. Make it a priority to meditate on and memorize the verses and acrostics throughout this book.

- "I have been crucified with Christ and I no longer live, but Christ lives in me. The life I live in the body, I live by faith in the Son of God, who loved me and gave Himself for me" (Galatians 2:20, NIV).

- "In Him lie hidden all the treasures of wisdom and knowledge" (Colossians 2:3).

- Remember the CROSS acrostic to help you live supernaturally in Christ:
  Concentrate on who you are as a new creation in Christ.
  Regard yourself as dead to sin and alive in Christ.
  Offer your body to God as an instrument of righteousness.
  Surrender your will continually to God.
  Stay dependent on Christ throughout the day.

Take Up Your Cross—Make it a habit to begin each day prayerfully meditating on the five principles of the CROSS acrostic. This is a prayer you can pray: "Heavenly Father, thank you that I am a new creation, dead to sin and alive in Christ. I present myself to You by offering my body as an instrument for righteousness. I surrender my will to You so that I can seek Your ways and accomplish Your purposes. I am dependent on You. Live Your life through me and empower me today. In Jesus' precious name, amen."

Act by Faith—Throughout the day, remember to apply the principles of the CROSS acrostic to your life. Thank God by faith that Christ is living His life through you. Remain sensitive to His leading and obedient to the prompting of the Holy Spirit.

PART II

Our Identity
in Christ

CHAPTER 4

Living as a Child of God

How would your life be different if you were adopted by the most powerful, virtuous, and wealthy person in the world? How would your self-image change because your father and new family were so prestigious? How would you feel about this person who lavished you with such favor?

The adoption offer has been made, but not by some world-famous human. The Creator and Sovereign Ruler of the universe has chosen you to be His dearly loved child.

God's Word gives this wonderful promise, "When the right time came, God sent His Son, born of a woman, subject to the law. God sent Him to buy freedom for us who were slaves to the law, so that He could adopt us as His very own children. And because you Gentiles have become His children, God has sent the Spirit of His Son into your hearts, and now you can call God your dear Father. Now you are no longer a slave but God's own child. And since you are His child, everything He has belongs to you" (Galatians 4:4–7).

One night, a house caught fire. It was the home of an orphaned boy and his grandmother. As the flames quickly spread throughout the house, the boy was trapped upstairs. His grandmother attempted to rescue him, but she died in the flames. Fortunately, a man who saw the fire heard the boy's cries. He climbed up an iron drainpipe to the lad's window. With the boy clinging to his neck and a firm grip on the drainpipe, he carefully lowered himself and the boy to safety.

A few weeks later, a public hearing was held to determine who should have custody of the boy. A teacher, a farmer, and the town's wealthiest citizen all gave reasons why they should be chosen to give the boy a home. But the sad boy only stared at the floor.

Then a stranger walked to the front of the room and announced his desire to adopt the boy. He slipped his hands out of his pockets and held them up for the crowd to see. His palms bore hideous scars.

The boy cried out in recognition and leaped into the man's arms. This was the man who had saved the child's life! His hands had been searched when he climbed the hot iron pipe. As the boy nestled in his savior's arms, the other men walked away. Those marred hands had settled the issue.[1]

> WE ARE VERY IMPORTANT TO GOD BECAUSE WE ARE HIS DEARLY LOVED CHILDREN.

In the same way, our Savior's nail-pierced hands have settled the issue for us. Our Lord's sacrifice saved us and made us children of God. Jesus Himself described those who believe in Him as "children of God raised up to new life" (Luke 20:36).

As believers, we are not orphans who are homeless and without parents. We have an incredible parent—a loving Father who cares for us and provides for us each moment of every day. And we have a marvelous home waiting for us in eternity. Even now, we experience comfort, peace, and a sense of belonging through our Father's Spirit—the Holy Spirit—who has made our heart His home. We are very important to God because we are His dearly loved children.

FREE TO SOAR IN CHRIST

As a believer in Jesus Christ, you are a child of the Sovereign Ruler of the universe! Does your life reflect your noble heritage?

A story is told of a baby eagle that fell out of its nest and was found by a farmer who raised it with his chickens. The eagle watched the chickens peck at their food and began to live as they did, never attempting to fly.

One day, a naturalist passed by the barnyard and wondered why the king of the birds was confined with chickens. He longed to free this magnificent bird from such a limited existence, so he attempted to teach it to fly. At first, the bird would only run around the barnyard flapping its wings. Finally, the naturalist took the bird to a high mountain and lifted it toward heaven. "You are an eagle," he told the bird. "You belong to the sky. Stretch forth your wings and fly."

The eagle began to tremble. Finally, it spread its wings and, with a triumphant cry, soared into the sky.

In the following weeks and months, that eagle may have flown over its old barnyard and even remembered the chickens with nostalgia. But it never returned to live like a chicken.[2]

Like the eagle, many of us do not fully understand who we are in Christ. As a result, we do not experience the incredible blessings God has intended for us. Instead, we must see ourselves as our loving Father sees us. Listen to how much He loves us:

> Long ago, even before He made the world, God loved us and chose us in Christ to be holy and without fault in His eyes. His unchanging plan has always been to adopt us into His own family by bringing us to Himself through Jesus Christ. And this gave Him great pleasure (Ephesians 1:4,5).

God is not some distant architect of the universe who remains light years away pondering His creation. He is a loving, involved Father who desires an intimate relationship with us. If we truly comprehend how much God loves us, we will never be the same. He has an amazing plan for us both now and for eternity. Our self-worth will no longer be based on human success or status, but on who we are in Him.

God tells us in Galatians, "You are all children of God through faith in Christ Jesus" (3:26).

After Vonette and I had been married for several years, we learned that we were unable to have children. Of course, we were heartbroken. But the wife of a doctor told us that a young woman was offering her newborn boy for adoption. I will never forget the day I went to the hospital and held little Zachary for the first time. I lost part of my heart, we bonded so completely. It did not matter that he was not our biological child. We had chosen him, adopted him, and he was ours.

Because you are God's precious child, He has given you certain privileges. These will be yours forever. The acrostic CHILD will help you remember that God . . .

C *Conforms* you to Christ's character

H *Hears* you when you pray

I *Indwells* you with His Spirit

L *Loves* you unconditionally

D *Disciplines* you lovingly[3]

GOD CONFORMS YOU TO CHRIST'S CHARACTER

In Scripture we read, "Those whom [God] foreknew, He also predestined to become conformed to the image of His Son, so that He would be the firstborn among many brethren" (Romans 8:29, NASB).

At creation, God declared His marvelous plan for us. Genesis 1:26 reveals, "God said, 'Let us make man in our image, in our likeness'" (NIV). God intended human beings to reflect His character. What an amazing calling! But instead of being mirrors of our awesome Creator, Adam and Eve disobeyed God. Their fall into sin distorted human nature so the mirror was cracked almost beyond repair. Jesus, however, mirrored God's character perfectly. In Him, we have a new nature— His nature.

God wants us to give up our sinful desires and become more and more like His Son, Jesus Christ.

Ephesians 5:1 encourages us, "Be imitators of God, therefore, as dearly loved children" (NASB). All of us have watched children imitate their parents. A little girl will dress up in her mother's jewelry and high-heeled shoes. A young boy will pretend to hammer a nail or fix the car like his father. Children naturally mimic those they respect. So, too, God's children should imitate Him and deeply desire to reflect the spiritual image of our loving Savior.

We can do this only by inviting God to work in us. Just as a loving parent seeks to shape the character of his or her child, God works to mold us into the character of His Son. Paul explains, "God is working in you, giving you the desire to obey Him and the power to do what pleases Him" (Philippians 2:13).

God knows we cannot become like Christ through our own abilities or in our own strength so He lovingly and patiently shapes us, like an artist sculpting a masterpiece.

The great sculptor Michelangelo was chiseling a large block of stone when someone asked him how he created such beautiful statues. He answered, "The angel is caught inside the stone. I simply keep chipping away everything that isn't the angel."[4]

God is chipping away at our imperfections to release the beautiful creation He has birthed within us. The "sculpting" may be aided by difficult trials, gracious blessings, or inspiring Scripture.

God's holy Word commands, "Don't copy the behavior and customs of this world, but let God transform you into a new person by changing the way you think. Then you will know what God wants you to do, and you will know how good and pleasing and perfect His will really is" (Romans 12:2).

Our heavenly Father will do His part to conform us as we "imitate" our holy and loving Savior.

GOD HEARS YOU WHEN YOU PRAY

The Bible promises, "We can be confident that He will listen to us whenever we ask Him for anything in line with His will. And if we know He is listening when we make our requests, we can be sure that He will give us what we ask for" (1 John 5:14,15).

Day or night, God hears our every prayer. What a privilege! We have unlimited access to our almighty Creator God because we have placed our faith in His Son, Jesus Christ.

During the Civil War, a Union soldier who had lost his father and older brother in the war tried to gain an audience with President Abraham Lincoln. He wanted to ask the president for an exemption from military service so he could go home and help his mother and sister with spring planting. But he was told, "The president is a very busy man. Get back out there and fight the Rebs like a good soldier." Disheartened, he left and sat down on a park bench near the White House.

A small boy approached the soldier and asked him why he was so sad. The soldier poured out his heart to the boy. Then the boy took the soldier by the hand and said, "Come with me." He led him into the White House, past the guards, past the generals and high-ranking government officials. Then they entered the office where President Lincoln was discussing battle plans with his Secretary of State! The soldier was mystified at how this boy could walk unhindered into the president's office. Then President Lincoln looked up and said to the boy, "What can I do for you, Todd?"

Todd replied, "Daddy, this soldier needs to talk to you." This boy was Lincoln's son!

The soldier pleaded his case and was exempted from military service.[5]

Jesus' death and resurrection demolished the barrier separating us from God. As God's dearly loved children, we can approach our heavenly Father with all our joys and sorrows. As a child crawls up into his daddy's lap, so we, too, can climb into our Father's arms and tell Him all that is in our hearts. What an honor to have such an intimate relationship with our awesome Creator God and Father!

As you talk to your heavenly Father, remember that prayer also involves listening to Him. It is exciting for me when I stop during my prayer to ask, "Lord, do you have anything to say to me?" As I listen, He speaks to me.

Many times in my life God has spoken to me, never audibly, but with resounding clarity in my mind. One occasion was during the third week of my first forty-day fast. I was reading the account of King Hezekiah in the Old Testament. Thirty days after he was crowned king, he cleaned out the temple, which his father had defiled with idols. Hezekiah then wrote a letter inviting people throughout Judah and Israel to come and celebrate the Passover in Jerusalem.

As I meditated on these Scriptures, the Holy Spirit impressed upon my heart that I should write a letter inviting Christian leaders to come fast and pray for revival in America and the world. I wrote the letter, and more than six hundred people from various denominations and parachurch organizations came. We had a wonderful, joyful experience, and God met us in a special way.

God speaks to us in many ways. It may be through His Word, circumstances in our lives, or the counsel of godly believers. But many times it is through the still, small voice of the Holy Spirit in our hearts.

GOD INDWELLS YOU WITH HIS HOLY SPIRIT

The Bible explains, "Because you are sons, God sent the Spirit of His Son into our hearts, the Spirit who calls out, 'Abba, Father'" (Galatians 4:6, NIV).

Our heavenly Father gave us the Holy Spirit as a seal of our relationship with Him. Ephesians 1:13,14 explains, "When you believed in Christ, He identified you as His own by giving you the Holy Spirit, whom He promised long ago. The Spirit is God's guarantee that He will give us everything He promised and that He has purchased us to be His own people."

We are so special to God that He permanently marked us as belonging to Him. The Holy Spirit has been placed within us as proof of God's calling in our lives. As the Holy Spirit resides within us, He teaches, guides, and empowers us. In John 16, Jesus describes the Holy Spirit as our Counselor and the Spirit of truth. Jesus also promises that the Holy Spirit will be with us forever. He will make the things of God known to us, and He will glorify Christ.

The Spirit even helps us pray. Paul writes, "The Holy Spirit helps us in our distress. For we don't even know what we should pray for, nor how we should pray. But the Holy Spirit prays for us with groanings that cannot be expressed in words. And the Father who knows all hearts knows what the Spirit is saying, for the Spirit pleads for us believers in harmony with God's own will" (Romans 8:26,27).

Often when we come before our loving Father in prayer, we do not really understand His will or our needs. We only know that we feel hurt or confused or dissatisfied with our situation and the world's solutions. The Holy Spirit knows God's will. He can penetrate our conscience, search our hearts, and show us what is best. But we must make sure no sin gets in the way of the Holy Spirit working in our life.

When our older son Zachary was a little boy, we bought him an electric train. I never had one as a child, so I was as excited to play with the train as he was. One day while I operated the controls and he chased the train around the track, it stopped running! I could not figure out what was causing the problem. I took the train apart and put it back together. I pushed the plug in and out of the socket. Nothing worked. Then I saw that a small piece of metal—a "no left turn" sign —had fallen across the tracks. When I lifted it off the tracks, the train started running. A little sign had short-circuited the power.

That is what sin does. It disrupts the flow of God's power to us. So we must remove it by confessing it to God. I call that process Spiritual Breathing: exhaling the impure and inhaling the pure.

Exhale—Confess

The Bible explains, "If we say we have no sin, we are only fooling ourselves and refusing to accept the truth. But if we confess our sins to Him, He is faithful and just to forgive us and to cleanse us from every wrong" (1 John 1:8,9). Confession means that we agree with God concerning our sins. This involves at least four considerations:

1. Agree that your sin is wrong and grievous to God. Be sure to actually name specific sins.

2. Acknowledge that God has already forgiven you through Christ's death on the cross for your sins.

3. Demonstrate your repentance by changing your attitude and behavior.

4. If you have wronged others, seek to make things right.

Inhale—Appropriate by Faith

Now that you, through confession, have exhaled the sin that interrupted your relationship with God, inhale the fullness of the Holy Spirit by faith. Claim Ephesians 5:18 and ask the Spirit to fill you with His power and love. Then enjoy a renewed fellowship with your heavenly Father as you are controlled and empowered by His Holy Spirit moment by moment. And remember, although your sin may grieve God and short-circuit the Spirit's power, no sin can ever change or jeopardize God's love for you.

GOD LOVES YOU UNCONDITIONALLY

The Holy Scriptures tell us, "See how very much our heavenly Father loves us, for He allows us to be called His children, and we really are!" (1 John 3:1).

God's love does not depend on what we do. It depends on who He is. In the Bible's famous love chapter, 1 Corinthians 13, we read, "Love never gives up, never loses faith, is always hopeful, and endures through every circumstance" (v. 7). This is God's love for us.

The story is told of a prince and his family who were captured by King Cyrus of Persia. When they were brought before the great monarch, he asked the prince, "What will you give me if I release you?"

The prince answered, "Half of my wealth."

"And if I release your children?"

"Everything I possess."

"And if I release your wife?"

"Your majesty," the prince replied, "I will give myself."

King Cyrus was so moved by the prince's devotion that he released all of them. As the prince and his family were returning home, the prince commented to his wife, "Wasn't Cyrus a handsome man?"

"I didn't notice," his wife said with a smile. "I could only keep my eyes on you—the one who was willing to give himself for me."[6]

Our supreme God and Creator gave Himself for us. His Son, Jesus, declared in John 15:13, "Greater love has no one than this, that one lay down his life for his friends" (NIV). God demonstrated His commitment to us by taking on human form and dying for us. What love!

The Bible reveals four aspects of God's amazing, perfect love. We will call them Love's Four U's.

Untiring Love: The prophet Jeremiah declares, "Long ago the Lord said to Israel: 'I have loved you, My people, with an everlasting love. With unfailing love I have drawn you to Myself'" (Jeremiah 31:3). It is this same unfailing love that God demonstrates to us, His children. Our heavenly Father loves us even when our "terrible two's" last a lifetime!

Unselfish Love: To save us, God did not sacrifice His life savings or His lifetime ambition, but the life of His Son. The Bible teaches, "God showed how much He loved us by sending His only Son into the world so that we might have eternal life through Him. This is real love. It is not that we loved God, but that He loved us and sent His Son as a sacrifice to take away our sins" (1 John 4:9,10).

Unfathomable Love: If the universe were one big measuring cup, it still would not be big enough to hold God's love. Paul imparts this blessing in Ephesians 3:17–19, "May your roots go down deep into the soil of God's marvelous love. And may you have the power to understand, as all God's people should, how wide, how long, how high, and how deep His love really is. May you experience the love of Christ, though it is so great you will never fully understand it. Then you will be filled with the fullness of life and power that comes from God."

Unstoppable Love: Nothing in the past, present, or future can separate us from God's amazing love. Paul writes in Romans 8:38,39, "I am convinced that nothing can ever separate us from His love. Death can't, and life can't. The angels can't, and the demons can't. Our fears for today, our worries about tomorrow, and even the powers of hell can't keep God's love away. Whether we are high above the sky or in the deepest ocean, nothing in all creation will ever be able to separate us from the love of God that is revealed in Christ Jesus our Lord."

That is the depth of God's love for you, His dear child. His unconditional love never grows weary and is never motivated by selfish desires. His love is beyond comprehension, and it never ends. How blessed we are to be loved by our marvelous Creator God and Father!

GOD DISCIPLINES YOU LOVINGLY

The Bible tells us in Proverbs, "My child, don't ignore it when the Lord disciplines you, and don't be discouraged when He corrects you. For the Lord corrects those He loves, just as a father corrects a child in whom he delights" (Proverbs 3:11,12).

Just like earthly children, God's children must experience discipline. Discipline is necessary to mature and grow in character. God lovingly disciplines us so we will become more mature in our walk with Him.

God's discipline is for our good. The Bible explains, "Our fathers disciplined us for a little while as they thought best; but God disciplines us for our good, that we may share in His holiness. No discipline seems pleasant at the time, but painful. Later on, however, it produces a harvest of righteousness and peace for those who have been trained by it" (Hebrews 12:10,11, NIV).

Parents who care about their children discipline them. Proverbs 13:24 states, "If you refuse to discipline your children, it proves you don't love them; if you love your children, you will be prompt to discipline them." I fell in love with our two sons, Zac and Brad, the first time I saw them. I love them even more today, although they are now mature adults. When they were young, I spanked them when they were disobedient. I am sure that I shed more tears while I was spanking them than they did. Each time I would explain that I disciplined them because I loved them. After I finished spanking them, I would ask, "Why did I spank you?"

They would reply, "Because you love me."

The only way children learn to control their emotions, share with others, treat people with respect, and speak politely is through discipline and example. Our heavenly Father provides both. God has given us the perfect example in Jesus Christ.

Character is vitally important to God so He tenderly pulls the weeds, cuts off the dead flowers, and prunes the branches in the garden of our blossoming character. Yes, the process can be painful. But the result will be a character that is wise, mature, content, and pleasing to God. This loving, painstaking process demonstrates the difference between God's discipline and Satan's accusations. Satan belittles us so we will give up, but God corrects us so we will grow up.

Imagine for a moment a display case filled with junk. You have some lovely things you want to place inside, but first you must clean out the worthless items.

As Christians, we are God's display cases. He uses discipline to remove our sin and pride so He can fill us with His beauty. This process can be painful for the moment, but will be productive for eternity. The result will be righteousness, peace, and other fruit of the Spirit.

Our Father is the Ruler of the universe! How thankful we should be for the wonderful privilege of being His children. As His offspring, we can enjoy His love, care, and commitment as we pursue intimacy with Him by faith.

Romans 8:15–17 declares, "So you should not be like cowering, fearful slaves. You should behave instead like God's very own children, adopted into His family—calling Him 'Father, dear Father.' For His Holy Spirit speaks to us deep in our hearts and tells us that we are God's children. And since we are His children, we will share His treasures—for everything God gives to His Son, Christ, is ours, too."

God wants us, His dearly loved children, to be blessed by His incredible treasures!

We will explore these spiritual riches in the next chapter, where we discuss our identity as heirs of God.

Life Application

Thank Your Heavenly Father—Thank God that you are His dearly loved child and that He is at work in your life to conform you to the character of Christ. Praise Him that He is always listening and hears you when you pray. Express your gratitude for His Holy Spirit within you who guarantees that you are His and empowers you in your Christian walk. Thank God that He loves you unconditionally and brings discipline into your life as needed so that you will mature in Christ and be conformed to His image.

Renew Your Mind—Memorize and meditate upon the following verses and acrostic:

- "God has sent the Spirit of His Son into your hearts, and now you can call God your dear Father" (Galatians 4:6).

- "To all who received Him, to those who believed in His name, He gave the right to become children of God" (John 1:12, NIV).

- The acrostic CHILD will help you remember that God...
  Conforms you to Christ's character
  Hears you when you pray
  Indwells you with His Spirit
  Loves you unconditionally
  Disciplines you lovingly

Reflect on Your New Life in Christ—In prayer, ask the Holy Spirit to fill your mind with images that reflect the truth that you are now a child of God. Imagine yourself the child of the Sovereign Ruler of the universe, your heavenly Father. Picture yourself embraced and totally surrounded by His loving presence. By faith, believe God for the practical demonstration of this amazing truth in your life.

Share the Blessings—Prayerfully think of someone you can introduce to your heavenly Father and loving Savior so they, too, can be adopted into His family.

CHAPTER 5

Living as an Heir of God

*H*ave you ever wondered what it would be like to receive a letter informing you that you were the heir to a vast fortune? Perhaps you have dreamed of inheriting a sprawling mansion filled with exquisite antiques. Or maybe your choice would be a gleaming sports car or a priceless art collection.

Most of us have fantasized about suddenly coming into a large amount of money. Yet each of us has received a letter promising an inheritance far more valuable and enduring than any material wealth.

This letter is the Bible. The Bible tells us in Galatians 4:7 that as God's children, we are His heirs. "Now you are no longer a slave but God's own child. And since you are His child, everything He has belongs to you." We are God's heirs, not because of our own righteousness, but because of His grace.

Chinese writer and minister Watchman Nee recounts a time when a new Christian came to see him. The man was deeply distressed. "No matter how much I pray, no matter how hard I try, I simply cannot seem to be faithful to my Lord," he complained. "I think I'm losing my salvation."

Nee replied, "Do you see this dog here? He is my dog. He is housetrained; he never makes a mess; he is obedient; he is a pure delight to me. Out in the kitchen I have a son, a baby son. He makes a mess, he throws his food around, he fouls his clothes, he is a total mess. But who is going to inherit my kingdom? Not my dog; my son is my heir.

You are God's heir because it is for you that He died."[1]

As heirs, we have inherited riches and the promise of blessings. The Bible reveals, "This is the secret plan: The Gentiles have an equal share with the Jews in all the riches inherited by God's children. Both groups have believed the Good News, and both are part of the same body and enjoy together the promise of blessings through Christ Jesus" (Ephesians 3:6).

God's Word also tells us that these riches are priceless and incorruptible. "God has reserved a priceless inheritance for His children. It is kept in heaven for you, pure and undefiled, beyond the reach of change and decay" (1 Peter 1:4).

Thanks to our wonderful Savior, we have an abundant inheritance. But many of us still live like spiritual paupers. Why is that?

First, we may be *unaware* of what we have.

Once during a speaking engagement in Switzerland, I stayed at a beautiful hotel, compliments of the conference host. Each day, as I walked through the lobby, I passed the hotel's lavish dining room and smelled the wonderful aromas of delicious entrees and desserts. But I was determined to save money, so I bought fruit, cheese, and crackers from a local market and lived on that all week. As I was packing to leave, my host asked me how I had enjoyed the cuisine. I stared at him in amazement. He had not informed me upon my arrival that my meals were provided along with my room! The hotel had one of the finest chefs in the entire country. I could have eaten like a king, but instead I subsisted on crackers and cheese.

How true this is of us! If we are unaware of our wonderful inheritance, we will miss out on a bountiful spiritual banquet which has been prepared for us. Satan loves to keep us in the dark. He will do anything to prevent us from fully experiencing the blessings we inherit as God's dearly loved children. He will try to convince us that the treasure is worthless. Or, he will sow seeds of insecurity and guilt so we feel undeserving of such a great inheritance. But we must not believe his lies! We must believe our loving heavenly Father who reveals the truth to us in His Word.

The second reason many of us live like spiritual paupers is that, although we are *aware* of our spiritual inheritance, we simply do not *believe* it.

The Scriptures urge us to "follow the example of those who are going to inherit God's promises because of their faith and patience" (Hebrews 6:12). Faith releases God's riches. The treasures of heaven that we inherit are claimed by faith here on earth.

Imagine for a moment that a distant relative has included you in his will. As part of the execution of that will, money is placed into a bank account for you, and you are notified of that fact. But you reason, "It can't be true!" So you never bother to write a check against that account. Although you have the inheritance, you do not benefit from it because you lack the faith and willingness to claim it.

How tragic! But we have a solution. As children of God, we must *be aware of our spiritual inheritance and claim it by faith*. Then we will experience the abundant spiritual riches God has for His children.

This inheritance is both present and future. I am told of a wealthy person who divided his inheritance into two parts for his children. He is giving them some of their inheritance now. For example, he helped his son start a business, and he helped his daughter purchase a condominium. They will receive additional money from time to time as they demonstrate that they can handle it well. But the bulk of their estate will come later.

In the same way, increasing spiritual maturity and faith release increasing measures of our spiritual riches. The riches begin the moment we become Christians, but the full riches of our relationship with God will be revealed in heaven.

But what are the riches we have inherited? The acrostic HEIR will help you remember that God endows you with...

H   *Holy* glory

E   *Eternal* life

I   *Infinite* spiritual blessings

R   *Royal* authority in Christ's kingdom

GOD ENDOWS YOU WITH HOLY GLORY

The Word of God promises, "Now if we are children, then we are heirs—heirs of God and co-heirs with Christ, if indeed we share in His sufferings in order that we may also share in His glory" (Romans 8:17, NIV). As children of God, we will share in His glory.

In the Old Testament, to enjoy God's glory was to enjoy His presence. And the glory of God is wondrous to behold! Exodus 19:16–19 describes the glory of the Lord descending upon Mount Sinai when God gave the people of Israel the Ten Commandments:

> On the morning of the third day there was thunder and lightning, with a thick cloud over the mountain, and a very loud trumpet blast. Everyone in the camp trembled. Then Moses led the people out of the camp to meet with God, and they stood at the foot of the mountain. Mount Sinai was covered with smoke, because the LORD descended on it in fire. The smoke billowed up from it like smoke from a furnace, the whole mountain trembled violently, and the sound of the trumpet grew louder and louder. Then Moses spoke and the voice of God answered him (NIV).

God bestows this same amazing power and glory upon us, His dearly loved children. We experience this marvelous glory in several ways:

First, we share Christ's glory by *being molded into His image.* Paul explains, "God knew His people in advance, and He chose them to become like His Son, so that His Son would be the firstborn, with many brothers and sisters. And having chosen them, He called them to come to Him. And He gave them right standing with Himself, and He promised them His glory" (Romans 8:29,30).

Second, we partake in God's amazing glory by *representing Him in the world.* Jesus prayed to God about His followers, "I have given them the glory that You gave Me, that they may be one as we are one: I in them and You in Me. May they be brought to complete unity to let the world know that You sent Me and have loved them even as You have loved Me" (John 17:22,23, NIV).

Third, someday, we will experience Christ's glory by *having a glorified body like Christ's.* When Jesus returns, our weak, mortal bodies will be transformed into glorious resurrected bodies. The Bible promises, "Our earthly bodies, which die and decay, will be different when they are resurrected, for they will never die. Our bodies now disappoint us, but when they are raised, they will be full of glory. They are weak now, but when they are raised, they will be full of power" (1 Corinthians 15:42,43).

And last, we will someday share Christ's glory by *reigning with Him.* Jesus promises His followers, "Just as my Father has granted Me a

Kingdom, I now grant you the right to eat and drink at My table in that Kingdom. And you will sit on thrones, judging the twelve tribes of Israel" (Luke 22:29,30).

God has generously endowed us with His holy glory, but there is something we must do. The Bible records in Romans 8:17 that in order to share Christ's glory, we must share His sufferings. Those who suffer for Christ will share in His glory. Suffering does not sound appealing, but the trials and difficulties we face in life become our training ground.

Picture the talented athletes who compete in the Olympics. These men and women endure the physical and emotional pain of training and competing, hoping for the glory of a medal. Their Olympic medal is in doubt, but our glorious inheritance is assured. They buffet their bodies for a medal that will perish, but we exercise our faith through suffering to win a greater award in God's eternal kingdom. As Paul declares, "I consider that our present sufferings are not worth comparing with the glory that will be revealed in us" (Romans 8:18, NIV).

Recently, I met Pastor Young, a man the Lord has mightily used in the underground churches in China. These churches represent some 50 million people. For most of his adult life, Pastor Young has been persecuted for his faith. He was imprisoned, beaten, and tortured to the point that the bones of his legs were so pulverized he could not walk. One day he called out to God, "Oh, God help me. I don't know how much more of this I can take."

In that glorious instant, he was healed and able to walk again! Although he lives in hiding and his life is always at risk, he travels around China mobilizing Christians to introduce people to Christ. When I saw him, Pastor Young was radiant, rejoicing over the privilege of suffering for Jesus.

We are being molded into the image of our holy Savior. We represent our mighty God in this world, and someday we will have resurrected bodies and reign with Christ. Praise God for bestowing His radiant glory upon us!

GOD ENDOWS YOU WITH ETERNAL LIFE

The Bible assures us, "God so loved the world that He gave His only Son, so that everyone who believes in Him will not perish but have eternal life" (John 3:16). Because of the selfless sacrifice of God's Son, Jesus Christ, we have inherited eternal life.

But what is eternal life? Jesus explains in His prayer to His Father, "This is eternal life: that they may know You, the only true God, and Jesus Christ, whom You have sent" (John 17:3, NIV). Eternal life is essentially a relationship with our Creator. Sin separated us from God. In fact, eternal *death*—or hell—is eternal separation from God who is all light, all truth, all love. How horrible! But thanks to our loving Savior, the barrier of sin has been removed, and we can experience the bliss of deep fellowship with God forever. This is eternal life!

HOW WE LIVE THIS TEMPORAL LIFE WILL AFFECT HOW DEEPLY WE ENJOY ETERNITY.

Eternal life is a gift from God. Paul explained in his letter to Titus, "[God] declared us not guilty because of His great kindness. And now we know that we will inherit eternal life" (Titus 3:7). According to Ephesians 2:8,9, "God saved you by His special favor when you believed. And you can't take credit for this; it is a gift from God. Salvation is not a reward for the good things we have done, so none of us can boast about it."

Like any friendship, our relationship with God can deepen and mature. So, too, our experience of eternal life can grow and become more abundant. One commentary illustrates this point with the analogy of attending a concert. As the symphony orchestra plays, everyone in the audience enjoys the beautiful music. However, those who have taken the time to study music, and perhaps even play a musical instrument, will more deeply appreciate the concert. Those who have nurtured a love and understanding for music will more fully enjoy the performance.[2]

In a similar way, the Bible makes it clear that how we live this temporal life will affect how deeply we enjoy eternity.

As Romans 2:7 promises, "He will give eternal life to those who persist in doing what is good, seeking after the glory and honor and immortality that God offers." Eternal life is an abundant, meaningful life that begins the moment we receive Christ and lasts forever. Are you secure in your eternal relationship with almighty God? (If you have any doubts, read Appendix A, which explains how you can enter into a personal relationship with Christ.) What a blessing, both now and for eternity, to know our loving God and gracious Savior.

GOD ENDOWS YOU WITH INFINITE SPIRITUAL BLESSINGS

Paul exclaims in Ephesians 1:3, "How we praise God, the Father of our Lord Jesus Christ, who has blessed us with every spiritual blessing in the heavenly realms because we belong to Christ."

Recently, I had the privilege of addressing a distinguished audience in Florida's state capitol. In the midst of the program, a woman told her story. God has led her to adopt children who are unwanted. Most of them have been abused, have fetal alcohol syndrome, or are crack babies. She brings these children into her home and loves them. She teaches them that they are children of God—princesses and princes of the kingdom. She even has a ceremony where she shakes hands with each child and addresses them, "I greet you, Prince Philip. I greet you, Princess Anne. You are a child of God." She takes children without parents and children of drug addicts, then teaches them that they are heirs of God and individuals of great worth. Before they knew nothing but neglect and deprivation, but now they have a loving mother and a promising future.

We have a wonderful heavenly Father who enjoys lavishing love and blessings upon His dear children. As heirs of God, we have inherited redemption, forgiveness, eternal life, and so much more.

Paul lists many of the abundant blessings we have inherited in the first chapter of Ephesians. Overcome by God's goodness, he declares, "So we praise God for the wonderful kindness He has poured out on us because we belong to His dearly loved Son. He is so rich in kindness that He purchased our freedom through the blood of His Son, and our sins are forgiven" (vv. 6,7).

Truly, God has generously bestowed on His children numerous blessings that are infinite in their scope and meaning. We are redeemed, we are forgiven, and, as we discussed in the last section, we have eternal life. But there is more.

Because we are redeemed, we have inherited Christ's holiness. "Long ago, even before He made the world, God loved us and chose us in Christ to be holy and without fault in His eyes" (Ephesians 1:4).

The Christian life is a process of becoming, in our experience, what we already are in God's sight.

We have also inherited the spiritual blessing of wisdom. "[God] has showered His kindness on us, along with all wisdom and understanding" (Ephesians 1:7,8).

This wisdom comes from the Holy Spirit, who indwells us and is a pledge of our inheritance. The Bible declares, "The Spirit is God's guarantee that He will give us everything He promised and that He has purchased us to be His own people. This is just one more reason for us to praise our glorious God" (Ephesians 1:14). What an amazing privilege to have God's Spirit within us to empower and direct our lives.

Since we are heirs of God, we are also co-heirs with Christ and we share in the amazing power of Jesus' name. Jesus told His disciples, "You can ask for anything in My name, and I will do it, because the work of the Son brings glory to the Father. Yes, ask anything in My name, and I will do it!" (John 14:13,14).

As heirs, we also share in Christ's victory. The Bible tells us in 1 John 4:4, "You belong to God, My dear children. You have already won your fight with these false prophets, because the Spirit who lives in you is greater than the spirit who lives in the world." Thanks to our abundant inheritance, we are truly more than conquerors through our Lord Jesus Christ (Romans 8:37).

But how do we tap into these blessings? I am reminded again of Galatians 2:20 where Paul says, "I have been crucified with Christ and I no longer live, but Christ lives in me. The life I live in the body, I live by faith in the Son of God, who loved me and gave Himself for me" (NIV).

We release these many blessings by surrendering our will to God in faith. When we surrender our own desires and offer our heart, soul, and mind irrevocably to God, He lavishes His spiritual blessings on us. Jesus demonstrated the attitude we should have when He taught His disciples the Lord's Prayer. This beautiful model instructs us to pray: "May your will be done here on earth, just as it is in heaven" (Matthew 6:10).

GOD ENDOWS YOU WITH ROYAL AUTHORITY IN CHRIST'S KINGDOM

Paul testifies in his letter to Timothy, "I am willing to endure anything if it will bring salvation and eternal glory in Christ Jesus to those God has chosen. This is a true saying: If we die with Him, we will also live with Him. If we endure hardship, we will reign with Him" (2 Timothy 2:10–12). As heirs of God, we will someday reign with Him.

The New Testament is filled with promises that God's children will reign in God's kingdom. Jesus declares in the Sermon on the Mount, "God blesses those who realize their need for Him, for the Kingdom of Heaven is given to them" (Matthew 5:3). In the letters to the churches in the Book of Revelation, Jesus gives this wonderful promise, "To all who are victorious, who obey Me to the very end, I will give authority over all the nations. They will rule the nations with an iron rod and smash them like clay pots. They will have the same authority I received from My Father, and I will also give them the morning star!"[3] (Revelation 2:26–28).

Notice the phrase "to all who are victorious, who obey Me to the very end." Although our salvation and entrance to God's kingdom is a gift, ruling with Christ depends on our obedience—our enduring until the end no matter the consequence. Therefore, if we meet God's conditions, we will someday reign with Christ.

Three famous Jews of ancient times demonstrated such obedience—Shadrach, Meshach, and Abednego. They lived in Babylon as captives and faced a terrible choice: bow down to an idol or be thrown into a fiery furnace.

These three men demonstrated godly character. They were determined not to bow down to the idol even though they did not know whether God would deliver them. But God brought them out of that fiery furnace without even the smell of smoke on them. Truly, safety consists not in the absence of danger but in the presence of God. As a result, Shadrach, Meshach, and Abednego lived out their days ruling as administrators over the province of Babylon.

As followers of Christ, we may also suffer for His sake and His kingdom. We may not come out of the furnace unscathed. But one thing we know: God will be with us and the final victory is His. Someday, Christ will reward our faithful endurance by appointing us to reign with Him.

In the famous "sheep and goats" illustration, Jesus promises the kingdom to those who live out their faith in love: "Then the King will say to those on the right, 'Come, you who are blessed by My Father, inherit the Kingdom prepared for you from the foundation of the world. For I was hungry, and you fed Me. I was thirsty, and you gave Me a drink. I was a stranger, and you invited Me into your home. I was naked, and you gave Me clothing. I was sick, and you cared for Me. I was in prison, and you visited Me'" (Matthew 25:34–36).

Our faith response to God's abundant inheritance should be to obey God and develop a heart like His. We should serve and give to others because of our love for Christ. Then, we will lay up treasures in heaven.

In the Gospel of Luke, Jesus tells the parable of a rich fool. This man raised wheat and other crops, and he did it very well. Soon he had such a great harvest that he scarcely knew what to do with it all. So he thought, "I'll tear down my old barns and build the biggest storehouses anyone has ever seen. And I'll fill them with grain. I'll have enough to last me the rest of my life, so from now on I'll be able to take life easy, eat, drink, and be merry!" But that night, he died and his abundant harvest did not benefit him at all!

The worldly pleasures of this life are fleeting, but loving and serving others in the power of the Holy Spirit will result in eternal treasures. The person who seeks happiness may never find it, but the person who loves and serves others in Christ's name always finds it. The law of sowing and reaping still works today. And, as Revelation so richly portrays, we who invest in God's kingdom will reign with Him: "The throne of God and of the Lamb will be there, and His servants will worship Him. And they will see His face, and His name will be written on their foreheads. And there will be no night there—no need for lamps or sun—for the Lord God will shine on them. And they will reign forever and ever" (Revelation 22:3–5).

God has given us a glorious inheritance. Ultimately, that inheritance is Christ. As children of God, we share in His holy glory; we live in intimate fellowship with Him; we enjoy infinite spiritual blessings; and, someday, we will reign with Him forever.

We are God's beloved children and heirs. But we are also His saints. We will discuss this amazing truth in the next chapter.

Life Application

Renew Your Mind—Commit the following verses and acrostic to memory:

- "Now you are no longer a slave but God's own child. And since you are His child, everything He has belongs to you" (Galatians 4:7).

- "Since we are His children, we will share His treasures—for everything God gives to His Son, Christ, is ours, too. But if we are to share His glory, we must also share His suffering" (Romans 8:17).

- The HEIR acrostic will help you remember that God endows you with...
  Holy glory
  Eternal life
  Infinite spiritual blessings
  Royal authority in Christ's kingdom

Take Up Your Cross—Concentrate on the truth that you are now an adopted child and dearly loved heir of the Sovereign Ruler of the universe. Prayerfully remember the five principles of the CROSS acrostic as they apply to your new identity: "I praise you, heavenly Father, that I am a new creation—Your adopted child and heir. Thank You that I am dead to sin and alive in Christ, so I can share in Your Holy glory and enjoy infinite spiritual blessings. I offer my body as an instrument of righteousness and surrender my will to You. Empower my life to help bring glory to Your eternal kingdom. And may I remain dependent on You moment by moment. In the matchless name of Jesus. Amen."

Act by Faith—Go through the day with the confidence that you are truly God's dearly loved child and heir. Embrace this amazing truth as a way of life. As you encounter different situations, ask yourself, "Because I am a child and heir of God, what should I be thinking? What should I be saying? What should I be doing?"

CHAPTER 6

Living as a Saint with a New Nature

*H*ave you noticed how often cities, waterways, and landmarks are named for saints? There is Saint Louis, the Saint Lawrence Seaway, and Mount Saint Helens. Many churches around the world bear the name of an apostle or another person considered especially holy. Rome boasts of Saint Peter's Basilica and London of Saint Paul's Cathedral. Most of us are familiar with legends about famous saints, such as Saint George slaying a deadly dragon or Sir Thomas More courageously standing up to Henry VIII. And occasionally when a person acts in an especially loving or unselfish way, we remark, "That person is a real saint."

But would any of us have the courage to add our name to this list of revered notables? Would any of us dare to call *ourselves* a saint?

Paul, under inspiration of the Holy Spirit, repeatedly referred to Christians as saints. He began his epistle to the Philippians with these words: "To all the saints in Christ Jesus at Philippi" (Philippians 1:1, NIV). To *all* the saints. He was not writing to a select few, but to the entire church at Philippi.

But how can this be? If you were to honestly examine the thoughts that pass through your mind each day, the words that you speak, or the things that you do, they probably would be far from saintly. Yet your distinction as a saint does not depend on your performance. We are called saints because of the wonderful sacrifice of God's Son, Jesus Christ, who shed His blood on the cross for our sins.

On May 21, 1946, in Los Alamos, a young scientist named Louis Slotin diligently prepared for an atomic test. Before this important test could be conducted in the waters of the South Pacific, he needed to determine the critical mass—the amount of U-235—necessary to begin an atomic chain reaction. He had conducted that same experiment several times before. Each time, he would push the two hemispheres of uranium together. Then just as the mass became critical, he would push them apart with a screwdriver. But on this day, just as the material became critical, the screwdriver slipped! The two hemispheres of uranium came too close, and the room was filled with a bluish haze.

Without thinking of his own safety, Slotin tore the two hemispheres apart with his bare hands, interrupting the chain reaction. By placing himself in the center of the deadly nuclear reaction, he saved the lives of the seven other people in the room.

As he waited to be taken to the hospital, Slotin calmly told his companion, "You'll come through all right. But I haven't the faintest chance myself." Nine days later he died in agony.[1]

Almost two thousand years ago, Jesus Christ took upon Himself sin's most concentrated "radiation" and endured an agonizing death. By this act, He broke the chain reaction. Christ's sacrifice and triumphant resurrection broke the power of sin in our lives and made us right with God. Because of His sacrifice, our nature has been transformed and our identity has been changed. We are no longer sinners, but saints.

The words for "saint" used in both the Old and New Testaments can also be translated as God's "holy ones," or "those who are called." These words refer to those who have a relationship with God. Saints are people who belong to God and are set apart for His purposes.

The New Testament applies the term "saint" to all true believers. It is not reserved for those who face a martyr's death or live especially holy lives. The term "saint" includes even those who are struggling spiritually. For example, many of the Corinthian believers struggled with sin. Yet notice how Paul begins his letter to them: "To the church of God which is at Corinth, to those who have been sanctified in Christ Jesus, saints by calling, with all who in every place call upon the name of our Lord Jesus Christ, their Lord and ours" (1 Corinthians 1:2, NASB).

If you are a true believer, Jesus Christ has sanctified you, and you, too, are a saint!

But perhaps you, like many of us, suffer from a distorted spiritual self-image. Most of us do not see ourselves as saints. We see ourselves as sinners. You may say, "I'm a sinner because I sin." But that is not true! What we do does not define who we are.

For example, fish and people both swim, but they are very different. Fish are cold-blooded creatures that have gills and fins and are designed to live in water. Humans are warm-blooded beings who have lungs and legs and are created to live on land. Fish spend their days swimming, sleeping, and eating, but people—through imagination, intellect, and ingenuity—talk on telephones, fly in airplanes, and a few have even walked on the moon.

Fish and people have very little in common. The same is true of saints and sinners. Although sinners sin and saints sin at times, by nature they are nothing alike. You must begin to see yourself as God sees you. If you have a distorted view of your spiritual identity, you will not recognize or reach your spiritual potential in Christ.

Consider for a moment how this principle operates in other areas of life. Before 1954, no athlete had run a mile in less than four minutes. But once Sir Roger Bannister broke that barrier, the world realized it could be done. Other athletes soon accomplished the same feat.

God wants you to realize that you are a saint who can live a holy life. Let's look at five reasons why God calls you a saint. The acrostic SAINT will help you remember that God...

S	*Sees* you as completely righteous in Christ
A	*Accepts* Christ's payment for all your sins
I	*Imparts* righteousness into your character and conduct
N	*Neutralized* the power sin had over you
T	*Tolerates* no condemnation of you[2]

GOD SEES YOU AS COMPLETELY RIGHTEOUS IN CHRIST

Paul testifies in Philippians 3:8,9, "I consider everything a loss compared to the surpassing greatness of knowing Christ Jesus my Lord, for whose sake I have lost all things. I consider them rubbish, that I may gain Christ and be found in Him, not having a righteousness of my own that comes from the law, but that which is through faith in Christ—the righteousness that comes from God and is by faith" (NIV).

Across the world, people attempt to be righteous by regularly attending a church, temple, synagogue, or mosque. Others endure physical hardships, perform pilgrimages, or contribute money. But human righteousness will never attain right standing with our holy Creator. As Isaiah declares, "When we proudly display our righteous deeds, we find they are but filthy rags" (Isaiah 64:6).

We are saints not because we live perfect lives, but because we have been forgiven and cleansed through Christ's sacrifice on the cross. When God looks at us, He does not see our sin. He sees Christ's righteousness!

The powerful minister Henry A. Ironside recalls a time he preached in a small town in Washington. While there, he was the guest of friends who raised sheep. It was lambing season. One morning he watched the new lambs play in the meadow. One lamb especially caught his attention. It appeared to have six legs and its fleece hung loosely from his body. When the preacher mentioned this curiosity, one of the herders caught the lamb and brought it to him. Then the mystery was revealed. Draped across the lamb was the fleece of another lamb which had died from a rattlesnake bite. The "odd-looking" lamb was an orphan, and although the herders had tried to convince the dead lamb's mother to take care of the orphan, the old ewe refused because she did not recognize the lamb's smell. It was not until the herders skinned her own lamb and draped the fleece over the living lamb that she adopted the orphaned lamb as her own.[3]

Jesus sacrificed His life and covered us with His blood so we could be forgiven of our sins. When God looks at us, He sees the righteousness of His perfect, beloved Son. Because of Christ, God is willing to adopt us as His own.

As we explored in Chapter 3, seeing ourselves as God sees us is an essential step to living in Christ. We have been redeemed, forgiven, and changed. No matter how polite or civilized we were before we became Christians, at our core we were sinners. No amount of good works or finishing school could change that. We were predisposed to sin. But God removed our sinful nature and gave us a new nature—Christ's nature.

Now we are made new! If God sees us as righteous, who are we to view ourselves any differently? Once we understand our righteousness in Christ by faith, we will be able to live a victorious life in Christ. Only then can we fulfill the command God gave to Israel through Moses, "You must be holy because I, the LORD your God, am holy" (Leviticus 19:2).

GOD ACCEPTS CHRIST'S PAYMENT FOR ALL YOUR SINS

The Bible explains, "You were dead because of your sins and because your sinful nature was not yet cut away. Then God made you alive with Christ. He forgave all our sins. He canceled the record that contained the charges against us. He took it and destroyed it by nailing it to Christ's cross" (Colossians 2:13,14).

When Christ died on the cross, He did not pay for just the small sins or only some of your sins. God took all of your sins—past, present, and future—and nailed them to Christ's cross.

Shortly after Vonette and I started Campus Crusade for Christ at UCLA, I met a very wealthy man. He owned five newspapers and seemingly had it all. But in reality, his life was in chaos. He was an alcoholic. He had already been married and divorced twice. Now his current marriage was on the rocks.

One night, he and his wife accompanied me to a church service. When I gave the invitation to receive Christ, he and his wife slipped out the door. But later, as we walked to the car, he asked me if it was too late for them to receive Christ. We drove home, got down on our knees, and they invited Christ into their hearts.

From that point on, he began to read his Bible for hours. He never took another drink of alcohol. And he became one of the most influential businessmen I have ever known. He generously spent a large part of his wealth to promote the Presidential prayer breakfast and sponsor World Vision banquets for needy children. He ministered with me on skid row and in jails. God mightily used him to reach thousands of leading businessmen for Christ. Truly, his sins were forgiven and he became a new creature.

How marvelous that all of our sins have been washed away because of the sacrifice of our loving Savior. The Bible proclaims, "Now your sins have been washed away, and you have been set apart for God. You have been made right with God because of what the Lord Jesus Christ and the Spirit of our God have done for you" (1 Corinthians 6:11).

GOD IMPARTS RIGHTEOUSNESS INTO YOUR CHARACTER AND CONDUCT

Scripture teaches that the power to be holy comes from God. "Now may the God of peace make you holy in every way, and may your whole spirit and soul and body be kept blameless until that day when our Lord Jesus Christ comes again. God, who calls you, is faithful; He will do this" (1 Thessalonians 5:23,24).

Shortly after Saint Augustine's dramatic conversion to Christianity, he was strolling down a street in Milan, Italy. A prostitute he had known intimately in his wild, pre-Christian days accosted him. She called to him, but he kept walking.

"Augustine," she called again, "it is I!"

Without slowing down, Augustine replied, "Yes, but it is no longer I."

How true! Because each of us is a new creation, we no longer are compelled to commit the sins we have in the past. Because of our Savior's sacrifice and the power of the Holy Spirit who lives within us, we have a choice. We do not have to sin.

Imagine for a moment that your old life is a garden filled with weeds. God wants to plant and cultivate holiness there. The new life He offers is a beautiful garden bursting with color and enticing fragrances. But you believe, "It's no use bothering with my garden. I have always been a weed patch, and I will never be anything else." This wrong thinking keeps you from blossoming into the lush garden God desires you to be.

Your Master Gardener has planted righteousness within you. The more you allow Him to fertilize it with His Word and water it with His Spirit, the more it will flourish and blossom into every corner of your heart and life.

Paul declared, "This is my prayer: that your love may abound more and more in knowledge and depth of insight, so that you may be able to discern what is best and may be pure and blameless until the day of Christ, filled with the fruit of righteousness that comes through Jesus Christ—to the glory and praise of God" (Philippians 1:9–11, NIV). Ask God to produce an abundant harvest of righteousness in the garden of your life.

There is something else this Master Gardener has done for us…

GOD NEUTRALIZED THE POWER SIN HAD OVER YOU

In Scripture we find this marvelous Emancipation Proclamation from sin, "Now you are free from the power of sin and have become slaves of God. Now you do those things that lead to holiness and result in eternal life" (Romans 6:22).

As a saint, sin no longer has power over you.

Suppose you have a job and your boss is fired. Then you are assigned to report to a new supervisor. Suddenly, your old boss shows up and starts telling you what to do.

Are you going to obey him? Of course not! Your old boss has no authority over you! You can ask your new boss to deal with this person for you.

Sin and Satan are like that old boss. They have no authority. They have been fired! And Jesus, your new boss, is always available to deal with them when you ask Him.

As saints in Christ, we are new creatures. Sin no longer has power over us. As we learned earlier through the CROSS acrostic, we are to regard ourselves as dead to sin and alive in Christ.

The Scriptures encourage us, "[Christ] died once to defeat sin, and now He lives for the glory of God. So you should consider yourselves dead to sin and able to live for the glory of God through Christ Jesus" (Romans 6:10,11).

A seminary student had been learning about the concept of being dead to sin in one of his classes. One night when he was alone at the funeral home where he worked part-time, he decided to prove the point to himself once and for all. In a nearby room lay a cadaver that was being prepared for a viewing the following day. The dead man was known to be an alcoholic. His widow had even tearfully admitted that his habit had greatly hastened his death.

The student pulled from his backpack a can of beer he had bought for the experiment, and crept into the room. Suddenly, he jumped up and yelled at the dead body. The body did not flinch. The student then waved the can of beer in front of the dead body. Nothing. He even opened the can and placed it on the man's chest. No hand reached up to grab the beer. The body in the casket was dead. It could not respond.

The clamor and seduction of sin is all around us. Daily we are confronted with temptation. When we believe that we are dead to sin and

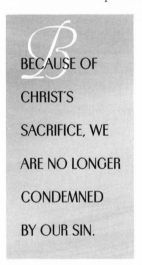

BECAUSE OF CHRIST'S SACRIFICE, WE ARE NO LONGER CONDEMNED BY OUR SIN.

draw upon the power of the Holy Spirit, we can live a victorious, overcoming life (Galatians 5:16,17). We can move from the experience of living in bondage to sin as described in Romans 7 to the hope of victory described in Romans 8.

The Word of God promises, "Remember that the temptations that come into your life are no different from what others experience. And God is faithful. He will keep the temptation from becoming so strong that you can't stand up against it. When you are tempted, He will show you a way out so that you will not give in to it" (1 Corinthians 10:13).

I memorized this verse as a young Christian. I shudder to think what my life would be like now if I had not claimed this promise on thousands of occasions through the years. Each time I am tempted, I ask the Holy Spirit to cleanse my mind of any evil thoughts with the precious blood of Jesus. I invite Him to fill me, empower me, and control me. I ask Him to orchestrate my thinking so I will think holy thoughts and not continue to be plagued by satanic attacks. It always works. God is faithful to lead each of us out of any temptation if we rely on Him.

GOD TOLERATES NO CONDEMNATION OF YOU

The Bible assures us, "There is no condemnation for those who belong to Christ Jesus" (Romans 8:1). Because of Christ's sacrifice, we are no longer condemned by our sin. As saints, we have been freed from eternal death, which is the consequence of sin. We can now enjoy complete forgiveness. Everything we have done in the past—and every thought, word, and deed in the future—is forgiven. Christ paid for all of our sins, once and for all.

But many of us still feel condemned. That is because of the great accuser, Satan. He enjoys reminding us of our failures and weaknesses. Even when we have confessed our sin to God and turned from our sinful ways, Satan still tries to make us feel guilty. As a result, we often wallow in false guilt—guilt over sins already forgiven or guilt for something God does not even consider as sin. Why does Satan do this? He knows that if we are discouraged by feelings of inadequacy and guilt we will not be able to live a victorious and fruitful life for Christ.

But our merciful God does not listen to the accusations of Satan. He sees you as holy, and He wants to bring you into a full experience of that holiness. But you must cooperate with Him. You must open the gate to your inner garden and give the Master Gardener full access. How do you do this?

The answer is contained in the CROSS acrostic from Chapter 3. To give God free rein in your life, you must offer your body to God as an instrument of righteousness and surrender your will to Him continuously.

Henrietta Mears, a dearly loved Bible teacher who greatly encouraged me in the Lord, inspired her students with the following analogy:

> A bird is free in the air. Place a bird in water and he has lost his liberty. A fish is free in the water, but leave him on the sand and he perishes. He is out of his realm. So, young people, the Christian is free when he does the will of God and is obedient to God's commands. This is as natural a realm for God's child as the water is for the fish, or the air for the bird.

You will not experience contentment by following your own will. You will be like a fish gasping for air on the beach. As Christians, we reach our fullest potential when we are in the center of God's will. There is no greater fulfillment than being in the will of God. Only there will we experience complete satisfaction. That is where we belong.

Daily surrender your heart, mind, soul, and life to God to be used for His glorious purpose. Seek first His kingdom. Then you will experience the reality of being set apart for Him; you will be called holy;

and you will fully understand what it means to be His saint.

In the Old Testament, the Lord instructed Moses to attach a plate of pure gold to Aaron's turban as he ministered in the Tabernacle. Inscribed on the plate were the words, "Holy to Yahweh." Because of the marvelous sacrifice of our loving Savior, Jesus Christ, we, too, have the words "Holy to Yahweh" sealed on our foreheads. We also minister as God's holy priests. Revelation 1:6 proclaims, "[Christ] has made us His kingdom and His priests who serve before God His Father. Give to Him everlasting glory!"

If we acknowledge our true identity—that we are saints—and live accordingly, we will be like the people described in Psalm 1:1–3:

> Oh, the joys of those who do not follow the advice of the wicked, or stand around with sinners, or join in with scoffers. But they delight in doing everything the Lord wants; day and night they think about His law. They are like trees planted along the riverbank, bearing fruit each season without fail. Their leaves never wither, and in all they do, they prosper.

When we delight in God and do His will, we are like trees along a riverbank bearing luscious fruit each season without fail. We are also the kind of people who can best minister to other believers and reach the world for Christ. We will explore this part of our supernatural identity in the next chapter when we learn what it means to be a member of Christ's body.

Life Application

Thank Your Heavenly Father—Thank God that He has set you apart as His saint! Praise Him that He sees you as righteous because you have been clothed in Christ's perfect righteousness. Thank Him that He is developing in you a noble character and holy conduct. Express your gratitude because you now have the power to resist the temptation to sin. And worship Him who protects you from all condemnation.

Renew Your Mind—Memorize the following verse and acrostic:

- "I consider everything a loss compared to the surpassing greatness of knowing Christ Jesus my Lord, for whose sake I have lost all things. I consider them rubbish, that I may gain Christ and be found in Him, not having a righteousness of my own that comes from the law, but that which is through faith in Christ—the righteousness that comes from God and is by faith" (Philippians 3:8,9, NIV).

- The SAINT acrostic will help you remember that God...
  Sees you as completely righteous in Christ
  Accepts Christ's payment for all your sins
  Imparts righteousness into your character and conduct
  Neutralized the power sin had over you
  Tolerates no condemnation of you

Reflect on Your New Life in Christ—Picture yourself first standing before God in the rags of your own righteousness. Then watch as those dirty rags are removed and all the wrong and hurtful things you have done in your life are washed away. Then, see Christ's gleaming white robe of righteousness draped around you. You are clean. You are set apart. You are a saint!

Share the Blessings—Encourage the members of your Bible study group or local church with the truth that they are special people set apart for God's glory—a community of saints!

CHAPTER 7

Living as a Member of the Body of Christ

*I*n a recent poll, 81 percent of Americans agreed that "an individual should arrive at his or her own religious belief independent of any church or synagogue." In fact, one respondent named Sheila stated, "I can't remember the last time I went to church. But my faith in myself has carried me a long way. It's 'Sheila-ism.' Just my own little voice."[1]

Individualism and autonomy are two characteristics cherished by most Americans and numerous cultures around the world. We pride ourselves on being independent and self-sufficient. But is this how our loving Father wants us to live out our faith? Previously we explored the wonderful blessings of being a child of God. But as God's children, do you and I have a need for spiritual siblings or family? Does Jesus Christ want us to "go it on our own" or to belong to a community of believers?

Perhaps we can learn a lesson from one of God's most amazing creations.

Towering along California's northern coastline are the largest living things on earth—the majestic redwood trees. These mighty monarchs pierce the sky at heights of 300 feet and boast a circumference of more than 40 feet. The Grizzly Giant tree—the largest of the sequoias

—is more than 2,500 years old. One would think that trees this large and ancient must have massive root systems that plunge hundreds of feet into the earth. However, this is not so. A redwood's roots are actually quite shallow, lying barely below the soil. The secret to the sequoias' strength is that these majestic trees grow only in groves so each tree's roots can intertwine with the roots of the trees near it. When the strong winds blow, they hold each other up![2]

JUST LIKE THE CROSS, OUR IDENTITY IN CHRIST HAS BOTH A VERTICAL AND A HORIZONTAL ASPECT.

In a similar way, our wonderful God created us to need others. He did not intend for us to live in isolation, and He does not want us to live out our Christian faith alone.

Just as the cross has a vertical and a horizontal piece, our identity in Christ has both a vertical and a horizontal aspect. As believers, we are related to God, but, like the mighty redwoods, we are also connected to each other. We belong to the community of believers. We are part of one spiritual family, which the Bible compares to a body. In 1 Corinthians 12:27, Paul explains, "All of you together are Christ's body, and each one of you is a separate and necessary part of it."

As members of the body of Christ, our identity has three dimensions:

■ Each of us is *distinctive*. We have a unique and significant role to play in the body of Christ.

■ Each of us is *dependent*. We need and are needed by the other members.

■ Each of us must be *directed*. We must work together under orderly leadership for the good of the whole.

Consider the following illustration.

A study was conducted to discover how members of the different sections of a symphony orchestra perceive each other. Surveying members of eleven major orchestras produced these interesting results: Percussionists were seen as "insensitive, unintelligent, and hard-of-hearing, yet fun-loving." String players were considered "arrogant, stuffy, and unathletic." "Loud" was the main adjective used to describe the brass players. And the woodwinds were viewed as "quiet and meticulous, though a bit egotistical."[3] If the members of the orchestra are truly so different, how do they produce such beautiful music?

An orchestra is composed of many different instruments, and the musicians playing them have very *distinctive* personalities and perceptions of each other. At the same time, each orchestra member is *dependent* upon the others when they perform. If they set their differences aside and are *directed* by the conductor, they can make magnificent music together. But if they ignore the conductor and do their own thing, all they will produce is a terrible noise.

Understanding our three-dimensional identity as members of Christ's body can help us make beautiful music instead of a terrible noise. Although each of us is *distinctive*, we must *depend* on each other and allow Christ to *direct* us.

Christ's purpose for His body is to mature us as believers and reach the world through us. We cannot accomplish this alone. Only by working together in community can we be Christ's body—His hands and feet—ministering to the world He loves.

Let us look at six aspects of our identity as members of Christ's body. The acrostic MEMBER will help you remember that God...

M   *Made* you part of His spiritual family

E   *Equipped* you with spiritual gifts for ministry

M   *Matched* you with specific needs in the body of Christ

B   *Baptized* you into one body for unity

E   *Enlisted* you to build up others in Christ

R   *Redeemed* you to love others[4]

GOD MADE YOU PART OF HIS SPIRITUAL FAMILY

The Bible tells us, "You Gentiles are no longer strangers and foreigners. You are citizens along with all of God's holy people. You are members of God's family" (Ephesians 2:19).

What an amazing privilege that God has chosen us to be part of His family!

Vonette and our sons are my immediate physical family. But I have a large extended family as well. The same is true of each of us spiritually.

Our immediate spiritual family is the local body of believers where we fellowship and worship. But we are also part of an extended family—the universal church—all believers everywhere for all time. No matter our nationality, race, gender, politics, or denomination, we are *blood relatives*. We are related by the blood of Christ, which was shed for us when He died on the cross for our sins.

It is said, "Blood is thicker than water." Our blood relation through Christ should be thicker than any earthly differences. Knowing that God specially chose each of us for His spiritual family should make us feel valued and loved, and should also cause us to appreciate all of our "brothers and sisters in Christ." When we realize how privileged we are to be part of God's family, we will begin to treat our spiritual family with love and respect. Then our local "body" will become a safe, loving community where we experience a sense of belonging and God's holy presence.

To have this type of community, spiritual "family time" is important. The Bible declares, "Let us not neglect our meeting together, as some people do, but encourage and warn each other, especially now that the day of His coming back again is drawing near" (Hebrews 10:25).

Our God knows that we need to be fed and encouraged by our fellow believers. One of the ways we maintain an intimate relationship with Christ is by staying vitally connected to the body of Christ. Imagine an ear sitting off by itself trying to hear. Equally ridiculous is the belief that we do not need to be part of a community of believers. Just as we need the love, support, and nurture of our physical family, we need the same from our spiritual family. This is where we can encourage each other, grow to maturity, learn family values, and discover our gifts.

GOD EQUIPPED YOU WITH SPIRITUAL GIFTS FOR MINISTRY

According to the Scriptures, "God has given gifts to each of you from His great variety of spiritual gifts. Manage them well so that God's generosity can flow through you" (1 Peter 4:10).

God has generously bestowed spiritual talents and abilities on each of us so that together we can fulfill the amazing plan God has for His church in this world and the next.

Paul explains, "He is the one who gave these gifts to the church: the apostles, the prophets, the evangelists, and the pastors and teachers. Their responsibility is to equip God's people to do His work and build up the church, the body of Christ" (Ephesians 4:11,12).

God is not concerned how our gifts compare to another believer's spiritual abilities. He cares about how well we use what He has given us. Jesus illustrates this truth in the parable of the talents. A man entrusted three servants with various talents or measures of money. One servant received five talents, another two, and a third servant one.

The first two servants doubled their talents and earned their master's approval. He was pleased because they had faithfully invested what they had been given. But the third servant buried his talent and did nothing with it. Consequently, his talent was taken away and given to the one who had ten talents (Matthew 25:14–30).

In the same way, our mighty God has graciously and generously bestowed abilities and resources upon us. But He does not want us to squander them or let them sit idle. God does not give us spiritual gifts to glorify ourselves. He wants us to use them for *His* glory as we minister to others.

Unfortunately, even the most wonderful gift, improperly used, can do more harm than good.

The concept of a good gift gone bad is brought home by the Christian physician and author Dr. Paul Brand. In one of his books, he recalls how a patient came to him with severe spastic twitching in his neck. A group of muscles was out of control in its use of the "gift" of motion. While movement is normally helpful to the body, this uncontrolled motion in the neck was horribly disruptive. It ultimately required surgical intervention.[5]

God does not want this to happen with our spiritual gifts. He wants us to use them under Christ's direction for the good of Christ's body. To do so, we need to *discover* and *develop* our gifts. We can do this by learning about our gifts in the Bible and asking other believers what they perceive to be our strengths.

Ask yourself: When I spend time with other Christians, what needs do I notice first? What tugs at my heart? This can be an indicator of your spiritual gifts. But be careful. Do not become so worried about discerning or using your spiritual gifts that you lose your willingness to serve. It is through service that your spiritual gifts are revealed and developed. And remember, the body of Christ needs the gifts and service of every member.

GOD MATCHED YOU WITH SPECIFIC NEEDS IN THE BODY OF CHRIST

The Scriptures explain our role in the church this way: "We will hold to the truth in love, becoming more and more in every way like Christ, who is the head of His body, the church. Under His direction, the whole body is fitted together perfectly. As each part does its own special work, it helps the other parts grow, so that the whole body is healthy and growing and full of love" (Ephesians 4:15,16).

THE BODY OF CHRIST NEEDS THE GIFTS AND SERVICE OF EVERY MEMBER.

Every believer has a vital part to play in Christ's body. The Bible explains, "In fact, some of the parts that seem weakest and least important are really the most necessary" (1 Corinthians 12:22).

In March 1981, President Reagan was shot. We all recognize how important the president of our country is, especially in times of war or economic crisis. Yet while he was hospitalized for several weeks, the government went on. That event probably had no impact on your daily life.

However, several years later, the garbage collectors in Philadelphia went on strike. The city was a mess! Trash began to pile up until the rotting garbage became a health hazard. If you lived in Philadelphia during that strike, I am sure you felt the impact of your garbage collector's absence.

The office of the presidency is highly esteemed and vitally important, yet even he is dependent on his garbage collector!

In a similar way, the roles in the family of God that are less visible are vitally needed to support the more visible work of pastors, teachers, and evangelists. Think back to the human body. We rarely pay any attention to our kidneys or liver, but if they malfunction, our skin and hair will show it and our whole body will eventually suffer. Instead of envying those with the most visible positions, we must faithfully develop and use the gifts we have to fulfill the unique purpose

God has for each one of us.

Nicolo Paganini, the famous violinist, willed his cherished violin to the city of Genoa on one condition—that the instrument never be played. But his request was tragic, because a violin is not to be viewed, but played. In fact, the precious wood of a violin shows little wear if it is used and handled. However, set aside and never touched, his violin began to decay. Today, the beautiful, mellow-toned instrument sits worm-eaten in its beautiful case, without value except as a relic.[6]

Like that beautiful violin, each member of the body of Christ is precious, but we must each play our part. Ephesians 2:10 explains, "We are God's masterpiece. He has created us anew in Christ Jesus, so that we can do the good things He planned for us long ago."

Christ gave each of us gifts for a purpose. We must use our abilities and resources, or they, like that violin, will decay, and we will miss out on the blessings of service to our Master.

If our goal is God's glory, we will delight in the ministry He has given us. And we will work together in *unity*.

GOD BAPTIZED YOU INTO ONE BODY FOR UNITY

The Bible declares, "Some of us are Jews, some are Gentiles, some are slaves, and some are free. But we have all been baptized into Christ's body by one Spirit, and we have all received the same Spirit" (1 Corinthians 12:13).

Our marvelous Creator does not want differences in personalities, backgrounds, worldly status, or spiritual gifts to create discord in the body of Christ. God wants His family to live in unity. Ephesians 4:3 challenges us, "Always keep yourselves united in the Holy Spirit, and bind yourselves together with peace."

Our wise heavenly Father has given us abilities and resources to "equip God's people to do His work and build up the church, the body of Christ, until we come to such unity in our faith and knowledge of God's Son that we will be mature and full grown in the Lord, measuring up to the full stature of Christ" (Ephesians 4:12,13).

We all have a particular role in God's divine economy, but we are not fulfilling that role unless we have a spirit of cooperation and partnership. The Bible explains it this way: "Just as our bodies have many parts and each part has a special function, so it is with Christ's body. We are all parts of His one body, and each of us has different work to do. And since we are all one body in Christ, we belong to each other, and each of us needs all the others" (Romans 12:4,5).

Modern medicine has only strengthened this biblical analogy. The human body is a marvel of "unity in diversity," beginning at the cellular level.

We now know that each human body is a vast array of different cells all working together in concert. Malfunction of even a few cells soon affects nearby cells and may cause serious illness, such as cancer.

Because of the interdependence of its parts, the human body needs direction, which is the function of the brain. Likewise, Christ—the head of the church—directs His body. As each distinct member of Christ's body follows His direction, the spiritual family will be united in harmony.

Imagine what would happen if your liver said, "I don't want to function anymore because I can't stand the kidneys?" You would be in big trouble. In fact, the biggest argument people make against Christianity is the way we condemn and criticize each other. This is not a coincidence. One of Satan's favorite schemes is to promote dissension among believers. He does not want the church to live in unity because he is frightened by the potential power and effectiveness of a unified body of believers. So he sows criticism, envy, and discord—anything to fracture godly harmony and unity.

But God wants us to experience a unity that is divine. Listen to Jesus' prayer for us: "My prayer for all of them is that they will be one, just as You and I are one, Father—that just as You are in Me and I am in You, so they will be in Us, and the world will believe You sent Me" (John 17:21).

The path to unity is humility, submission, and forgiveness. Paul urges us, "Is there any encouragement from belonging to Christ? Any comfort from His love? Any fellowship together in the Spirit? Are your hearts tender and sympathetic? Then make me truly happy by agreeing wholeheartedly with each other, loving one another, and working together with one heart and purpose. Don't be selfish; don't live to make a good impression on others. Be humble, thinking of others as better than yourself" (Philippians 2:1–3).

If we are humble, we will have no problem submitting to those in the church whom God has placed in authority over us. Also, we will be willing to forfeit some of our own desires to meet the needs of other members of our spiritual family. This attitude of submission promotes unity. Paul instructs the church at Ephesus, "Submit to one another out of reverence for Christ" (Ephesians 5:21, NIV).

Forgiveness is also essential to establishing unity in God's spiritual family. Paul writes, "You must make allowance for each other's faults and forgive the person who offends you. Remember, the Lord forgave you, so you must forgive others" (Colossians 3:13). Because everyone in God's spiritual family is still very human, disagreements and wrong-doing will arise. When they do, we must remember how much God has forgiven us, and, in appreciation, bestow the same forgiveness on others so healing can take place.

Every time we pray with an unforgiving attitude toward someone, we condemn ourselves because Jesus instructs us to pray, "Forgive us our debts, as we have also forgiven our debtors" (Matthew 6:12, NIV). Through the years, I have encountered people who have had a discordant influence in my life and ministry. But always, as I have chosen to love them by faith, God has helped me to build bridges that have resulted in making friends out of enemies.

By demonstrating humility, submission, and forgiveness, we follow Christ's example. And we will be better able to fulfill God's plan for us.

GOD ENLISTED YOU TO BUILD UP OTHERS IN CHRIST

The Bible exhorts, "Think of ways to encourage one another to outbursts of love and good deeds" (Hebrews 10:24).

How often do any of us encourage and challenge our Christian brothers and sisters to live a life of love and good deeds? Yet God has called us to do just that. Our heavenly Father knows that His spiritual family will be healthy only if each member lovingly compels the others to become more Christlike and to accomplish God's plan for them.

Proverbs 27:17 provides wise insight, "As iron sharpens iron, a friend sharpens a friend." Just as two pieces of iron rubbed together produces sharp and effective tools, so we refine each other as we pray, worship, and serve together. Too often, Christian brothers and sisters tear each other down with criticism and petty rivalries. But God wants everything about our lives—what we say and how we act—to encourage fellow Christians in Christ.

In the CROSS acrostic, we learned that we must offer our body to God as an instrument of righteousness. Offering all that we have and are to God also means dedicating ourselves to the welfare of God's church. Our presence in God's spiritual family can produce either love or hatred, unity or discord. If we live and speak in a righteous manner, we will be an example of godly living to all around us. And if we consciously season our speech with love and encouragement, we will positively inspire those God has placed within our sphere of influence.

Henry Ford was once quite discouraged. His newly built combustion engine was criticized and ridiculed because most mechanical experts of his day believed that the "horseless carriage" would be powered by electricity, not gasoline.

One evening, he attended a dinner where Thomas Edison was seated several chairs away. As Ford explained his engine to the men near him, Edison overheard and moved closer. Finally, Edison asked Ford to make a sketch of the engine. After studying the drawing, Edison suddenly banged his fist on the table. "Young man," he said, "that's the thing! You have it!"

Ford later stated, "The thump of that fist upon the table was worth worlds to me."[7]

God wants us to build up and affirm our brothers and sisters in Christ. We are to admonish—warn, advise, and urge—other believers as we worship together.

Colossians 3:16 declares, "Let the word of Christ dwell in you richly as you teach and admonish one another with all wisdom, and as you sing psalms, hymns and spiritual songs with gratitude in your hearts to God" (NIV). As we feed on the Word of God, we are to exhort each other with God's truth and wisdom. What should our motivation be? Gratitude for all the wonderful blessings God has given us.

In 1953, a British expedition set out to climb Mount Everest, the highest mountain in the world. Two in that expedition—Sir Edmund Hillary and Tenzing Norgay—were the first to scale this formidable mountain. However, they could not have accomplished such a feat without the entire crew, and especially the selflessness of two climbers in their expedition. Two in the crew almost reached the summit, but ran out of daylight. When they abandoned their quest, they left their extra oxygen tanks behind so that others could use them. Two days later, Hillary and Norgay reached the peak. But on their return down the mountain, they ran out of oxygen. If they had not found the oxygen tanks the other members of their crew had left behind, Hillary and Norgay would not have lived to tell of their grand accomplishment.[8]

As we travel together on the amazing adventure of the Christian life, we are always to consider the needs of our fellow believers, not just our own. The body of Christ has an amazing purpose, and we cannot fulfill God's calling by ourselves. We must work together and stimulate each other to Christlike behavior as we live for Him.

To do this, we must honestly examine ourselves. Ask yourself: Do my words and deeds encourage the people in my local church? Do I spur others to love and good deeds, or do I criticize and tear others down?

Keep in mind the words of Hebrews 3:13: "Encourage one another daily, as long as it is called Today, so that none of you may be hardened by sin's deceitfulness" (NIV).

GOD REDEEMED YOU TO LOVE OTHERS

The Bible proclaims, "You can have sincere love for each other as brothers and sisters because you were cleansed from your sins when you accepted the truth of the Good News. So see to it that you really do love each other intensely with all your hearts" (1 Peter 1:22).

God wants the members of His spiritual family to love each other. Jesus told His disciples that love would be a hallmark of His church. "I am giving you a new commandment: Love each other. Just as I have loved you, you should love each other. Your love for one another will prove to the world that you are My disciples" (John 13:34,35).

Calvin Hunt was an alcoholic and a drug addict. He worked during the day and got high at night and on weekends. He often slept all night in a neighbor's doghouse because he was too ashamed to go home. Seeing his wife and children was a painful reminder of how he had failed them and how desperate his life had become.

But his wife prayed for him, as did the members of her church. One night while she and the children were at a prayer meeting, Calvin sneaked into their apartment to take a shower, put on clean clothes, and eat. As he lay down for a nap, he heard what sounded like people weeping. He checked the closets and under the bed, but no one was there.

Unnerved, he hurried to the church to find his wife. As he entered the sanctuary, the same sound of weeping greeted him. There in intense prayer were Calvin's wife and members of her church. Many of these people had never met him, yet they had been weeping and praying over him for an hour. Their love helped bring Calvin to a new and abundant life in Christ.[9]

When members of the body of Christ love each other, they reflect Christ to the world.

Consider the following illustration. At many amusement parks and other tourist attractions you can find painted on placards the faceless body of a muscle man, a voluptuous beauty, or even a clown. Many of us have had our pictures taken standing behind such painted frames. As we place our head on the body of some bulging cartoon figure, the image can be hilarious because it is such a mismatch.

But ask yourself this: If the world could see Christ's head on your local body of believers, would it look out of place? Or would people marvel at the fit and be drawn to Him?

We read in 1 John 4:12, "No one has ever seen God. But if we love each other, God lives in us, and His love has been brought to full expression through us."

In 1889, a tower was built for an international exposition. The citizens of the city called the structure "monstrous" and demanded it be torn down as soon as the exposition was over. Yet from the start, the architect believed in his creation and boldly defended it against those who wanted to destroy it. He believed the tower was destined for greatness.

Today this tower is considered one of the architectural wonders of the modern world, and it is the primary landmark of Paris, France. The architect was Alexandre Gustave Eiffel, and the tower, of course, is the Eiffel Tower.[10]

Jesus has designed a unique structure that He greatly loves and champions. In the past, He entrusted this unique entity to an unlikely group of disciples. Today He has committed it to our care. Outsiders might view this creation as "monstrous" and believe that we are incapable, but Jesus knows that His structure is destined for greatness.

What is this amazing structure? The church. The body of Christ began with the early disciples and stretches into eternity. It cannot be destroyed. Jesus promises His followers, "Upon this rock I will build my church, and all the powers of hell will not conquer it" (Matthew 16:18).

What a privilege to be members of the body of our Lord! How we should cherish our place in His spiritual family.

The next time you attend your local church, see it through the eyes of your loving Father. Commit yourself to use the gifts God has given you to build up your brothers and sisters and promote unity. And above all, determine to love the wonderful community of believers God has chosen.

The church has an amazing future. It is the beautiful bride of Christ, and someday we will spend eternity with our wonderful bridegroom. On that day, a huge crowd in heaven will shout, "Let us be glad and rejoice and honor Him. For the time has come for the wedding feast of the Lamb, and His bride has prepared herself" (Revelation 19:7).

We will discuss more about our amazing calling in the next chapter when we explore our identity as citizens of Christ's kingdom.

Life Application

Renew Your Mind—Commit the following verses and acrostic to memory:

■ "Since we are all one body in Christ, we belong to each other, and each of us needs all the others" (Romans 12:5).

■ "I am giving you a new commandment: Love each other. Just as I have loved you, you should love each other. Your love for one another will prove to the world that you are My disciples" (John 13:34,35).

■ The MEMBER acrostic will help you remember that God...
Made you part of His spiritual family
Equipped you with spiritual gifts for ministry
Matched you with specific needs in the body of Christ
Baptized you into one body for unity
Enlisted you to build up others in Christ
Redeemed you to love others

Take Up Your Cross—Prayerfully meditate on the five principles of the CROSS acrostic: "Heavenly Father, thank You that I am a new creation and a specially gifted part of Your body. I praise You that I am dead to sin, so jealousy and discord have no power over me. Instead, I offer my body as an instrument of righteousness to promote love and unity. I surrender my will to You, willing to sacrifice my personal desires for the needs of others. Empower me with Your Holy Spirit, I pray. Amen."

Act by Faith—You are a part of an amazing community that spans all nationalities and has an eternal destiny. Invite the Holy Spirit to make this truth real in your life and ministry. Ask God to show you specific needs you can meet in your local church. Pray that He will direct you to people whom you can encourage and disciple. Ask the Holy Spirit to expose anything in your life that promotes divisiveness or disunity. Confess anything that displeases Him, and always look for ways to demonstrate your love to your brothers and sisters in Christ.

CHAPTER 8

Living as a Citizen of Christ's Kingdom

*E*ach of us is a citizen of at least one country, yet most of us do not truly appreciate what citizenship means.

Webster's Dictionary defines citizen as "a native or naturalized member of a state or nation who owes allegiance to its government and is entitled to its protection." We became a citizen by being born in a certain country or by having a country legally adopt us. And because we are citizens, our nation protects our rights and our very lives. But sometimes it is necessary for us to change our citizenship because we are so opposed to our nation's policies and actions.

Albert Einstein was born in Ulm, Germany, and published his most important papers and theories as a German citizen. However, in 1914, after spending several years in Switzerland, he did not renew his German citizenship because he disagreed with his homeland's aims in World War I. Then in 1932, he moved to the United States to escape the rise of fascism in Germany. Can you imagine what would have happened if this extraordinary mind had remained a citizen of Germany during World War II? If his allegiance had been to Hitler and his brilliance had been harnessed to promote Hitler's aim of world dominance? Or perhaps the Nazis would have judged him merely by his Jewish ethnicity and, consequently, would have killed one of the greatest minds of the 20th century in a gas chamber. Instead, he was able to further develop and promote his revolutionary scientific theories while living in safety in the United States. And after the war, he even played an influential role in establishing the nation of Israel.

Another facet of our identity in Christ is that we are citizens of Christ's kingdom. Scripture says, "Our citizenship is in heaven" (Philippians 3:20, NIV). Adoption by God brings an automatic change in our citizenship.

The Bible explains, "[The Father] has rescued us out of the darkness and gloom of Satan's kingdom and brought us into the kingdom of His dear Son" (Colossians 1:13, TLB).

Fortunately, we are not illegal aliens who hope to sample a few blessings of Christ's glorious kingdom before we are discovered and deported. No, we are full citizens, therefore we can enjoy all the rights of our heavenly citizenship.

Because we are citizens of Christ's kingdom, we have a new assurance that God will care for us and supply all our needs. A country takes care of its citizens. The military defends them; the police protect them; and the state educates them. But the Sovereign Ruler of our heavenly kingdom takes care of us even more.

Jesus taught His disciples in the Sermon on the Mount, "Do not worry, saying, 'What shall we eat?' or 'What shall we drink?' or 'What shall we wear?' For the pagans run after all these things, and your heavenly Father knows that you need them. But seek first His kingdom and His righteousness, and all these things will be given to you as well" (Matthew 6:31–33, NIV). Our mighty Lord promises to provide for the citizens of His eternal kingdom.

The honor of citizenship endows us with many rights and privileges, but it also demands certain duties on the part of each citizen. A nation demands allegiance from its citizens. Each day, school children pledge allegiance to the country's flag. And some of us have been called to demonstrate our allegiance by fighting for our country in a time of war.

As Christians, our *allegiance* must be to Christ and His kingdom rather than to the things of this world. Jesus says of His followers, "They are not part of this world any more than I am" (John 17:16). Therefore, the following description should no longer apply to us: "There are many whose conduct shows they are really enemies of the cross of Christ. Their future is eternal destruction. Their god is their appetite, they brag about shameful things, and all they think about is this life here on earth" (Philippians 3:18,19). As children of God, our allegiance is to a kingdom that will endure forever. Our behavior should demonstrate our princely heritage. Paul admonished the church in Colosse, "Since you have been raised to new life with Christ, set your sights on the realities of heaven, where Christ sits at God's right hand in the place of honor and power. Let heaven fill your thoughts. Do not think only about things down here on earth" (Colossians 3:1,2).

If we understand our identity as citizens of Christ's kingdom, we will live differently here on earth. A glorious example of this is the prophet Daniel.

When Daniel was a young man, King Nebuchadnezzar captured Jerusalem, demolished the Temple, and destroyed the city. Daniel was taken to Babylon as a slave where he spent the rest of his life in exile.

Although he lived in Babylon, Daniel knew he was first and foremost a citizen of God's kingdom. He understood where he must place his highest allegiance. As a result, he was salt and light to the greatest pagan rulers of his time.

Let us consider seven aspects of citizenship in Christ's kingdom. The acrostic CITIZEN can help you remember that God...

C   *Chose* you for Christ's unshakable kingdom

I   *Installed* you as a priest in Christ's holy kingdom

T   *Told* you, in the Bible, the secrets of Christ's kingdom

I   *Illuminated* you to be Christ's light to the world

Z   *Zealously* freed you from Satan's kingdom of darkness

E   *Entrusted* you with the keys to Christ's kingdom

N   *Named* you as an ambassador for Christ's kingdom[1]

GOD CHOSE YOU FOR CHRIST'S UNSHAKABLE KINGDOM

The Bible states this wonderful promise, "Long ago, even before He made the world, God loved us and chose us in Christ to be holy and without fault in His eyes" (Ephesians 1:4).

Do you remember those anxious days of childhood when we waited to be picked to play baseball, kickball, or some other sport? Two of our peers would scrutinize the line-up and decide who they wanted on their team. How we hoped we would be chosen!

The amazing truth is that we have been chosen, and not by some childhood peer. Our awesome Creator selected each of us to be part of His eternal kingdom! Jesus told His followers, "So don't be afraid, little flock. For it gives your Father great happiness to give you the Kingdom" (Luke 12:32).

Our loving heavenly Father has chosen us to be His children and to enjoy Christ's unshakable kingdom. And this is not just any kingdom. Earthly kingdoms come and go, but Christ's kingdom is supreme above all others and will last for all eternity.

Daniel prophesied about Christ's eternal kingdom:

> In my vision at night I looked, and there before me was one like a son of man, coming with the clouds of heaven. He approached the Ancient of Days and was led into His presence. He was given authority, glory and sovereign power; all peoples, nations and men of every language worshiped Him. His dominion is an everlasting dominion that will not pass away, and His kingdom is one that will never be destroyed (Daniel 7:13,14, NIV).

How wonderful that our incredible Creator chose us to be citizens of Christ's unshakable kingdom!

GOD INSTALLED YOU AS A PRIEST IN CHRIST'S HOLY KINGDOM

Scripture tells us, "You are a chosen people. You are a kingdom of priests, God's holy nation, His very own possession. This is so you can show others the goodness of God, for He called you out of the darkness into His wonderful light" (1 Peter 2:9).

In Old Testament times, priests would enter God's holy temple and offer sacrifices to atone for the sins of the people of Israel and themselves. King David appointed priests to sing and play instruments in worship to the glorious Lord of Hosts. Often, Levites, such as Ezra the scribe, taught the people God's Word and commands.

In the same way, we, as God's chosen ones, are to offer our worship, ourselves, and all we possess to our holy Lord.

How our glorious Creator enjoys the praises of His people! Our worship is a sweet sacrifice to Him. The Word of God declares, "Through Jesus, therefore, let us continually offer to God a sacrifice of praise—the fruit of lips that confess His name" (Hebrews 13:15, NIV). The psalmist proclaims, "Shout with joy to God, all the earth! Sing to the glory of His name; offer Him glory and praise!" (Psalm 66:1,2, NIV).

Our God also wants us to give ourselves and all we possess to Him in holy worship. As the third point of the CROSS acrostic explains, we do this by offering our body to God as an instrument of righteousness.

This is what Paul means when he exhorts believers in Romans 12:1, "Dear brothers and sisters, I plead with you to give your bodies to God. Let them be a living and holy sacrifice—the kind He will accept. When you think of what He has done for you, is this too much to ask?"

Offering our bodies means committing to the Lord and His work all that we are and have. This is a pleasing sacrifice that we can offer to our gracious God. As priests, we are to place ourselves and our possessions on the altar before our Lord as love offerings, dedicating everything to Him for His use and service.

> AS PRIESTS, WE ARE TO PLACE OURSELVES AND OUR POSSES-SIONS ON THE ALTAR BEFORE OUR LORD.

As priests in Christ's kingdom, we can also mediate for others through intercessory prayer. In the same way that the priests of the Old Testament came before God with the sins and needs of the people of Israel, we can come before our Lord in prayer with the needs of others. The Bible declares, "Pray at all times and on every occasion in the power of the Holy Spirit. Stay alert and be persistent in your prayers for all Christians everywhere" (Ephesians 6:18).

Not only has God installed us as priests in Christ's kingdom, but we are also the temple of God! Paul challenged the believers in Corinth with these words, "Do you not know that your body is a temple of the Holy Spirit, who is in you, whom you have received from God?" (1 Corinthians 6:19, NIV). God has chosen every believer to be a temple in which He lives.

Because the Holy Spirit lives within us, we have constant access to our glorious Father. This is a privilege the priests of the Old Testament never knew. Only once a year could the high priest enter the holiest part of the temple, called the Holy of Holies, to offer a sacrifice for the people. We have access to our holy God every moment of every day!

Scripture says, "You have caused them to become God's kingdom and His priests. And they will reign on the earth" (Revelation 5:10).

Daniel fulfilled the priestly role of all believers. He lived a holy life and served as a mediator between God and people. The Bible tells us he was a man of prayer. He prayed specifically for the restoration of the Jewish people. We can assume he also prayed for the nonbelievers around him. And he delivered God's messages to the pagan kings of his day.

As believers, we are also called to be priests and mediators. Our purpose in the world is to talk to God about people and to people about God. We are called to live holy lives that demonstrate our love for God and our allegiance to Christ's kingdom. We can do this because our mighty God has revealed His word and insights, not only to Old Testament prophets like Daniel, but to you and me as well.

GOD TOLD YOU, IN THE BIBLE, THE SECRETS OF CHRIST'S KINGDOM

Jesus told His disciples, "You have been permitted to understand the secrets of the Kingdom of Heaven, but others have not" (Matthew 13:11).

Because we are citizens of Christ's kingdom, God enables us to see reality through the truth of His Word and His Holy Spirit.

Before the government of the Soviet Union collapsed, I visited Moscow and other prominent cities of that country several times. To protect Soviet citizens from the influences of the West, the government carefully monitored the information people received about their nation and the rest of the world. Often I would hear the misconceptions generated by this propaganda: that they were the chosen people, that their economy was much stronger than America's, that Americans were backward and deprived. However, because I was a visitor I had the benefit of information outside that closed system, and I was able to see the propaganda for the lies they were.

The same is true in the moral realm around us. We are bombarded with propaganda every day through advertisements, billboards, radio, television, and newspapers. But because we have been given the Word of God and the Holy Spirit, we are able to see the propaganda of this world system as the lies they truly are.

Because we are citizens of heaven, we can differentiate between reality and illusion. When the media tries to define our identity by our yearly salary or the kind of car we drive, we can recognize this as a lie to be rejected. We will not be deceived by the current cultural mantra or the latest opinion poll if we study God's Word and allow the Holy Spirit to enlighten us.

During Daniel's lifetime, the king's wise men and astrologers did not know the one true God or His ways. So when King Nebuchadnezzar had troubling prophetic dreams, they could not help him. But Daniel was able to explain the mystery of the dreams to Nebuchadnezzar because God revealed the truth in response to Daniel's prayers. Daniel's insights were a mighty testimony to this pagan king.

Many of the wise men of the world today do not understand God's secrets anymore than the astrologers of Daniel's day. But God will reveal His truth and wisdom to us if we study the Scriptures and pray.

We have a choice. Are we going to look at life from God's perspective or allow our feelings and what the world believes to determine our perception?

God has revealed the truth in His Word, and He wants us to share this reality with others for His glory, just as Daniel did.

GOD ILLUMINATED YOU TO BE CHRIST'S LIGHT TO THE WORLD

Jesus declared, "You are the light of the world—like a city on a mountain, glowing in the night for all to see" (Matthew 5:14).

Because we are citizens of Christ's kingdom, God wants our very presence in the world to radiate His truth and His character to those around us.

We are citizens of heaven, but we still live in a world dominated by the kingdom of darkness. Jesus frequently calls Satan the "prince of this world" (John 12:31; 14:30; 16:11). So how are citizens of Christ's kingdom supposed to live in a world dominated by Satan's deceptions?

We find the answer in the book of Philippians: "Do everything without complaining or arguing, so that you may become blameless and pure, children of God without fault in a crooked and depraved generation, in which you shine like stars in the universe as you hold out the word of life" (Philippians 2:14–16, NIV).

When we allow Christ to live in and through us, our character will be transformed. As a result, our behavior should demonstrate God's supernatural love, power, and grace to those around us. In this way, our thoughts, speech, and actions will shine God's truth to the nonbelieving world.

Jesus proclaims, "Let your light shine before men, that they may see your good deeds and praise your Father in heaven" (Matthew 5:16, NIV). When we recognize our divine citizenship and act accordingly, our life should be a beacon of light to those around us—no matter where we are.

From a young age, Sara Wright wanted to be a missionary to Africa. She believed this to be God's highest calling in her life. In preparation, she completed a B.A. in languages and trained to be a nurse. On weekends, she would drive into the Kentucky mountains to share Christ and tend to the medical needs of the poor who lived there. While she ministered among these people, she contracted tuberculosis.

Because of her health problems, the mission board informed Sara that she could not go to Africa. She was devastated, but she did not become bitter. In the sanitarium where she was recovering from TB, she started a Bible study, and several women came to know the Lord. Sara had always hoped to someday marry, but she did not live aimlessly while waiting for a husband. When she was released from the sanitarium, she attended Columbia Bible College and then moved to Mississippi to teach Bible in the public schools. For over 35 years, she taught children from elementary school to high school about God and His Word. Although she never married and never had children of her own, the Lord gave her thousands of spiritual children and grandchildren. Near the end of her service on this earth, her hometown celebrated a "Miss Wright Day" in appreciation for her fruitful life—all because she radiated God's truth and character wherever God led her.

This is the power of the Holy Spirit. This is the power of living in Christ as a result of embracing our new identity and amazing destiny.

Though Daniel was chosen for service in King Nebuchadnezzar's kingdom, he recognized a higher calling. First and foremost, he was chosen to serve the King of kings. He dared to be different.

God honored his obedience. Daniel thrived physically and excelled in wisdom and learning. He became a walking example of God's goodness and greatness.

Daniel was a shining light of godliness and integrity in a dark, pagan world. King Nebuchadnezzar recognized that "the spirit of the holy gods" was in him. Years later, when the Persians conquered the Babylonians, a group of jealous officials wanted to get rid of Daniel. But his character was so pure that they could find no grounds to attack his integrity.

Like Daniel, we should reflect God's holiness to those around us. The Word of God declares, "You were once darkness, but now you are light in the Lord. Live as children of light" (Ephesians 5:8, NIV).

And you are free to do so because . . .

GOD ZEALOUSLY FREED YOU FROM SATAN'S KINGDOM OF DARKNESS

We began this chapter with a wonderful promise from God's Word: "[The Father] has rescued us out of the darkness and gloom of Satan's kingdom and brought us into the Kingdom of His dear Son" (Colossians 1:13, TLB).

Because we are citizens of Christ's kingdom, sin and Satan no longer have any authority over us.

As Christians, we are under new headship. As we mentioned in Chapter 6, we have a new ruler. Thanks to our glorious Savior, we are free from the power of the prince of this world.

The Bible explains, "Because God's children are human beings— made of flesh and blood—Jesus also became flesh and blood by being born in human form. For only as a human being could He die, and only by dying could He break the power of the Devil, who had the power of death" (Hebrews 2:14).

Because of Jesus Christ's selfless sacrifice, we do not need to listen to Satan's lies or give in to his temptations because he has no power over us. We learned earlier in the CROSS acrostic that we should regard ourselves as dead to sin and alive in Christ. We can regard ourselves as dead to sin and Satan's power because we no longer belong to the kingdom of darkness.

Daniel lived in Babylon, but he was not a prisoner of its beliefs. He lived by biblical values and worshiped His Creator—even when he was thrown into a den of lions for his allegiance to God.

The world may also pressure us to abandon God's way and God's values. Society may threaten us with ferocious lions—like job loss or social rejection—if we refuse. Although we may have to suffer for a time, God's kingdom is eternal and His rewards are abundant. What a privilege to be set free from the dominion of darkness and brought into the kingdom of light!

GOD ENTRUSTED YOU WITH THE KEYS TO CHRIST'S KINGDOM

Jesus promises His followers: "I will give you the keys of the Kingdom of Heaven. Whatever you lock on earth will be locked in heaven, and whatever you open on earth will be opened in heaven" (Matthew 16:19).

What an amazing promise! Because we are citizens of Christ's kingdom, we have been granted spiritual authority.

Jesus told His disciples in Matthew, "All authority in heaven and on earth has been given to me" (Matthew 28:18, NIV). Scripture describes our amazing Savior this way: "[Christ] existed before God made anything at all and is supreme over all creation. Christ is the One through whom God created everything in heaven and earth. He made the things we can see and the things we can't see—kings, kingdoms, rulers, and authorities. Everything has been created through Him and for Him" (Colossians 1:15,16).

Our glorious Lord rules a supreme kingdom, and He has bestowed His authority upon us. What spiritual authority have we been given in Christ's kingdom?

First, we have been given the authority of Christ to overcome the evil one. Paul writes in 2 Corinthians 10:4, "The weapons we fight with are not the weapons of the world. On the contrary, they have divine power to demolish strongholds" (NIV).

Second, we have been given authority to govern the church and discipline those who persist in sin. Jesus taught in Matthew 18:18, "I tell you the truth, whatever you bind on earth will be bound in heaven, and whatever you loose on earth will be loosed in heaven" (NIV).

Third, we have been given authority to announce the forgiveness of sins. After Jesus' resurrection, He appeared to His disciples and made this promise, "If you forgive anyone's sins, they are forgiven. If you refuse to forgive them, they are unforgiven" (John 20:23). Jesus does not say that we can determine who enters the kingdom and who does not. But we can declare that someone has been forgiven of their sins if they have truly placed their faith in Christ. We can also say with certainty that anyone who has not received Christ will spend eternity in hell.

Lastly, we who hold the keys to the kingdom have the authority to bring others to Christ! What a wonderful privilege to lead others into the kingdom of light! That is what it means to be an ambassador of Christ.

GOD NAMED YOU AS AN AMBASSADOR FOR CHRIST'S KINGDOM

The Bible explains, "We are Christ's ambassadors, and God is using us to speak to you. We urge you, as though Christ Himself were here pleading with you, 'Be reconciled to God!'" (2 Corinthians 5:20).

An ambassador is an authorized representative of a ruler or government. He does not speak in the authority of his own name, but on behalf of his country or king, and his responsibility is to faithfully represent the concerns of his king or nation to those to whom he is sent. We are God's ambassadors, and our mission is to tell others about Christ's wonderful kingdom.

Jesus gave His disciples and all believers a Great Commission, which we find in the Gospel of Matthew: "Jesus came to them and said, 'All authority in heaven and on earth has been given to me. Therefore go and make disciples of all nations, baptizing them in the name of the Father and of the Son and of the Holy Spirit, and teaching them to obey everything I have commanded you'" (Matthew 28:18–20, NIV).

God wants to draw people to Himself through His believers. Everywhere we go, we are to represent our amazing King and Savior.

Dr. Charles Malik was the Lebanese ambassador to the United Nations. In 1959, he served as president of the United Nations General

Assembly. With an earned doctorate from Harvard University and more than fifty honorary doctorates from many of the world's most prestigious universities, Dr. Malik was truly one of the great intellectual and spiritual giants of our century.

It was my privilege to hear this dear friend speak to a group of world leaders in Washington, D.C. I was deeply touched by his strong witness for the Lord Jesus when he said, "Only those who stay close to Jesus Christ can help others who are far away. The needs of the world are much deeper than democracy and progress. The deeper need of the world belongs to the sphere of the mind, heart, and spirit —a spirit to be penetrated with the light and grace of Jesus Christ."

AS CITIZENS OF GOD'S KINGDOM, WE ARE DRAPED WITH ALL THE PRIVILEGES AND PROTECTION OF OUR MAGNIFICENT GOD.

He went on to say, "I really do not know what will remain of civilization and history if the accumulated influence of Jesus Christ, both direct and indirect, is eradicated from literature, art, practical dealings, moral standards, and creativeness in the different activities of mind and spirit." Then he concluded with this profound statement: "The heart of the whole matter is faith in Jesus Christ."

Following his address, I approached him to say, "Many political leaders speak of God, the Bible, and prayer in a general way, but I have never heard one in your position speak so powerfully and so convincingly of your faith and love for Jesus Christ."

His response moved me deeply. "I am sobered by the words of our Lord: 'Whosoever therefore shall confess Me before men, him will I confess also before My Father which is in heaven. But whosoever shall deny Me before men, him will I also deny before my Father which is in heaven'" (Matthew 10:32, KJV).

Dr. Malik was an ambassador to the United Nations, but more important, he was an ambassador for Christ. Like Dr. Malik, we are to be excited about our wonderful Lord. In the words of Paul, "Everywhere we go we talk about Christ to all who will listen" (Colossians 1:28, TLB).

Jesus proclaims, "The righteous will shine like the sun in the kingdom of their Father. He who has ears, let him hear" (Matthew 13:43, NIV). What blessings are ours because we are citizens of Christ's glorious kingdom!

Many years ago, a violent coup erupted in a Latin American country. In the midst of the bloodshed, the rebels arrested an American citizen and sentenced him to die. As the man stood before a firing squad, a United States officer draped an American flag around his compatriot. "If you shoot this man," the officer shouted, "you will fire through the American flag and incur the wrath of a whole nation." The revolutionary in charge let the man go.[2]

As citizens of God's kingdom, we are draped with all the privileges and protection of our magnificent God. Any person or spiritual force that wishes to harm us will incur the wrath of almighty God. What a blessing to belong to His kingdom!

The only proper response for this amazing privilege is gratitude. The Bible declares, "Since we are receiving a kingdom that cannot be shaken, let us be thankful, and so worship God acceptably with reverence and awe" (Hebrews 12:28, NIV).

Our mighty God has granted us a new identity because of the sacrifice of His Son, Jesus Christ. In the preceding chapters, we have discussed the fact that each of us is a child of God, an heir of God, a saint with a new nature, a member of the body of Christ, and a citizen of Christ's kingdom. Hopefully, you now have an accurate understanding of who you are in Christ—your amazing identity—and the wonderful plan He has for you.

In the next section, we will begin to uncover the impact this new identity should have on your everyday life as you think, speak, and behave like Jesus.

Life Application

Thank Your Heavenly Father—Thank God that He has chosen you as a citizen of Christ's kingdom. Praise Him that He has made you a priest and revealed His thoughts and plans to you in the Bible. Express your gratitude to Him that you have been freed from the power of Satan and given the keys to Christ's kingdom of light. Praise Him for naming you His ambassador.

Renew Your Mind—Memorize the following verses and acrostic:

- "We are citizens of heaven, where the Lord Jesus Christ lives. And we are eagerly waiting for Him to return as our Savior" (Philippians 3:20).

- "He has rescued us from the one who rules in the kingdom of darkness, and He has brought us into the Kingdom of His dear Son. God has purchased our freedom with His blood and has forgiven all our sins" (Colossians 1:13,14).

- The CITIZEN acrostic will help you remember that God…
  Chose you for Christ's unshakable kingdom
  Installed you as a priest in Christ's holy kingdom
  Told you, in the Bible, the secrets of Christ's kingdom
  Illuminated you to be Christ's light to the world
  Zealously freed you from Satan's kingdom of darkness
  Entrusted you with the keys to Christ's kingdom
  Named you as an ambassador for Christ's kingdom

Reflect on Your New Life in Christ—Picture yourself being liberated from a country of darkness and cruelty and led into a nation of freedom and light. Envision Jesus greeting you, His arms outstretched in welcome. As He embraces you, experience the acceptance, safety, and love of finally being home.

Share the Blessings—Is there someone in your life who needs to be set free from the darkness and gloom of Satan's kingdom? As an ambassador of Christ, share with them the good news that they, too, can enter Christ's kingdom of love and light.

PART III

Our Life
in Christ

CHAPTER 9

Thinking with the Mind of Christ

"I think, therefore I am."

When the 17th century French philosopher Rene Descartes penned this statement as proof of his own existence, he made an important point. Central to each person's being and actions is what he or she thinks. Long before Descartes was born, God gave us this truth in His Word, "As he thinks within himself, so he is" (Proverbs 23:7, NASB).

Consider Adolph Hitler, whose anti-Semitic and fascist beliefs led to World War II and the destruction of millions of lives. Mother Teresa's conviction that even the poorest are precious in the sight of God caused her to dedicate her life to ministering to the sick, the dying, and the destitute in the slums of Calcutta. Her self-sacrifice has confirmed the value of every human being and has inspired millions to demonstrate respect and compassion to those less fortunate than themselves.

In the preceding chapters, we discovered the amazing truth of our precious, remarkable identity as children of God, heirs of God, saints with a new nature, members of the body of Christ, and citizens of Christ's kingdom. Understanding more about who we are in Christ enables us to live by the truth that we belong to Him. This new kind of living begins with our mindset as we commit ourselves to think with the mind of Christ.

An anonymous author penned, "Let the mind of the Master be the

117

master of your mind." This should be our goal as children of God and followers of Christ.

Before you and I became Christians, we could not comprehend spiritual truths. But now Christ lives in us through the Holy Spirit. Scripture tells us, "We can understand these things, for we have the mind of Christ" (1 Corinthians 2:16).

Although God in His grace has given us the mind of Christ, we still may not think like Christ in our daily habits and routine. To do so, our minds must be reprogrammed or renewed.

The Bible urges us, "You must no longer live as the Gentiles do, in the futility of their thinking" (Ephesians 4:17, NIV). In Romans, Paul admonishes, "Don't copy the behavior and customs of this world, but let God transform you into a new person by changing the way you think. Then you will know what God wants you to do, and you will know how good and pleasing and perfect His will really is" (Romans 12:2).

The Holy Spirit is the agent who renews our mind. He does this through the Word of God. The process is continuous as we cooperate with Him.

Imagine for a moment that your mind is a closet in need of a spiritual spring cleaning. You find things in the closet that are useless or even hurtful to your walk with the Lord. The useful items may be buried under so much junk that they are hard to find. God wants to clean out and reorganize your mental closet. He wants to get rid of the garbage and clutter. He wants biblical truths easy to access. He wants to make room to add more godly insights with the passing of time.

But we must cooperate in that process. We must give God free reign in the closet and not throw in more trash that could hinder His work.

As you immerse yourself in the truth of who you are in Christ, your thinking should change radically. Continually remind yourself that you are a child of God, an heir of God, a saint with a new nature, a member of the body of Christ, and a citizen of Christ's kingdom. Your new, supernaturally transformed self-image should dramatically change the thoughts you think. Let's explore five principles of thinking that are consistent with your new self-image. You can remember them by the acrostic THINK:

T	*Test* your thoughts to see if they are from God.
H	*Hold* fast to God's truth and perspective.
I	*Inquire* of God for guidance, wisdom, and insight.
N	*Nurture* your mind with Scripture.
K	*Keep* your mind fixed on what is true and holy.

TEST YOUR THOUGHTS TO SEE IF THEY ARE FROM GOD

Scripture puts it this way, "We demolish arguments and every pretension that sets itself up against the knowledge of God, and we take captive every thought to make it obedient to Christ" (2 Corinthians 10:5, NIV).

We must not allow untamed thoughts to run wild in our mind. Instead, through the enabling of the Holy Spirit, we must reject any thought that does not honor God.

I grew up on a ranch in Oklahoma, and we imported wild horses from the ranges of Wyoming and Montana. It was my privilege to have a father who was a superb horseman. He taught his five sons how to break and ride wild broncos.

An untamed horse can throw you off or take you where you do not want to go. Untamed thoughts can do the same thing. They can take you where you do not want to go and throw you off spiritually. This is because what we think will eventually determine our actions.

One of the most infamous criminals of the 20th century was Ted Bundy. He confessed to sexually assaulting and brutally murdering thirty-six women across the nation. In 1989, before being executed in Starke, Florida, Bundy asked Dr. James Dobson, president of Focus on the Family, to talk with him. In this interview, Bundy stated that his murderous rampage was fueled by an addiction to violent pornography. He explained how filling his mind with obscene material eventually made him want to act out what he had read or seen. His interest in "soft" porn gradually led to a fascination with more graphic pornography. Finally his thoughts incited him to murder.[1]

Jesus clearly understood the power of impure thoughts. In the Sermon on the Mount, He told His followers to guard their thoughts because "anyone who even looks at a woman with lust in his eye has already committed adultery with her in his heart" (Matthew 5:28). As children of our glorious Creator God and Savior, we must control our thought life through the power of the Holy Spirit, so we will reflect the mind of Christ.

HOLD FAST TO GOD'S TRUTH AND PERSPECTIVE

Our awesome God tells us in His Word, "'My thoughts are completely different from yours,' says the Lord. 'And My ways are far beyond anything you could imagine. For just as the heavens are higher than the earth, so are My ways higher than your ways and My thoughts higher than your thoughts'" (Isaiah 55:8,9).

To think with the mind of Christ, we need to look at life through the lens of God's Word.

On July 17, 1999, the nation was gripped by a terrible tragedy. While flying at night near Martha's Vineyard, John F. Kennedy, Jr., lost his bearings, and the plane carrying him, his wife, and her sister plunged into the Atlantic Ocean. In the agonizing investigation that followed, a possible cause of the horrible accident emerged. It was explained that as an amateur pilot, John F. Kennedy, Jr. was trained only to fly by sight. However, on a foggy night, his vision proved useless. Experts speculate that to compensate, Kennedy attempted to rely on his senses, became disoriented, and the plane crashed into the ocean. Perhaps if he had known how to use and trust the instrument panel rather than rely solely on his senses, this devastating tragedy could have been avoided.

In a similar way, we cannot always trust our senses or feelings because they can be misleading. In the midst of a complex and dark world, we must believe and follow the timeless, inspired Word of God. It is our instrument panel. It reveals the truth about God, ourselves, and our circumstances. To avoid terrible tragedy, we must trust the Bible rather than our feelings. If God says something is true, we need to accept it no matter what our senses or emotions tell us.

In the famous story *The Wizard of Oz*, Oz was called the Emerald City because the whole city was green. Or so the people thought. But actually, the wizard had tricked them. He made sure everyone who entered the city put on a pair of special glasses that were tinted green. The city was not "emerald" at all. The colored glasses distorted reality!

The world likewise distorts God's truth. We will not be able to experience reality unless we take off the world's colored glasses and put on God's clear lenses—His point of view as revealed in the Bible.

How do we understand God's point of view? It begins by simply asking Him for His truth in our situation.

INQUIRE OF GOD FOR GUIDANCE, WISDOM, AND INSIGHT

Scripture says, "Trust in the Lord with all your heart; do not depend on your own understanding. Seek His will in all you do, and He will direct your paths. Don't be impressed with your own wisdom. Instead, fear the Lord and turn your back on evil. Then you will gain renewed health and vitality" (Proverbs 3:5–8).

To think with the mind of Christ, we must ask God for His wisdom and direction.

King Solomon, who penned Proverbs 3, knew about inquiring of God. When he succeeded his father David as king of Israel, he felt overwhelmed by the task of governing God's people. One night, the Lord came to him in a dream and told Solomon to ask for whatever he wanted and God would give it to him. Solomon asked God for wisdom. He acknowledged that he needed God's guidance to rule Israel. God not only granted his request, but He was greatly pleased by Solomon's choice.

God's Word promises, "If you need wisdom—if you want to know what God wants you to do—ask Him, and He will gladly tell you. He will not resent your asking. But when you ask Him, be sure that you really expect Him to answer, for a doubtful mind is as unsettled as a wave of the sea that is driven and tossed by the wind" (James 1:5,6).

God is pleased when we ask Him for wisdom, which is readily available to us in His powerful Word, the Bible. We know He will answer our request because Scripture promises, "This is the assurance we have in approaching God: that if we ask anything according to His will, He hears us. And if we know that He hears us—whatever we ask—we know that we have what we asked of Him" (1 John 5:14,15, NIV).

NURTURE YOUR MIND WITH SCRIPTURE

King David proclaimed, "I have hidden Your word in my heart, that I might not sin against You...Oh, how I love Your law! I think about it all day long. Your commands make me wiser than my enemies, for

Your commands are my constant guide. Yes, I have more insight than my teachers, for I am always thinking of Your decrees" (Psalm 119:11, 97–99).

We develop the wisdom and thoughts of Christ by filling our hearts and minds with the Word of God. Our amazing triune God is the source of all wisdom, and He has revealed His heart and character in the Bible. When we interact with this amazing book and allow God's truth to permeate our minds and souls, we cannot help but be changed. As we invite the Holy Spirit to speak to us through the pages of God's wonderful Word, we begin to love what God loves and see reality as He does.

The Bible will also point out areas in our thoughts that are not Christlike. This process can be compared to the way paint is purified. The paint we buy contains impurities that are not apparent to the eye. If this paint is applied to a surface, these impurities may appear unexpectedly, causing an imperfect finish. For this reason, professional house painters pour their paint through a metal grid. This grid strains out the impurities so they will not mar the painted surface.

Like that paint, our thoughts have hidden impurities. God uses His Holy Word to strain them out. The Bible is a grid—a divine brain purification system. As we spend time meditating on God's Word, the Holy Spirit will convict us of these "impurities" and develop in us a mind that dwells on what is true—not illusions, sinful passions, or lies.

When thoughts come to my mind which do not honor the Lord, it is my practice to ask that the blood of Jesus shed on the cross for my sins cleanse every impurity from my mind. I ask the Holy Spirit to take control of my mind so I will think only God's thoughts. And each day, I consciously practice Spiritual Breathing—exhaling the impure, and inhaling the pure truth of God's Holy Spirit and Word.

KEEP YOUR MIND FIXED ON WHAT IS TRUE AND HOLY

God commands us to discipline our mind in order to change its focus. The Bible prescribes the following exercise program for a healthy thought life: "Fix your thoughts on what is true and honorable and right. Think about things that are pure and lovely and admirable. Think about things that are excellent and worthy of praise" (Philippians 4:8).

Television, magazines, advertisements, and the Internet bombard us with the immoral, the violent, and even the obscene. But God wants our minds to dwell on what is righteous, pure, and admirable.

The Scripture says, "Let the Lord Jesus Christ take control of you, and don't think of ways to indulge your evil desires" (Romans 13:14). God will empower us to do what He commands. Good mental habits are crucial. An ungodly thought life can have far-reaching negative effects.

None of us would jump off a high building because we understand the danger. The earth's gravity would immediately smash us into the ground.

The consequences of our thought life are not always so immediate, but they can be just as serious. What we allow into our minds and what we think about will ultimately shape who we are.

As one critical observer put it:

> Sow a thought, and you reap an act;
> Sow an act, and you reap a habit;
> Sow a habit, and you reap a character;
> Sow a character, and you reap a destiny.[2]

Our thoughts shape our attitudes toward God and others. In turn, our attitudes shape our values—the ideals we consider important and by which we live.

To fix your mind on Christ, ask yourself, "What attitudes and values reflect the mind of Christ?" The life of Jesus and His teachings reveal godly attitudes and values that God wants us to adopt.

Let us look at six attitudes. Three are attitudes toward God and three are attitudes toward others. Each attitude leads to a beneficial, godly value which contradicts a harmful worldly value.

Right Attitudes Toward God

First, Jesus wants us to have an attitude of love and reverence for God. When He was asked which commandment was greatest, Jesus replied, "You must love the Lord your God with all your heart, all your soul, and all your mind" (Matthew 22:37).

If we love and revere God, we will value what is in heaven rather than what is on earth. God will be our first love. This was not the case with the rich young ruler. You may recall Jesus asked him to sell his possessions, give his money to the poor, and follow Him. But the man walked away. He could not do it. His first love was his worldly wealth.

Second, Jesus wants us to have an attitude of dependence on God. Jesus said, "Yes, I am the vine; you are the branches. Those who remain in Me, and I in them, will produce much fruit. For apart from Me you can do nothing" (John 15:5).

If we depend on God, we will value God-reliance rather than self-reliance.

Depending on God means relying on Christ, just like branches hold fast to a vine. As the branches are sustained by abiding in the vine, so we will draw nourishment and strength from Him. We will invite our marvelous Savior to think, speak, and live through us. Then, we will do His will, not ours.

Third, Jesus wants us to have an attitude of submission to God. Christ Himself is the most powerful example. Consider His attitude in the Garden of Gethsemane as He faced an excruciating death on the cross. Scripture tells us, "He went on a little farther and fell face down on the ground, praying, 'My Father! If it is possible, let this cup of suffering be taken away from Me. Yet I want Your will, not mine'" (Matthew 26:39).

An attitude of submission means that we surrender completely to God. As a result, we are willing to do what He wants regardless of the cost—just as Jesus did when He died on the cross for us.

An attitude of submission leads us to value biblical ethics rather than situational ethics. Perhaps you are tempted to cheat on your income taxes to have extra money. Perhaps you are considering an abortion because it seems easier than bringing a child into the world. But God's ways are best, and they do not change based on our inconvenience or discomfort. Rather than trying to explain away God's standards whenever they are hard to follow, we must remain faithful to the clear moral standards in the Bible.

Right Attitudes Toward Others

If we have the right attitudes toward God, He will change our attitudes toward others. Let us consider three attitudes Jesus wants us to have toward others.

The first is an attitude of humility and servanthood. The Bible says, "Be humble, thinking of others as better than yourself. Don't think only about your own affairs, but be interested in others, too, and what they are doing" (Philippians 2:3,4).

This attitude helps us value others' interests rather than self-interests. Again, Jesus is our example.

The mother of James and John came to Jesus seeking greatness for her sons. She asked if these two disciples could sit on either side of Jesus in His kingdom. Jesus told her that greatness comes from serving others, even as He came to serve and die for us.

Second, Jesus wants us to have an attitude of gentleness. In the Sermon on the Mount, Jesus says, "God blesses those who are gentle and lowly, for the whole earth will belong to them" (Matthew 5:5).

This attitude helps us value God's sovereign power to change people rather than our power to influence them. The Bible commands us to pray for others, do good to them, and love them—even if they are our enemies. Jesus modeled this attitude in His life, ministry, and death.

Jesus also modeled a third attitude toward others: an attitude of grace and forgiveness. Jesus says, "God blesses those who are merciful, for they will be shown mercy" (Matthew 5:7). And He warns believers: "If you forgive those who sin against you, your heavenly Father will forgive you. But if you refuse to forgive others, your Father will not forgive your sins" (Matthew 6:14,15).

This attitude helps us value reconciliation rather than revenge. When the prodigal son in Jesus' famous parable returned to his father, the father had every right to treat him harshly. The son had acted disgracefully, squandered his inheritance, and insulted his father. Yet the father welcomed his wayward son back with open arms and a joyous celebration. So, too, we must humble ourselves to seek healing and restoration instead of revenge.

The powerful hymn penned by Kate B. Wilkinson proclaims this prayer: "May the mind of Christ, my Savior, live in me from day to day, by His love and power controlling all I do and say."[3]

When Christ lives in us and controls our thoughts, we see ourselves, others, and our circumstances as He sees them. We experience true reality because the Creator of all truth—the God who encompasses all truth—reveals it to us. His love and power will influence all we think, say, and do. Truly, our thoughts and attitudes shape our values, and our values shape our lifestyle for good or evil.

In the next chapter, we will continue our discussion on our life in Christ when we explore the importance of speaking with the words of Christ.

Life Application

Renew Your Mind—Memorize the following verses and acrostic:

■ "Don't copy the behavior and customs of this world, but let God transform you into a new person by changing the way you think. Then you will know what God wants you to do, and you will know how good and pleasing and perfect His will really is" (Romans 12:2).

■ "Fix your thoughts on what is true and honorable and right. Think about things that are pure and lovely and admirable. Think about things that are excellent and worthy of praise" (Philippians 4:8).

■ The THINK acrostic will help you remember to:
Test your thoughts to see if they are from God.
Hold fast to God's truth and perspective.
Inquire of God for guidance, wisdom, and insight.
Nurture your mind with Scripture.
Keep your mind fixed on what is true and holy.

Take Up Your Cross—Prayerfully meditate on the five principles of the CROSS acrostic: "I praise You, Holy Father, that I am a new creation with the mind of Christ. Thank You that I am dead to sin so I do not need to dwell on tempting thoughts. Instead, I offer my mind and body as instruments of righteousness. I surrender my will to You, drawing upon Your strength, wisdom, and power to think supernaturally. Fill my mind with Your thoughts, my Lord and Savior. Amen."

Act by Faith—Take charge of your thought life by monitoring what goes into your mind. Carefully consider what you view on television, the Internet, in movies, and magazines. If you are tempted to dwell on godless, lustful thoughts, replace them by filling your mind with what is noble and true. Read the Bible, listen to uplifting music, and associate with people who encourage you in the Lord, rather than contribute to your worldly temptations.

CHAPTER 10

Speaking with the Words of Christ

*I*n this age of the Internet, cell phones, electronic media, and fax machines, communication is a highly valued commodity. Words bombard us everyday via the computer, radio, television, and print media. Rarely are we free from the tyranny of words.

Although the number of words passed over telephone lines and computer networks increases every year, their quality has not. In fact, many would argue that most of the words with which we come into daily contact are neither uplifting nor encouraging. Unfortunately, even Christians are not immune from the trend to emphasize volume and speed of communication over the content of our words.

We are also not exempt from using words to hurt or degrade others.

A story is told of a 16th century priest, Saint Philip Neri, who heard the confession of a young woman who was known to gossip. He wanted to show her the danger of her ways, so he gave her an unusual penance. He ordered her to scatter bird feathers all over town. When she had done so, he instructed her to go back and pick them up. She protested that this was impossible because the wind had blown the feathers far and wide. She could never retrieve them all.[1]

The wise priest was pointing out that the same is true of words. Once we scatter them, we can never get them all back. That is why it is so important to be careful about what we say.

Words can have tremendous power. In the first chapter of John, Christ Himself is called "the Word": "In the beginning the Word already existed. He was with God, and He was God…The Word became human and lived here on earth among us. He was full of unfailing love and faithfulness. And we have seen His glory, the glory of the only Son of the Father" (John 1:1,14). Our glorious risen Savior is God's powerful Word—His revelation—in flesh.

The power of words was also demonstrated when our awesome God created the world. Genesis 1:3 declares, "God said, 'Let there be light,' and there was light." Our mighty God *spoke* creation into being.

We also can speak things into being. Our words can create harmony or discord, happiness or discouragement, a positive or negative self-image in another. What we say can have a tremendous effect for either good or evil, so we must be careful.

Our Lord will judge each word we speak. Jesus taught His disciples, "I tell you this, that you must give an account on judgment day of every idle word you speak. The words you say now reflect your fate then; either you will be justified by them or you will be condemned" (Matthew 12:36,37).

Scripture warns us, "The tongue is a small thing, but what enormous damage it can do" (James 3:5).

The Serpent's lies in the Garden of Eden tempted Eve to disobey God and led to humanity's Fall. Hitler's words of hate spawned World War II and genocide. Jim Jones's deceptive words led more than 900 followers of his false religion to commit suicide in Jonestown, Guyana. The negative power of words can be seen on the stage of world history and in our individual lives.

What we say can hurt others even when no harm is intended. I remember as a small child overhearing a neighbor say some negative things about me. Those words affected my self-image for years.

But words can also have a tremendous power for good, especially when they echo the heart and character of Christ. Peter said of the words of Jesus, "You alone have the words that give eternal life" (John 6:68).

No words have had more impact for good than God's Word. This is what the Bible says about its power to influence us: "All Scripture is inspired by God and is useful to teach us what is true and to make us realize what is wrong in our lives. It straightens us out and teaches us to do what is right. It is God's way of preparing us in every way, fully equipped for every good thing God wants us to do" (2 Timothy

3:16,17). My study of the Word over the past years has confirmed the truth of this passage in many ways.

Scripture says, "Let the words of Christ, in all their richness, live in your hearts and make you wise. Use His words to teach and counsel each other. Sing psalms and hymns and spiritual songs to God with thankful hearts" (Colossians 3:16).

So how do you and I speak with the words of Christ? To help answer this question, give yourself the "3 M Test":

- What is my *motive?*
- What is my *message?*
- What is my *manner?*

First, what is my motive? The Bible indicates what our motive for speech should be: "Speaking the truth in love, we will in all things grow up into Him who is the Head, that is, Christ" (Ephesians 4:15, NIV).

Everything we say should be motivated by love. The Bible's famous love chapter, 1 Corinthians 13, lists characteristics that help define love. We can apply them to loving speech as well: "Love is patient and kind. Love is not jealous or boastful or proud or rude. Love does not demand its own way. Love is not irritable, and it keeps no record of when it has been wronged" (1 Corinthians 13:4,5). Each characteristic of love is an act of the will which takes precedence over how we feel. By faith, we can choose these qualities to be a reality in our lives. Speaking in love means we want our words to benefit, bless, and build up others so they will be the best they can be for God.

Second, what is my message?

In the Old Testament Book of Zechariah, God said to His people, "This is what you must do: Tell the truth to each other" (Zechariah 8:16). Our message must be truthful. When we speak to each other, we need to be honest.

A vital part of speaking the truth in love is to seek the Holy Spirit's leading and not rush God's timing. Our loving Lord never reveals more truth than we can bear. But in our zeal, we may mistakenly do this with others.

My friend Dick Day has a marvelous illustration of this principle. He compares our sins to three sizes of fruit: grapefruits, oranges, and lemons. When we first become Christians, God begins to refine us by working on our grapefruits. In time, He moves on to our oranges, and, finally, to our lemons. But we must be careful not to get ahead of God and have someone focus on their lesser sins while God wants them to deal with more major sins.

Our loving God in His wisdom usually points out the larger areas that need growth in our lives before He convicts us of smaller areas needing refinement. We must be sensitive to how God is working in the lives of others.

The third question is: What is my manner?

In the Bible, we read this about Jesus, "All who were there spoke well of Him and were amazed by the gracious words that fell from His lips" (Luke 4:22).

Like Jesus, our manner of speech should be gracious. This means that what we say should demonstrate kindness, love, and courtesy. It should also be controlled. Elsewhere, Scripture explains, "We all make many mistakes, but those who control their tongues can also control themselves in every other way" (James 3:2).

Our speech should flow out of our supernatural identity in Christ. We are children of God, heirs of God, saints with a new nature, members of the body of Christ, and citizens of Christ's kingdom. Our speech should reflect our divine heritage. Let us look at five guidelines the Bible provides for controlling our tongue. You can remember them by the acrostic SPEAK:

S *Stifle* the impulse to speak hastily or foolishly.

P *Pray* about what to say, especially in difficult situations.

E *Encourage*, exhort, and edify others in love.

A *Avoid* foolish, boastful, obscene, hurtful, or false speech.

K *Keep* your ears open and be quicker to listen than to talk.

STIFLE THE IMPULSE TO SPEAK HASTILY OR FOOLISHLY

The Bible tells us in Proverbs, "The godly think before speaking; the wicked spout evil words" (Proverbs 15:28).

If the character of Christ is to be evident in our speech, we must think before we speak.

How many times have you said something that you wished you

could take back?

In a small village church, an altar boy accidentally dropped a carafe of wine while serving the priest at Sunday mass. Angered, the priest slapped him on the cheek and shouted, "Leave the altar and never come back!" That boy was Josip Broz Tito, who later became the Communist leader of Yugoslavia.

How different that boy's life might have been if he had never heard those words. What regrets we would avoid if we would only pause a moment before we release a torrent of words.

Our tongue is like the steering wheel of a car. Both are small, but both can steer us wrong and create disastrous results, especially if we are reckless or impulsive in the way we handle them. Consider what happens when a car starts to skid. Our impulse is to turn the steering wheel in the opposite direction from which the car is sliding. But safety experts tell us this will not work because it may cause the car to spin out of control. Our best chance to regain control is to steer into the skid. If we follow our impulse, we are more apt to crash the car. But if we think before we act, we will save ourselves and those who are with us from harm.

The same is true of controlling our tongue. When we find ourselves in a hostile or difficult situation, our impulse may be to lash out or say something we will later regret. But if we think before we speak, we can avoid much grief.

PRAY ABOUT WHAT TO SAY, ESPECIALLY IN DIFFICULT SITUATIONS

Scripture urges us, "Don't worry about anything; instead, pray about everything. Tell God what you need, and thank Him for all He has done" (Philippians 4:6).

When we do not know what to say or when we are afraid of what we might say, there is only one answer—prayer!

The prophet Daniel understood this truth. King Nebuchadnezzar commanded the execution of all the wise men in Babylon because none were able to interpret his dream. Although Daniel had not been given a chance to answer the king's request, he also was slated to die. Daniel asked three friends to join him in prayer for the interpretation of the dream. God revealed the dream's meaning and Daniel explained it to the king. Instead of a death sentence, Daniel was rewarded with a high government position.

Do you have difficulty communicating with a spouse, parent, or child? Is there a person whom God is calling you to lovingly confront? Have you developed unhealthy patterns of insulting or criticizing others? Whatever your situation, ask God to show you areas where your speech does not reflect His character and ask Him to give you the right words to speak in love.

ENCOURAGE, EXHORT, AND EDIFY OTHERS IN LOVE

Scripture says, "A wise man's heart guides his mouth, and his lips promote instruction. Pleasant words are a honeycomb, sweet to the soul and healing to the bones" (Proverbs 16:23,24, NIV).

If we wish to speak like Christ, our words should build up and affirm others.

A story is told about a man who was always being badgered by his wife to meet her perfectionistic standards. He was finally so beaten down by her nagging that he asked her to make a list of her expectations, which she did. Soon after, she died. Months later, he met and married someone else, and his new marriage seemed blissful by comparison.

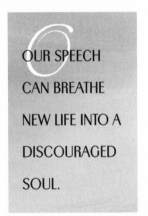

OUR SPEECH CAN BREATHE NEW LIFE INTO A DISCOURAGED SOUL.

One day, he found the old list of demands his first wife had written. To his astonishment, he realized that in his second marriage, he was meeting all of these expectations, although his second wife never demanded anything from him. What made the difference? The man concluded it was this: His first wife was constantly saying, "I hate it when…" But his new wife's constant comment was, "I just *love* it when…"[2]

How wonderful to be around people who are encouraging, whose words are seasoned with grace and love. Each of us can be that kind of person. As we allow Christ to live in and through us, our speech can breathe new life into a discouraged soul. For Jesus told His disciples, "The very words I have spoken to you are spirit and life" (John 6:63).

AVOID FOOLISH, BOASTFUL, OBSCENE, HURTFUL, OR FALSE SPEECH

The Bible urges us, "Don't use foul or abusive language. Let everything you say be good and helpful, so that your words will be an encouragement to those who hear them...Get rid of all bitterness, rage, anger, harsh words, and slander, as well as all types of malicious behavior...Obscene stories, foolish talk, and coarse jokes—these are not for you" (Ephesians 4:29,31; 5:4).

Speaking the words of Christ means avoiding words that demean, desecrate, and destroy.

One day in the mid-18th century, Josiah Wedgwood, famous for his beautiful Wedgwood pottery, escorted a nobleman through a tour of his factory. Accompanying them was a young boy who was one of Wedgwood's employees. The nobleman was excessively vulgar—telling irreverent jokes and spewing profanities. At first, the young boy was shocked at the nobleman's behavior, but then he became fascinated by the man and laughed at his jokes.

This made Wedgwood deeply upset. At the end of the tour, the nobleman admired an exquisite vase of unique and rare beauty. As he reached for it, Wedgwood knocked the vase to the floor. The nobleman was incensed because he wished to purchase it for his collection. Wedgwood replied, "Sir, there are other ruined things more precious than a vase which can never be restored. You can never give back to that young man, who just left us, the reverence for the sacred things which his parents have tried to teach him for years. You have undone their labor in less than half an hour!"[3]

Oh, if we would only realize the damage that can be caused by thoughtless, profane, and hurtful words.

The Bible compares our tongue to a spark that can burn down a forest.

For many years, Campus Crusade for Christ's headquarters was nestled in the mountains of San Bernardino, California. In that area, forest fires are a very present danger. In November 1980, the Panorama fire raged for five days. The blaze burned a 23,800-acre path and left four people dead, 284 homes destroyed, and $40 million in damages. Six of our buildings and the entrance bridge were burned down. Thankfully, none of our staff were harmed, but the fire caused

$1 million of damage to our property. Imagine, hundreds of homes and lives devastated all because of one match carelessly thrown, or a small campfire not properly extinguished.

Throwing out words that are angry, hurtful, or otherwise ungodly can be like tossing a smoldering match onto dry brush. We may torch what is dear to us: our marriages, our friendships, or our unity as believers. That is why it is so important to pay attention to what we say ...and to listen to what *others* say.

To help you determine the merit of the words you are about to say, give yourself this four-question test:

- Is it the truth?
- Is it fair to all concerned?
- Will it build good will and better friendship?
- Will it be beneficial to all concerned?

Use these questions as guidelines to help you control you speech.

KEEP YOUR EARS OPEN AND BE QUICKER TO LISTEN THAN TO TALK

The Bible warns us, "He who answers before listening—that is his folly and his shame" (Proverbs 18:13).

If our speech is to resemble Christ's, we must be quick to listen and slow to speak.

On average, a person thinks about four times faster than he speaks. Therefore, many of us become impatient and rush into speaking before we have really heard what another person has said. But that can lead to disastrous results.

Being a good listener takes practice. It involves eye contact, patience, self-control, and above all humility. Listening puts into practice the Bible's admonition: "Don't be selfish; don't live to make a good impression on others. Be humble, thinking of others as better than yourself. Don't think only about your own affairs, but be interested in others, too, and what they are doing" (Philippians 2:3,4).

Surrendering our will to the Lord means being willing to lay aside our own agenda and desire for recognition to allow someone else to be heard. A little poem about a wise old owl says it well.

A wise old owl sat in an oak,
The more he heard the less he spoke;
The less he spoke the more he heard.
Why aren't we all like that wise old bird?[4]

As we allow Christ to live in and through us, our words should reflect the heart of our Savior. By committing ourselves to speak words that are consistent with who we are in Christ, our speech will have *constructive* benefits rather than *destructive* consequences.

Jesus told His disciples, "Heaven and earth will disappear, but my words will remain forever" (Mark 13:31). Christ's words are eternal, and they are eternally true.

Meditate on His words and allow them to take root in your heart. Jesus, who is the Word, is the source of all knowledge and the One who gave you the ability to speak. Rely on His strength to help you speak as you should, and draw upon His love to help you attentively listen to others.

Speech is a trigger that leads to action. What we think influences what we say, and what we say affects our behavior. As we think with the mind of Christ and speak with the words of Christ, we will then be able to behave with the character of Christ. This is the subject of the next chapter.

Life Application

Thank Your Heavenly Father—Thank God for sending His Word in flesh—Jesus Christ—to demonstrate how we should live and speak. Praise Him that He offers you the wisdom to know what to say and the self-control to know when to speak and when to remain silent. Thank Him that He is the best encourager and listener, and ask Him to help you be a compassionate listener to others.

Renew Your Mind—Memorize and meditate on the following verses and acrostic:

■ "Let your conversation be gracious and effective so that you will have the right answer for everyone" (Colossians 4:6).

■ "The godly think before speaking; the wicked spout evil words" (Proverbs 15:28).

■ The SPEAK acrostic will help you remember to:
Stifle the impulse to speak hastily or foolishly.
Pray about what you say, especially in difficult situations.
Encourage, exhort, and edify others in love.
Avoid foolish, boastful, obscene, hurtful, or false speech.
Keep your ears open and be quicker to listen than to talk.

Reflect on Your New Life in Christ—Read Ephesians 4:17—5:21. Write down several ways you can "put off the old self" through your manner of conversation. Now think of several situations where your patience is tried or you need to communicate something important. What words can you speak that will exhibit grace to those around you?

Share the Blessings—Is there someone to whom you spoke harshly? Did you gossip, tell an obscene story, or use hurtful words? Perhaps you did not listen as you should. Go to that person and ask forgiveness. Share with him or her about what you learned in this chapter. Then invite the Holy Spirit to speak the words of Christ through you!

CHAPTER 11

Behaving with the Character of Christ

he popular evangelist and preacher of the 19th century, Dwight L. Moody, said, "Character is what you are in the dark."[1]

How very true this is. When no one is watching and you believe no one will ever find out, what do you do? How do you behave?

Our world is hungry for people who exhibit integrity and honesty. All too few of our leaders and famous personalities display an upright character. Even many of our parents and elders falter. Yet God wants His children to reflect the character of Christ.

Paul Gustave Dore, a famous 19th century artist, lost his passport while traveling in Europe. When he reached a border crossing, he had no papers to prove who he was. Although he pleaded with the guard, he was not granted passage. Finally, the guard had an idea. Dore could prove his identity in another way.

The guard pointed to some nearby peasants and asked Dore to sketch them. Quickly, Dore penciled a masterful rendering of the peasants that confirmed his identity.[2]

Would our actions confirm our identity as followers of Christ? Scripture says, "We are God's workmanship, created in Christ Jesus to do good works, which God prepared in advance for us to do" (Ephesians 2:10, NIV).

As you understand who you are in Christ, your behavior should begin to live up to your amazing new identity. You are a child of God, an heir of God, a saint with a new nature, a member of the body of Christ, and a citizen of Christ's kingdom. Your new, supernatural self-image should dramatically transform your lifestyle and behavior.

Godly behavior has three characteristics. Ask yourself if your behavior would pass the "3 P Test."

- Is the *purpose* of your behavior to do God's will?

- Does the *power* for your behavior come from God?

- Does the *product* of your behavior glorify God rather than yourself?

First, is the purpose of your behavior to do God's will? Jesus set the example for us when He walked this earth in human form. Jesus said, "I have come down from heaven to do the will of God who sent Me, not to do what I want" (John 6:38). This same Jesus lives in and through us. His presence should create in us a desire to do what God

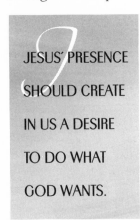

JESUS' PRESENCE SHOULD CREATE IN US A DESIRE TO DO WHAT GOD WANTS.

wants. Our all-knowing Father may lead us in unexpected ways, but remember that even small things people do can have a big impact —like a young boy's act of kindness toward a schoolmate he did not even know.

The boy, Steve, was walking home from junior high school when he noticed another boy who had tripped and fallen on the sidewalk. Books and other possessions were scattered around him. Steve helped the other boy, Bob, pick up his things and carry them home. The boys spent a few hours together playing games and watching TV. Over the next few years, they saw each other only sporadically, but just before high school graduation, Bob told Steve a long-kept secret.

Bob revealed why he had been carrying such an armload on that day long ago. He had emptied out his locker because that afternoon he was planning to commit suicide. But his pleasant hours with Steve made him reconsider. He realized how much he would miss if he killed himself, so he changed his mind. Steve's small kindness saved Bob's life.[3]

The second question to ask about your behavior is: Does its power come from God? We learn in Scripture that Paul had a thorn in the flesh. He asked God to remove it, but God did not: "Three different times I begged the Lord to take it away. Each time He said, 'My gracious favor is all you need. My power works best in your weakness.' So now I am glad to boast about my weaknesses, so that the power of Christ may work through me...For when I am weak, then I am strong" (2 Corinthians 12:8,9,10).

I make it a regular practice to get on my knees and pray, "Lord Jesus, I thank You that You live within me in all of Your mighty resurrection power. I invite You to walk around in my body, think with my mind, love with my heart, and speak with my lips. Continue the ministry of seeking and saving the lost through me as You came into the world to do 2,000 years ago."

All day long I draw on the supernatural resources of God. Sometimes I have been so weary from traveling and various engagements that I can hardly put one foot in front of the other. But God enables me to accomplish what I need to do. On different occasions, I have sat on a platform in a church service and was so tired that I unintentionally dozed off while people were singing. Then, even though I was very exhausted, I got up and preached with power. This has to be the touch of God. It certainly is not my doing. Which brings us to the third test of godly behavior.

Does the product of your behavior glorify God rather than yourself? Jesus said, "In the same way, let your good deeds shine out for all to see, so that everyone will praise your heavenly Father" (Matthew 5:16).

God can use ordinary people in extraordinary ways for His glory. Corrie ten Boom was a Dutch believer in Holland at the start of World War II. She and her family hid Jews in a secret room of their home. In time, they were caught, and were sent to a Nazi concentration camp.

Corrie had a small Bible she wanted to take inside the camp, but prisoners were being stripped and searched before they entered. She prayed and asked God to intervene in His power. As she was searched, she clutched her precious Bible in her hands. Although it was in plain sight, the guards never saw it. Later, God in His sovereignty used an infestation of fleas to keep the guards away from the barracks so Corrie could lead a Bible study in that awful concentration camp. As a result, she was able to share hope and love in a place filled with hate and despair.[4]

Corrie's purpose was to do God's will. She relied on God's power, and the product of her behavior glorified Him.

How can we act in ways that bring glory to God? How can we behave with the character of Christ in our everyday situations? Let us look at six guidelines for godly behavior. Each is linked to an aspect of our identity in Christ. As you read through these next pages, ask yourself if these characteristics are evident in your behavior. You can remember them by the acrostic BEHAVE:

B	*Bend* to God's holy will and loving discipline as His child.
E	*Esteem* your spiritual riches as an heir of God.
H	*Honor* God by your holiness as His saint.
A	*Apply* your gifts to serve others as a member of Christ's body.
V	*Voice* the gospel to others as a citizen of Christ's kingdom.
E	*Exhibit* faith in God in all circumstances as a vessel for Christ.

BEND TO GOD'S HOLY WILL AND LOVING DISCIPLINE AS HIS CHILD

Scripture says, "Obey God because you are His children. Don't slip back into your old ways of doing evil; you didn't know any better then" (1 Peter 1:14). Jesus proclaimed, "My nourishment comes from doing the will of God, who sent Me, and from finishing His work" (John 4:34).

If we are to behave with the character of Christ, we must trust and obey our loving heavenly Father.

A story is told of a loving father who was trying to save his daughter during a bombing raid in World War II. Fleeing a building that had just been hit and desperate for shelter, he spied a large hole from an earlier shell explosion. He leaped in, then lifted his arms to catch his child. The terrified girl cried out that she could not see him. He looked up and saw her silhouette illuminated by tracer lights and fire. The father called out to her, "I can see you. Jump!" When she heard the encouraging words of her father, she jumped into the safety of his arms.[5]

Our wise and all-knowing God sees us everyday, and He knows how to protect us from dangers—both spiritual and physical. When we bend to His will and discipline, we are jumping into His invisible arms. We are demonstrating our love and are trusting in His wisdom rather than relying on our own understanding.

As we daily surrender our plans and desires to our loving Father, we reflect the character of Jesus. In obedience to His Father, Jesus sacrificed everything. He gave up His life and took upon Himself the horror and guilt of our sins. This choice to obey was not easy, as His battle in Gethsemane reveals. The Bible describes His sweat as "drops of blood" as He pleaded, "Father, if You are willing, take this cup from Me; yet not My will, but Yours be done" (Luke 22:42, NIV).

ESTEEM YOUR SPIRITUAL RICHES AS AN HEIR OF GOD

Consider Paul's prayer for the Ephesians: "I pray that your hearts will be flooded with light so that you can understand the wonderful future He has promised to those He called. I want you to realize what a rich and glorious inheritance He has given to His people" (Ephesians 1:18).

If we want to exhibit the character of Christ, we must realize that what we value motivates what we do.

Often, we do not realize the value of what is in front of us. This is illustrated by a well-known poem, *The Touch of the Master's Hand*. An auctioneer holds up an old violin and asks for bids. The instrument is battered and scarred, and the bids are low—only a few dollars. But then, a gray-haired man strides to the front of the crowd. He takes the violin, dusts it off, tunes the strings, and plays an angelic melody. A hush falls over the crowd. When he finishes, the auctioneer holds up the violin again, but this time the bids are in the thousands! What was the difference? The touch of the master's hand.

The poem concludes with a beautiful comparison. Often we feel as worthless as that old violin, but the touch of our magnificent Creator and Master shows the infinite value of each battered soul.[6]

We can extend that analogy to spiritual riches. God offers us riches of infinite worth—forgiveness, wisdom, the power of the Holy Spirit, eternal life, and so much more. But sometimes we discount them and place more value on the shiny treasures of *this* world. Yet the fleeting riches of beauty, fame, power, or money do not compare with the eternal treasures our loving Father lavishly bestows upon us.

What we value—either God's abundant riches or the world's false treasures—will dictate our behavior. If we value money, our time will be dedicated to accumulating wealth. If we desire power or fame, we will act in ways to gain the world's approval. But if we value God's treasures and seek to store our treasures in heaven, "where they will never become moth-eaten or rusty and where they will be safe from thieves" (Matthew 6:20), we will live a life that pleases God. Jesus goes on to say, "Wherever your treasure is, there your heart and thoughts will also be" (Matthew 6:21).

As a young man, I was especially ambitious. I was a humanist and a materialist. As an unbeliever, the only way I measured success was in the accumulation of wealth. But with the passing of time, I began to learn about our great God and Savior, and I gave myself to Him. It was then that I began to experience true wealth—an intimate relationship with the One who created over a hundred billion galaxies. Now my desire is to know Him better and to daily invite Him to work through me to fulfill His purposes in my life and the world.

HONOR GOD BY YOUR HOLINESS AS HIS SAINT

The Bible urges us, "Be careful how you live among your unbelieving neighbors. Even if they accuse you of doing wrong, they will see your honorable behavior, and they will believe and give honor to God when He comes to judge the world" (1 Peter 2:12).

We honor God when we reflect the holy character of Jesus. Just as a child's good or bad behavior reflects on his or her parents, our behavior reflects on God, our heavenly Father.

My grandfather was a leading businessman in Oklahoma. He had a reputation for being as honest as Abraham Lincoln. On one occasion an oil venture did not go as he had hoped. The law did not require him to return the investors' money, but his integrity did. So he paid back each investor.

Many years later in 1948 as I was on my way home to Oklahoma to be married, I stopped in a city where my grandfather had lived for some time. I went into a jewelry store to buy gifts for my wedding party. I asked the gentleman if the store accepted out-of-state checks. He said, "No." Then as I was about to leave, he asked, "What's your name?"

When I replied, "Bill Bright," he asked, "Do you know a man by the name of Sam Bright?" I told him Sam Bright was my grandfather. Immediately, he said, "If you're like your grandfather, your check is good for anything you want in this store. He was the most honorable man I have ever known."

As Christians, we represent our loving Savior, and when we act with integrity, we bring glory to Him. God calls on us to "be holy, because I am holy" (1 Peter 1:16, NIV). We are God's saints so we should commit ourselves to live holy lives worthy of our calling.

APPLY YOUR GIFTS TO SERVE OTHERS AS A MEMBER OF CHRIST'S BODY

The Bible teaches us, "A spiritual gift is given to each of us as a means of helping the entire church" (1 Corinthians 12:7).

If we wish to exhibit the character of Christ, we must serve others. Jesus declares in Matthew 20:28, "Even I, the Son of Man, came here not to be served but to serve others, and to give My life as a ransom for many."

A few years ago, I planned to take Vonette to an especially elegant restaurant to celebrate our anniversary. I wanted to express to her in a tangible way how important she is to me. But then something caused me to change my mind, and she and I agreed to spend that evening serving meals to the homeless on skid row. That night as we ladled out food together side-by-side, our hearts were broken. These men and women were all visibly defeated. No one looked me in the eye. I soon realized that but for the grace of God, what had happened to them could happen to me. I began to weep. I served for an hour or so with tears streaming down my cheeks. Although it was a small act of service, God reminded me how important it is to demonstrate compassion to those less fortunate. And He showed me the importance of being a servant.

We are called to be servants to the poor, orphans, widows, and especially those in the family of God. When we cultivate an attitude of service, we promote unity in the church and build each other up in Christ.

VOICE THE GOSPEL TO OTHERS AS A CITIZEN OF CHRIST'S KINGDOM

Jesus said, "When the Holy Spirit has come upon you, you will receive power and will tell people about Me everywhere—in Jerusalem, throughout Judea, in Samaria, and to the ends of the earth" (Acts 1:8).

He declared about Himself, "The Son of Man came to seek and to save what was lost" (Luke 19:10). And elsewhere Scripture says, "You must never be ashamed to tell others about our Lord" (2 Timothy 1:8).

If we are to behave with the character of Christ, we must openly share the joy of our salvation to those around us.

The Book of Esther is about a young Jewish girl who was called upon to speak out for God. Esther was chosen Queen of Persia at a time when many Jews lived under Persian rule. An evil man named Haman convinced the king to order the death of all the Jews. When the king granted the request, he did not know that Esther was Jewish. Esther's uncle, Mordecai, asked her to go to the king and intervene on behalf of her people. But she knew that if she came into the king's presence without being invited, he could have her executed.

At first she hesitated. But Mordecai pointed out that God may have placed her in the palace for just this purpose. She asked her uncle to have the Jews join her in fasting and prayer. Then led by God, she spoke to the king. She found favor, and both she and her people were spared.

Esther's action saved thousands of her people. Each day, we come into contact with people who need to experience the salvation of God as much as those Jews did. When Jesus walked this earth, He boldly proclaimed the gospel to all who would listen. So, too, we have the honor and privilege of sharing the wonderful news that Jesus is the way for every person to be reconciled to their glorious God and Creator.

EXHIBIT FAITH IN GOD IN ALL CIRCUMSTANCES AS A VESSEL FOR CHRIST

Scripture encourages, "Consider it pure joy, my brothers, whenever you face trials of many kinds, because you know that the testing of your faith develops perseverance" (James 1:2,3, NIV).

If we are to reflect the character of Christ, we must prove faithful, regardless of our circumstances.

In the mid-1800s, a young couple in Glasgow, Scotland, gave birth to a beautiful baby boy. The baby developed an infection in his eyes that marred his vision. Although his parents and medical specialists fought heroically to reverse this condition, before George Matheson finished his coursework at Glasgow University, he was completely blind. His family was distraught.

But George was deeply committed to the Lord. Rather than becoming bitter, he drew upon his Savior's strength. Within a few years, he graduated with honors in philosophy, studied for the ministry, and became the pastor of one of the largest congregations in Edinburgh! In his memorable lifetime, he not only prepared numerous sermons, he also visited his many parishioners, continued his studies, and wrote twelve books and numerous articles.

How difficult it must have been for George and his parents when he first lost his eyesight. But God gave him the courage, perseverance, and resourcefulness to be victorious in spite of his handicap. And his faith grew ever stronger. After twenty years of blindness, he penned the beautiful hymn:

> O Love that will not let me go,
> I rest my weary soul on Thee!
> I give Thee back the life I owe
> That in Thine ocean depths its flow
> May richer, fuller be.[7]

God honors those who place their faith in Him. Queen Esther certainly grew in her faith, as did Abraham, Sarah, Moses, David, and many others mentioned in Hebrews 11, the Bible's Faith Hall of Fame. "By faith these people overthrew kingdoms, ruled with justice, and received what God had promised them...But others trusted God and were tortured, preferring to die rather than turn from God and be free ...All of these people we have mentioned received God's approval because of their faith" (Hebrews 11:33,35,39). God wants you and me to grow in our faith, too. Few of us will have to endure the torture and oppression mentioned in Hebrews 11, but all of us must persevere through the daily struggles of life.

One minister explains this concept through an analogy of a $1,000 bill. If our life were represented by a $1,000 bill, we must first lay that bill on the table and say, "Here's my life, Lord. I'm giving it all." But our walk with the Lord does not stop there. Rarely does God have us spend that thousand dollars all at once through one "blaze of glory"— one dramatic act for the kingdom of God. Instead, God sends us to the bank and has us cash in the $1,000 for quarters. Then we go through life serving our magnificent Lord by accomplishing small, everyday acts of obedience—putting out 25 cents here and 50 cents there.[8]

Your daily 50 cents might be faithfully taking care of an ailing parent or working on a struggling marriage. Perhaps a child is rebelling or finances are low. Each loving word you speak and every life you touch with the gospel of Christ is an investment to the glory of God.

As F. B. Meyer, an influential English clergyman and friend of D. L. Moody, wrote, "Don't waste your time waiting and longing for large opportunities which may never come, but faithfully handle the little things that are always claiming your attention."[9]

Whatever your situation, trusting in God is a dynamic witness that builds character—Christlike character.

Inviting Christ to live in and through us means our behavior should begin to mirror our wonderful Savior's divine nature. When we obey God, claim our spiritual inheritance, pursue holiness, serve others, witness, and exhibit faith, we are doing just that. As we imitate Christ, we will enjoy the peace, joy, and abundant blessings of a godly character.

And we shall also experience Christ's victory. We will explore this in the next chapter when we begin Part IV, "Our Victory in Christ."

Life Application

Renew Your Mind—Commit the following verses and acrostic to memory:

- "In the same way, let your good deeds shine out for all to see, so that everyone will praise your heavenly Father" (Matthew 5:16).

- "Obey God because you are His children. Don't slip back into your old ways of doing evil; you didn't know any better then" (1 Peter 1:14).

- The BEHAVE acrostic will help you remember to:
  Bend to God's holy will and loving discipline as His child.
  Esteem your spiritual riches as an heir of God.
  Honor God by your holiness as His saint.
  Apply your gifts to serve others as a member of Christ's body.
  Voice the gospel to others as a citizen of Christ's kingdom.
  Exhibit faith in God in all circumstances as a vessel for Christ.

Take Up Your Cross—Prayerfully meditate on the five principles of the CROSS acrostic: "Heavenly Father, I thank You that I am a new creation and free from the destructive behaviors of my old nature. I praise You that I am dead to sin, so I can resist any temptation to act in a way that dishonors Your Name. I offer my body as an instrument of righteousness and thank You that I will reap the rewards of a godly life—the greatest reward being Your pleasure. I surrender my will to You, depending on Your strength and power to live as I should. May my actions honor and exalt Christ, my Lord and Savior. Amen."

Act by Faith—Would you like to be known as a person of honest character and integrity? Each morning, ask God to empower you with the Holy Spirit so you will act as you should. Then as tempers flair or conflicts arise, ask God for direction and do not hesitate to admit your failings. Remember, only the power of Christ living in and through you can produce a Christlike character.

PART IV

Our Victory
in Christ

CHAPTER 12

Experiencing Supernatural Power

*T*he 100 Most Powerful People." This headline dominates the cover of a popular entertainment magazine. Inside, the editors rank film and television moguls and celebrities based on their financial resources and their ability to mastermind megaprojects and close multimillion-dollar deals.

As we read through the list of notables, many of us may feel a twinge of jealousy. How we wish we were powerful! If we only had more power we could change our circumstances, influence other people, or feel in control of our lives.

But are we so powerless? Is worldly power really what we need?

On a radiant New Year's morning in Pasadena, California, a beautiful float in the Tournament of Roses parade suddenly sputtered and stopped. It was out of gas. The entire parade came to a standstill until someone brought a few gallons of gasoline.

The irony of the situation was that the float represented the Standard Oil Company. This large corporation owned vast reserves of gas and oil, yet its float came to a grinding halt because it had run out of fuel.[1]

How similar this is to us when we fail to draw upon the vast reserves of our mighty Savior's power, which are so readily available to us through our new identity in Christ.

In the first few chapters of this book, we discovered that we are children of God, heirs of God, saints with a new nature, members of

151

the body of Christ, and citizens of Christ's kingdom. Once we were assured of our wonderful new identity, we saw how Christ living in and through us should influence how we think, speak, and behave. In this section, we will uncover the incredible victory that is possible when we understand our amazing identity and live accordingly. Because a supernatural self-image plus a Christlike lifestyle equals victory!

IT MAKES ALL THE DIFFERENCE

In the mid-1800s, an ordinary boy grew up in a small town in Massachusetts. His widowed mother struggled to provide for her nine children. At one point, the family was so poor that the children walked to church barefoot carrying their shoes and stockings so they would not wear out. But at the age of 17, this boy made a commitment to Christ in the back room of the shoe store where he worked. His life was changed. He began inviting everyone he could to his church. When he attempted to preach, one of the deacons assured him that he could serve God best by keeping silent. Another member praised the young man for his zeal, but recommended that he realize his limitations and not attempt to speak in public.

This average young man was Dwight L. Moody. He went on to preach to millions and to be used by God to draw thousands upon thousands into Christ's kingdom.

What made the difference in the life of this ordinary man? At the beginning of Moody's ministry, he accepted the challenge of a Mr. Henry Varley: "The world has yet to see what God will do with and for and through and in and by the man who is fully consecrated to Him." As Moody reflected on these wise words, he thought, "He said 'a man.' He did not say a great man, nor a learned man, nor a smart man, but simply 'a man.' I am a man and it lies within the man himself whether he will or will not make that entire and full consecration."[2]

That day D. L. Moody gave all of himself to his Savior and Lord. He invited Christ to live in and through him—and that made all the difference.

POWER FOR VICTORY

Our victory in Christ, like the victory D. L. Moody experienced, is possible only by living in Christ's power. His power is radically different from and superior to the power of the world. King David declared, "In

Your hands are strength and power to exalt and give strength to all" (1 Chronicles 29:12, NIV). Jeremiah exclaimed, "Ah, Sovereign LORD, You have made the heavens and the earth by Your great power and outstretched arm. Nothing is too hard for You" (Jeremiah 32:17, NIV). Our Lord is the one who healed the leper, gave sight to the blind, and raised the dead.

The natural vehicles of power in this world are wealth, authority, popularity, might, and influence. But God's power is supernatural. His power is not limited by our abilities, resources, or intelligence. He is not bound by time or any physical barriers. His power can be awesome, as displayed in the parting of the Red Sea, or serene, as demonstrated by the still, small voice of God.

If we depend on God, we also are no longer limited by the power of our natural resources. To be used by God, we do not need to graduate first in our class or make a large salary. His power is available to us for the everyday struggles of battling temptation and bad attitudes. At times, God's power will also produce supernatural healing or other miraculous answers to prayer.

Often, God may sovereignly use the world's sources of power for His purposes, as He did when He placed Esther in a place of authority to save the Jewish people. But God is not limited by our lack of wealth, influence, position, or prestige. In fact, Christ's power is made perfect in our weakness. That is why Paul exclaims, "I am glad to boast about my weaknesses, so that the power of Christ may work through me" (2 Corinthians 12:9).

God's greatest "power play" was the ultimate act of love, servanthood, and self-sacrifice—Christ's death on the cross and His glorious resurrection. This sacrificial act of supernatural power defeated death and Satan making it possible to have eternal fellowship with our all-powerful God.

If we understand who we are in Christ, we can access His power to reach our spiritual potential. Through Him, we can reach heights we could never attain on our own.

RESOURCES FOR SPIRITUAL POWER

Think about what happens when we board a plane. We say, "I am flying to my destination." But we are not doing the flying; the plane is. We are able to fly only because we are in the plane. If we stepped outside the door, we would plummet to the ground.

In the same way, we have no power in and of ourselves to live the Christian life. It requires supernatural power—Christ's power. We can have that power only when Christ lives in and through us. If we try to "step outside the plane" and live the Christian life in our own strength, we will fall.

Through the Holy Spirit, we have been given supernatural power to live a victorious life for Him. It is available to us from the moment we are born spiritually. The Bible assures us, "His divine power has given us everything we need for life and godliness through our knowledge of Him who called us by His own glory and goodness" (2 Peter 1:3, NIV).

Despite God's provision, we may suffer a power shortage in our lives. We may fail to understand the amount of power available to us. Or we may short-circuit the flow of that power in our lives by sin, unbelief, or a failure to spend time with God to prayerfully seek His will in His Word. These grieve and quench the Holy Spirit. But we can confess our sins and restore our fellowship with Him.

All believers have three resources for spiritual power:

- The Holy Spirit

- Scripture

- Prayer

As we discussed in Chapter 2, we are empowered by the Holy Spirit who indwells us. He is the source of all spiritual power. He gives us power to live a supernatural life and be fruitful for God. We see this in Paul's divinely inspired prayer for the Ephesians: "I pray that from His glorious, unlimited resources He will give you mighty inner strength through His Holy Spirit" (Ephesians 3:16).

In 1947, I was part of a seminary deputation team that spoke in a church in Los Angeles. People came up afterward and complemented us. They said, "Oh, you are wonderful. You will make fine ministers." But no one, as far as I know, was challenged to do anything for the Lord.

Later that year, while I was at Forest Home Conference Center in the San Bernardino Mountains, the Holy Spirit gave me insights that transformed my life in a supernatural way. For the first time I really understood what it meant to be filled with the Holy Spirit. I went back to that same church to speak, and when I gave the invitation, practically the whole church came forward weeping. I was speaking with the supernatural power of the Holy Spirit, which made all the difference!

We are also empowered by God's Word. The Holy Spirit empowers and transforms us with God's truth. Scripture says, "The word of God is full of living power. It is sharper than the sharpest knife, cutting deep into our innermost thoughts and desires. It exposes us for what we really are" (Hebrews 4:12).

Martin Luther's life was transformed by the power of God's Word. As a student and later as a monk, he suffered from fits of severe depression. We do not know what physiological or psychological factors may have been involved, but we do know that he was desperately seeking assurance of his salvation.

Although Luther poured himself into his studies, received a doctorate in theology, and became a professor of Scripture, his agony continued. Then one night, the Holy Spirit opened his eyes to the marvelous truth of Romans 1:17, "...the just shall live by faith" (KJV). Hope and peace filled his heart.

> THE HOLY SPIRIT GIVES US POWER TO LIVE A SUPERNATURAL LIFE AND BE FRUITFUL FOR GOD.

The Bible assured Luther that salvation was not determined by his own good works, but by faith in Christ—and the Reformation was born. God's truth from the Bible powerfully transformed Luther's life and the world.

We are also empowered through prayer. Prayer releases God's power in our lives. Scripture commands, "Devote yourselves to prayer with an alert mind and a thankful heart" (Colossians 4:2).

Shortly after its founding, Dallas Seminary faced a severe financial crisis. One morning, its founders met to pray knowing that at noon that very day all the creditors would foreclose. Harry Ironside, who was in that meeting, prayed, "Lord, we know that the cattle on a thousand hills are thine. Please sell some of them and send us the money."

As they prayed in the seminary president's office, a tall Texan showed up in the business office with a check in his hand. He explained that he had sold some cattle and had planned to use the money for a business deal, but the deal did not work out. He felt God wanted the money given to the seminary.

A secretary brought the check to the prayer meeting. The amount was exactly what the seminary owed. The president recognized the name on the check. He turned to Dr. Ironside. "'Harry,'" he said, "God sold the cattle."[3]

Prayer involves praising and thanking God, listening to Him, and seeking His will to accomplish His purposes. Obviously, it was God's purpose for Dallas Seminary to continue. Since that day, God has used this seminary to train tens of thousands of pastors, missionaries, teachers, and other ministers.

God wants us to use His power for His purposes today. Let's look at five reasons why God gives us power. With the acrostic POWER, you can remember that God gives you power to...

P   *Proclaim* the gospel boldly

O   *Overcome* evil forces in the world and spiritual realm

W   *Withstand* personal temptation and adversity

E   *Embrace* God's perfect will for your life

R   *Reflect* God's character

POWER TO PROCLAIM THE GOSPEL BOLDLY

Jesus explained to His followers, "When the Holy Spirit has come upon you, you will receive power and will tell people about Me everywhere—in Jerusalem, throughout Judea, in Samaria, and to the ends of the earth" (Acts 1:8).

God has empowered us to be His witnesses, even in the most difficult circumstances.

Paul and Silas traveled to Philippi to share the good news of Jesus' death and resurrection. But rather than rejoicing at the wonderful news of a right relationship with the only true God, the Philippian magistrates had Paul and Silas severely beaten and thrown in prison.

How did Paul and Silas respond? As they lay in their cell, their feet in stocks and their backs bloody, they did not hate their enemies or feel despair. Instead, they prayed, sang hymns, and proclaimed Christ to those around them. As a result, the jailer and his family were saved, and a great work began in Philippi.

This same Holy Spirit motivates and empowers believers today. On any given day, it is estimated that as many as 2,000 teams are showing the *JESUS* film in villages, cities, and universities around the world. These teams consist of courageous, godly men and women who in certain parts of the world risk their lives to share the wonderful message of Jesus Christ. Because these brave believers love God so much, they refuse to remain silent as long as there are people who have not heard the gospel. Many have been stoned; others have been poisoned; some even killed. These dedicated Christians have helped take the gospel through the *JESUS* film to more than 3.5 billion people.

Words apart from the power of God are simply words. But as we draw upon His power, the words of the gospel will penetrate the minds and hearts of those around us.

POWER TO OVERCOME EVIL FORCES IN THE WORLD AND SPIRITUAL REALM

The Bible explains, "Every child of God defeats this evil world by trusting Christ to give the victory. And the ones who win this battle against the world are the ones who believe that Jesus is the Son of God" (1 John 5:4,5).

God's power working in and through us surpasses all worldly and evil forces.

The Old Testament prophet Elijah relied on God's power to prevail against strongholds of deception. King Ahab had turned many of the people away from God to worship Baal.

But Elijah stood up to the king and hundreds of false prophets. He proposed a power demonstration. Two bulls would be placed on altars as sacrifices. Whoever consumed a bull by fire—Baal or the God of Israel—was God indeed.

The prophets of Baal cried out to their god, cut themselves, and danced around their altar, but nothing happened. Then Elijah ordered that the bull on the altar of the LORD be thoroughly soaked with water. As he prayed, God sent down fire from heaven and consumed the bull, as well as the surrounding wood, stones, and soil. When the Israelites saw this, they fell prostrate and cried, "The LORD is God! The LORD is God!" (1 Kings 18:39) As a result, the prophets of Baal were put to death, for their deception had been revealed.

Satan's primary weapon is deception. But the power of God's truth can defang the lies of the Serpent. Scripture says, "We are human, but we don't wage war with human plans and methods. We use God's mighty weapons, not mere worldly weapons, to knock down the Devil's strongholds. With these weapons we break down every proud argument that keeps people from knowing God. With these weapons we conquer their rebellious ideas, and we teach them to obey Christ" (2 Corinthians 10:3–5).

POWER TO WITHSTAND PERSONAL TEMPTATION AND ADVERSITY

God's Word assures us, "The temptations that come into your life are no different from what others experience. And God is faithful. He will keep the temptation from becoming so strong that you can't stand up against it. When you are tempted, He will show you a way out so that you will not give in to it" (1 Corinthians 10:13).

GOD'S POWER

IS STRONG

ENOUGH TO

HELP US RESIST

ANY TEMPTATION.

God's power is strong enough to help us resist any temptation.

When Jesus was tempted by Satan in the wilderness, He relied on the power of God's Word. He resisted Satan's propaganda by quoting Scripture. Satan offered Jesus the kingdoms of the world, tempted Him to use His power to satisfy His desires, and suggested that Jesus test God to prove His own deity. But Jesus withstood the temptation and chose to gain power God's way—by dying on the cross.

The power of God's Word is also available to you. The Spirit of the living Christ—the One who successfully resisted Satan in the wilderness—lives in you.

One young boy was asked what he did when he was tempted. He answered, "When I hear Satan come knocking at the door of my heart, I just say to the Lord Jesus, who lives within my heart, 'Lord Jesus, will You please go to the door?' And then, when the Lord Jesus opens the door, Satan draws away and says, 'Oh! Excuse me, I have made a mistake.'"[4]

You may be tempted by pornography, addictions, or other things that take you away from wholeheartedly loving and serving your wonderful Savior. Scripture warns, "Do not be deceived: God cannot be mocked. A man reaps what he sows. The one who sows to please his sinful nature, from that nature will reap destruction; the one who sows to please the Spirit, from the Spirit will reap eternal life" (Galatians 6:7,8, NIV). When you disobey God, you will reap consequences —broken hearts, missed opportunities, and shattered lives. But Christ in you is stronger than any temptation. When facing temptation, remember the many promises of Scripture and rely on the Holy Spirit to empower you. Then stand firm!

POWER TO EMBRACE GOD'S PERFECT WILL FOR YOUR LIFE

Through God's power, we can accomplish much more than the goals and plans possible by human means. Scripture promises, "Now glory be to God! By His mighty power at work within us, He is able to accomplish infinitely more than we would ever dare to ask or hope" (Ephesians 3:20).

Our mighty God empowers us to complete our life quest. Jesus' disciples learned this firsthand when He asked them to feed more than five thousand men, women, and children with five loaves and two fish.

Imagine feeding thousands of people with this little bit of food! The disciples thought it was impossible, but Jesus took their meager resources, blessed them, and gave them back to the disciples.

What happened? As the disciples obeyed the Lord and distributed the food, it multiplied. Everyone was fed. And there were twelve baskets of food left over!

How amazing to be used to bring about a miracle! We, too, can accomplish the Lord's mighty work when we allow Him to live in and through us.

Paul declares this marvelous truth, "We are God's masterpiece. He has created us anew in Christ Jesus, so that we can do the good things He planned for us long ago" (Ephesians 2:10).

If we place ourselves and all we have into God's hands, He will bless and multiply our efforts and resources to accomplish His purposes. He will empower us to accomplish what He desires in the fulfillment of His will—including living a godly life.

POWER TO REFLECT GOD'S CHARACTER

The Bible records Paul's divinely inspired prayer for the Colossians, "We also pray that you will be strengthened with His glorious power so that you will have all the patience and endurance you need" (Colossians 1:11).

God empowers us to become more like His holy Son.

Peter was strengthened with God's mighty power. He went from denying Christ three times to being a mighty leader of the early Church. Through the power of the Holy Spirit, he was used by God to bring 3,000 people to Christ at Pentecost, and he was the first to spread the gospel to the Gentiles. In the end, when Peter was martyred for his faith, he refused to die the same way as his glorious Savior, so the soldiers crucified him upside down. Although Peter began his journey with Jesus as an impulsive, rugged fisherman, he died a mirror of the One he so loved.

Peter is an example of how the power of God can be manifested in an ordinary person's life. Though he lacked worldly wealth and influence, he allowed himself to be a channel for God's power. Because of his yieldedness to God, he had a tremendous spiritual impact which continues today.

You and I may feel very ordinary at times, but Christ's power in us makes all the difference. Scripture promises, "Those who wait on the LORD will find new strength. They will fly high on wings like eagles. They will run and not grow weary. They will walk and not faint" (Isaiah 40:31).

One summer in the late 1800s, the composer Edvard Grieg vacationed in a small town in his native Norway. At the hotel where he stayed, a restless child sat down at the piano and attempted to play. The notes were broken and discordant, and the guests quickly became annoyed at the noise.

Suddenly, Grieg entered the room. Sensing the tension among the guests, he softly stole up behind the child, spread his arms on either side of her, and began to play. He wove such beautiful harmonies around her discordant notes that her mistakes were lost in the music of the master. When the piece was finished, Grieg presented the child to the audience and called for applause.[5]

Our amazing God masterfully weaves His power and grace around our fumbling efforts. Often we feel powerless, but we must always remember that the source of all power is the Master of the universe. His power is available to all who seek Him.

When Christ lives in and through us, the same power that raised Him from the dead is available to us. This power enables us to live a life of liberating freedom, which is the subject of our next chapter.

Life Application

Thank Your Heavenly Father—Thank your almighty Creator for making His power available to you. Praise Him that you can boldly live and speak the truth of the Good News to those around you. Thank Him that you do not need to fear Satan's power or his demons because God is infinitely more powerful. Express your gratitude for the power He gives you to overcome temptation and withstand the trials of life. Praise Him that as He empowers you to become more like Jesus, you will accomplish the purposes which He desires for your life.

Renew Your Mind—Commit the following to memory:

- "As we know Jesus better, His divine power gives us everything we need for living a godly life. He has called us to receive His own glory and goodness!" (2 Peter 1:3).

- "Now glory be to God! By His mighty power at work within us, He is able to accomplish infinitely more than we would ever dare to ask or hope" (Ephesians 3:20).

- The acrostic POWER can help you remember that God gives you power to...
  Proclaim the gospel boldly
  Overcome evil forces in the world and spiritual realm
  Withstand personal temptation and adversity
  Embrace God's perfect will for your life
  Reflect God's character

Reflect on Your New Life in Christ—Think of a time when you felt powerless. Now picture yourself in the same situation, having been filled with the mighty power of the Holy Spirit. How would your words and actions be different?

Share the Blessings—Is someone in your life feeling powerless? Tell him or her about our all-powerful God and the supernatural power that Christ offers.

CHAPTER 13

Enjoying Liberating Freedom

Freedom. Patriotic songs and history books extol its importance. Wars have been fought, lives lost, protests organized —all for the cause of freedom.

But what does it mean to live a life of freedom? Is freedom the license to do whatever we feel like doing? Is it the removal of obligations and responsibilities? Or is it something deep inside us that only our all-knowing Creator can provide?

In 1973, a somber crowd filled a stadium in Uganda to witness an execution. Three men were scheduled to die by firing squad. The men stood before the crowd with their hands cuffed and their feet chained.

A cleric who was granted permission to talk to the men before they died wondered what to say. Certainly the doomed men must be seething with rage. But as he approached the men, their expressions told a different story. Their faces were radiant! The men triumphantly proclaimed that each of them had received Jesus Christ as their Savior. Although they were in handcuffs and chains and were waiting to be killed, they knew they were free. Their sins were forgiven and they would be with Christ forever. They died, waving to the crowd of onlookers, their faces jubilant. They were humanly bound, but divinely liberated.[1]

These prisoners understood a tremendous truth. As Christians, we can experience liberating freedom regardless of our circumstances. The only true bondage is to sin and the only true freedom is in Christ.

Jesus Himself confirms this truth, "I assure you that everyone who sins is a slave of sin. A slave is not a permanent member of the family, but a son is part of the family forever. So if the Son sets you free, you will indeed be free" (John 8:34–36).

At the cross, Christ freed us from slavery to sin and death. The Scripture assures us, "Our old sinful selves were crucified with Christ so that sin might lose its power in our lives. We are no longer slaves to sin. For when we died with Christ we were set free from the power of sin. And since we died with Christ, we know we will also share His new life. We are sure of this because Christ rose from the dead, and He will never die again. Death no longer has any power over Him. He died once to defeat sin, and now He lives for the glory of God. So you should consider yourselves dead to sin and able to live for the glory of God through Christ Jesus" (Romans 6:6–11).

Jesus conquered sin and death by dying on the cross and rising again. As Peter proclaims, "Praise be to the God and Father of our Lord Jesus Christ! In His great mercy He has given us new birth into a living hope through the resurrection of Jesus Christ from the dead" (1 Peter 1:3, NIV).

SLAVERY OR FREEDOM

Before we met Christ, you and I were slaves in the sweatshop of sin. Our master was the Prince of Darkness. There was no way out, and our end was eternal damnation.

But Jesus bought our freedom with His blood. Scripture declares, "He has rescued us from the one who rules in the kingdom of darkness, and He has brought us into the Kingdom of His dear Son. God has purchased our freedom with His blood and has forgiven all our sins" (Colossians 1:13,14). There are only two kingdoms: the Kingdom of Christ and the kingdom of Satan. Everyone belongs to one of these two kingdoms. No matter how sophisticated, educated, or moral we might have been before meeting Christ, we were members of Satan's kingdom.

Salvation does not come from our own effort. The Word of God explains, "God saved you by His special favor when you believed. And you can't take credit for this; it is a gift from God. Salvation is not a reward for the good things we have done, so none of us can boast about it" (Ephesians 2:8,9). When we received Christ's gracious sacrifice for our sins, we were liberated from the clutches of that dark kingdom. Jesus welcomed us into His Father's family, the kingdom of righteousness. We are now children of God and joint heirs with Christ. And we are seated with Him in the heavenlies (Ephesians 2:6).

But our old nemesis, that evil Prince of Darkness, hates our new freedom. He wants to deceive us into a false bondage. He wants us to believe that we are still trapped in sin. However, Christ enables us to maintain our liberty through the power of His Spirit. Scripture explains, "Those who are dominated by the sinful nature think about sinful things, but those who are controlled by the Holy Spirit think about things that please the Spirit" (Romans 8:5).

CHRIST HAS CONQUERED SIN

Days after the American forces dropped atomic bombs on Nagasaki and Hiroshima, the Japanese surrendered. However, it took several weeks for news of the surrender to reach some of the concentration camps in Japan. Even after the war was over, prisoners in these camps continued to work, suffer, and die because they did not know the freedom that was theirs. In one place, an American general flew a helicopter into the camp and announced to the startled guards that they were now the ones to be in bondage—and the prisoners cheered![2]

How tragic that even though the peace treaty ensured the freedom of all Allied prisoners, many of them were still in bondage because they did not know that they were free. How true this is of us if we do not realize that Christ has set us free. The enemy has been defeated, and we can leave Satan's camp and kingdom.

To further illustrate the point, we can compare our situation as believers to a hearty oak that enjoyed a sunny spot in a neighborhood park. Then a vine sprouted and began to grow along its trunk. At first the vine seemed harmless, but over the years it grew so thick that the vine's creepers covered the lower half of the tree. The mass of tiny feelers was taking over the tree and threatening to squeeze the life out of it.

A gardener, seeing the danger, slashed the main trunk of the vine so it could no longer kill the tree. But the tangled mass of the vine's branches still twined around the tree.[3]

Christ has slashed the trunk of the sin-vine. But like the tree, we still have some branches of sin clinging to us. The Holy Spirit wants to clear them away, but Satan wants to make us believe those branches of sin are still alive and part of us. He wants to stunt our growth and keep us from fully experiencing our liberty.

Christ liberates us from the bondage of Satan's lies through the truth of His Word. Jesus said, "You will know the truth, and the truth will set you free" (John 8:32).

Let us look at seven areas of bondage and how God has set us free as explained in His holy, inspired, inerrant Word. With the acrostic FREEDOM, you can remember that God has set you free from...

F	*Fear* and worry
R	*Rejection* and inferiority
E	*Ego* and self-centeredness
E	*Envy* and bitterness
D	*Dependencies* and lusts
O	*Oppressive* guilt
M	*Meaninglessness* and despair

FREEDOM FROM FEAR AND WORRY

Anxiety about our health. Fears about loved ones being killed in an automobile accident or plane crash. Worry about our performance at work or school. Nervous anticipation about what may happen in the future. These gnawing concerns eat away at us and destroy our time, health, and happiness.

But why do we so easily become mired in fear?

Satan relishes crippling our lives with debilitating fear and worry. He lies to us, insinuating that we cannot fully trust and rely on God. He gleefully whispers in our ears that God is too busy, that He is unconcerned about our welfare. He tells us that we must handle everything in our own strength, or we are headed for disaster.

But these are lies! We must choose not to listen to them. For the truth is that we can depend on God because He is our Father and we are His dear *children* in whom He delights (Zephaniah 3:17).

Scripture explains, "You did not receive a spirit that makes you a slave again to fear, but you received the Spirit of sonship" (Romans 8:15, NIV).

God cares about us every moment of our lives. He will help us with any difficulty no matter how great or small. Our great God created over a hundred billion galaxies. The universe moves at a speed of a million miles an hour, yet He holds it all together by the word of His command. Certainly our awesome Creator can handle any problem or situation we face. We must only give our fears and worries to Him in obedience to His command: "Cast all your anxiety on Him, because He cares for you" (1 Peter 5:7, NIV).

Hudson Taylor, missionary to China and founder of China Inland Mission, wrote this kernel of wisdom: "Let us give up our work, our plans, ourselves, our lives, our loved ones, our influence, our all, right into God's hand; and then, when we have given all over to Him, there will be nothing left for us to be troubled about."[4]

How true this is! When we are free from fear and worry, we are able to live productive, joyful lives for God, for fear immobilizes, intimidates, destroys creativity, and even robs us of physical energy.

During the Napoleonic Wars, a French army of 18,000 soldiers surrounded a defenseless Austrian town. The town's inhabitants believed surrender was inevitable, but the old dean of the church reminded them that it was Easter. He begged them to hold services as usual and leave the dire situation in God's hands.

The town's leaders heeded his advice, and the dean went to the church to prepare for the services. The bells rang joyfully that Easter morning as the dean called the inhabitants to worship. But the French soldiers heard another meaning in the chimes. They concluded that the bells were ringing because the Austrian army had come to rescue the town. Before the bells had ceased to ring, the French army broke camp and vanished.[5]

Instead of concentrating on our fears, we should focus on being obedient to God and accomplishing the work He has for us. Then we will experience God's wonderful deliverance. The Bible promises, "Don't be afraid, for I am with you. Do not be dismayed, for I am your God. I will strengthen you. I will help you. I will uphold you with My victorious right hand" (Isaiah 41:10).

FREEDOM FROM REJECTION AND INFERIORITY

In this world of more than six billion people, it is easy to feel inferior and unimportant. In the bustle of everyday life, our self-image is often attacked with thoughts of "I'm not good enough" or "I don't matter."

Satan delights in such thoughts. In fact, he enjoys deceiving us into believing that we are unacceptable to God.

This is a lie. Because we have trusted in Jesus Christ, God not only accepts us; He has adopted us as His very own children. He loves us as much as He loves His only begotten Son, Jesus (John 17:23). The Bible teaches us that each of us is a beloved *child of God*. We are children of the King of the universe! And if God is for us, who can ever be against us? (Romans 8:31).

King David penned this beautiful promise, "You saw me before I was born. Every day of my life was recorded in your book. Every moment was laid out before a single day had passed. How precious are your thoughts about me, O God! They are innumerable!" (Psalm 139:16,17).

A story is told of a missionary couple who had labored in Africa for many decades and were returning home to America. When their boat docked in New York harbor, a band played and throngs of people lined the peer. But the celebration was not for them. President Teddy Roosevelt happened to be a passenger on that ship. He was returning from a safari in Africa, and he was the one the crowds had come to see.

This faithful couple was stepping back onto American soil after a lifetime of "sacrificial" service in a foreign land. Yet, as the wife remarked sadly to her husband, no one had come to welcome them.

With tears in his eyes, the husband turned to his wife and said, "Darling, we're not home yet." This couple's life of service was not for the approval of men, but for God.

We, too, must examine our motives. Who is our audience? Whose approval do we desire—God's or man's?

The Bible warns, "Cursed are those who put their trust in mere humans and turn their hearts away from the LORD. They are like stunted shrubs in the desert, with no hope for the future. They will live in the barren wilderness, on the salty flats where no one lives. But blessed are those who trust in the LORD and have made the LORD their hope and confidence. They are like trees planted along a riverbank, with roots that reach deep into the water. Such trees are not bothered by the heat or worried by long months of drought. Their leaves stay green, and they go right on producing delicious fruit" (Jeremiah 17:5–8).

When we seek God's approval, there is no fear of rejection, for He loves us as His dear children.

FREEDOM FROM EGO AND SELF-CENTEREDNESS

"The only sustaining love involvement is with yourself," the actress Shirley MacLaine declares.[6] Advertisements and advice columnists urge us to "look out for number one." But these attitudes are deceptions of Satan. He wants to undermine our relationship with God and others by directing our focus to ourselves.

The truth is, God designed us to be *members of Christ's body.* We are meant to be in fellowship with Him and other believers. The greatest blessings and honor come from serving God and others.

This is God's law: As we sow, we reap; as we give, we receive. That is why the sowing and giving of love is so paramount in God's plan. The Bible commands, "Don't be selfish; don't live to make a good impression on others. Be humble, thinking of others as better than yourself. Don't think only about your own affairs, but be interested in others, too, and what they are doing" (Philippians 2:3,4). God wants us to have a healthy self-image, but He also wants us to have a realistic understanding of our place in His marvelous creation.

> WE MUST EXAMINE OUR MOTIVES. WHO IS OUR AUDIENCE? WHOSE APPROVAL DO WE DESIRE— GOD'S OR MAN'S?

The naturalist William Beebe was a good friend of Teddy Roosevelt. After a full day at Sagamore Hill, the two would stroll out on the lawn and search the night sky for a spot of light near the Great Square of Pegasus. Then Teddy Roosevelt would recite: "That is the Spiral Galaxy in Andromeda. It is as large as our Milky Way. It is one of a hundred million galaxies.[7] It consists of one hundred billion suns, each larger than our sun." Then Roosevelt would turn to Beebe and grin, "Now I think we are small enough! Let's go to bed."[8]

President Teddy Roosevelt knew the virtue of humility. So did godly men like J. C. Penney, who built his merchandizing empire on the Golden Rule and gave most of his profit to Christian causes. There is great freedom in humility—freedom to serve others and freedom to enjoy God's honor when He bestows it on us. Scripture says, "Humble yourselves under the mighty power of God, and in His good time He will honor you" (1 Peter 5:6).

If a man truly has a correct view of God, he cannot have a big ego. Anyone who has had an intimate, divine encounter with God will inevitably say with Isaiah, "Woe to me!...For I am a man of unclean lips, and I live among a people of unclean lips, and my eyes have seen the King, the LORD Almighty" (Isaiah 6:5, NIV). Beware, the Scripture records and history confirms, "God sets Himself against the proud, but He shows favor to the humble" (James 4:6).

Our glorious Savior is our example. Although He was God, He humbled Himself by becoming a man and even dying for us! He told His disciples, "If any of you wants to be My follower, you must put aside your selfish ambition, shoulder your cross and follow Me. If you try to keep your life for yourself, you will lose it. But if you give up your life for My sake and the sake of the Good News, you will find true life" (Mark 8:34,35).

FREEDOM FROM ENVY AND BITTERNESS

"I wish I made the money he does."

"Why can't I drive a car like that? I deserve it."

"How come she always gets what she wants?"

"Life's just not fair!"

Do thoughts like these ever cross your mind? An afternoon stroll through a shopping mall, an update from an old school friend, or simply flipping through a catalog is enough to move many of us to envy.

But the Word of God declares, "Stay away from the love of money; be satisfied with what you have. For God has said, 'I will never fail you. I will never forsake you'" (Hebrews 13:5). And the tenth commandment is "Do not covet" (Exodus 20:17).

Satan enjoys sowing seeds of discontent in our lives. In fact, he likes to deceive us into believing that we have been cheated in life. He implants in our minds: If God is in charge, He must not be fair either!

But the truth is, we have no reason to feel cheated. We are *heirs of God*. We have a marvelous inheritance. Feeling cheated when others succeed or prosper only demonstrates that we value the wrong things.

Jesus taught, "Don't store up treasures here on earth, where they can be eaten by moths and get rusty, and where thieves break in and steal. Store your treasures in heaven, where they will never become moth-eaten or rusty and where they will be safe from thieves. Wherever your treasure is, there your heart and thoughts will also be" (Matthew 6:19–21).

God promises to provide all we need—not all we want! Contentment is perhaps one of God's greatest blessings. Paul writes, "Godliness with contentment is great gain" (1 Timothy 6:6, NIV).

Dwight L. Moody told a fable about an eagle who envied another bird who could fly higher than he could. One day, the eagle pointed out his rival to a hunter with a bow and arrow. "I wish you would shoot down that eagle up there," he said.

The hunter agreed to try, but said he needed feathers for his arrow. The eagle eagerly plucked out some of his own feathers and gave them to the hunter. The hunter shot the arrow, but it fell short of the eagle. The envious bird pulled out more feathers, but the arrows could not reach the rival bird because he was flying too high. The first eagle pulled out more and more feathers until finally he himself could not fly. The hunter then took advantage of the situation and killed the helpless bird.[9]

This fable illustrates an important truth. If you envy others, the one you hurt the most is yourself. Fortunately, if we follow the words of our wonderful Savior and allow Him to live in and through us, we will be set free from this destructive cycle of envy. As Jesus taught, "Seek first His kingdom and His righteousness, and all these things will be given to you as well" (Matthew 6:33, NIV).

FREEDOM FROM DEPENDENCIES AND LUSTS

Gossip, alcohol, smoking, food addictions, pornography. Do you feel trapped by a destructive habit? Are you tired of fighting it? Are you beginning to believe that you are a helpless sinner with no way out?

Satan, the father of lies, enjoys telling God's children that we will never conquer the cravings that enslave us. But the Bible says otherwise. Paul explains, "So I say, live by the Spirit, and you will not gratify the desires of the sinful nature. For the sinful nature desires what is contrary to the Spirit, and the Spirit what is contrary to the sinful nature. They are in conflict with each other, so that you do not do what you want. But if you are led by the Spirit, you are not under law" (Galatians 5:16–18, NIV; see also Romans 7).

In Christ we are *saints*. God sees us as holy, and He will work in and through us to accomplish what we cannot. The whole of the Christian life is a process of growing and maturing until we are finally conformed to the image of Christ. Then we will be what God already acknowledges us to be.

Many years ago, Vonette and I were walking down a shallow stream in Yosemite National Park with our two young sons. Because the rocks were slippery, I was holding our five-year-old son, Bradley, by the hand. Suddenly Brad slipped, and his feet went out from under him. I held him firmly until he regained his balance. As we continued on our walk, Brad looked up at me with an expression of gratitude and said, "Daddy, I'm sure glad you saved me from falling."

At that moment I was reminded how my heavenly Father has kept me from falling on many occasions. We walked in silence for a few minutes. Then Brad gazed up into my face again and said, "Daddy, I'm glad you're holding my hand." This time tears came to my eyes as I said to my Father in Heaven, "I'm so glad You hold me by the hand; I'm so prone to fall."

We can experience glorious freedom when we hold tightly to the hand of God. He is more powerful than the most powerful addiction. Remember, "God is working in you, giving you the desire to obey Him and the power to do what pleases Him" (Philippians 2:13).

FREEDOM FROM OPPRESSIVE GUILT

If we dwell on our failings, each of us has reasons to feel guilty. Perhaps we recently hurt our Christian witness at work or lost our temper with our spouse or children. Perhaps some past sin continues to haunt us. But that is not to be our focus! Satan, the great accuser, enjoys dredging up the past and focusing our attention on our shortcomings so we will be crippled by feelings of guilt.

God wants us, His dear children, to focus on Him and our new identity in Christ. We are new creatures, and we have been clothed in the righteousness of our glorious Savior. Isaiah declares, "I am overwhelmed with joy in the LORD my God! For He has dressed me with the clothing of salvation and draped me in a robe of righteousness" (Isaiah 61:10).

In Christ our sins are fully paid, and we are saints. The Scriptures assure us, "So now there is no condemnation for those who belong to

Christ Jesus. For the power of the life-giving Spirit has freed you through Christ Jesus from the power of sin that leads to death" (Romans 8:1,2).

The night before slavery was abolished in Jamaica in 1838, a large group of slaves gathered on the beach for a special ceremony. Before them was a large mahogany coffin and a deep hole. One by one, the soon-to-be-emancipated slaves placed symbols of their enslavement into the coffin: chains, leg-irons, padlocks, whips.

As midnight approached, the heavily laden coffin was lowered into the hole. Then the ex-slaves took up shovels and buried the coffin. As they did so, the group broke into joyous song: "Praise God from whom all blessings flow. Praise Him all creatures here below. Praise Him above ye heavenly host. Praise Father, Son, and Holy Ghost."[10]

Like those slaves, we, too, have been set free. God has buried all of our past wrongs and has freed us from guilt. When Satan tries to remind us of our sins and enslave us again with guilt, we must remember that we are forgiven, thanks to the death and resurrection of our wonderful Savior!

FREEDOM FROM MEANINGLESSNESS AND DESPAIR

Propelled by the doctrines of evolution and relativism, a pessimistic view of life has woven its way into the fabric of our society. Even we as Christians may be tempted to question whether our lives have any meaning or purpose. But this pessimism is a lie of Satan.

The truth is: We are *citizens of Christ's kingdom*. We have an amazing calling and a glorious purpose. God has appointed us as His ambassadors to proclaim His gospel through our words and our lives. There is no greater purpose or any greater adventure then serving our King. No wonder Jesus said, "I have come that they may have life, and have it to the full" (John 10:10, NIV).

In 1945 when I was a new Christian, God impressed upon me to do a film on the life of Jesus. I hoped to finance the film through my own business interests. But God, in His sovereignty, had led Vonette and me to invest the money we had to help start Campus Crusade for Christ.

Thirty-three years later, God moved in the hearts of a beloved couple, Bunker and Caroline Hunt, to underwrite the production costs for the *JESUS* film. As of January 1, 2000, this film has been viewed by over 3.4 billion people in 575 languages. Hundreds of millions have indicated salvation decisions. What an amazing work of God! All because a handful of people allowed Christ to work out His purposes through them. I have learned that God will always accomplish His will in His timing with greater results than we could have imagined. We have no reason to become disheartened with our current situation.

When you are tempted to become discouraged because of life's problems, allow the wonderful promises of Scripture to free you from despair: "The LORD hears His people when they call to Him for help. He rescues them from all their troubles. The LORD is close to the brokenhearted; He rescues those who are crushed in spirit. The righteous face many troubles, but the LORD rescues them from each and every one" (Psalm 34:17–19).

"Why am I discouraged? Why so sad? I will put my hope in God! I will praise Him again—my Savior and my God!" (Psalm 42:11). Meditating on God's promises frees our minds of dread and discouragement while filling our hearts with security and significance.

Imagine for a moment that you are the victim of a case of mistaken identity. You are arrested and convicted of a crime that someone else has committed. You needlessly spend years in jail until the truth is discovered and you are freed.

Many of us put ourselves in prison because we are mistaken about our identity in Christ. We may spend years in unnecessary bondage because we fail to believe the truth or apply it in our lives. But if we recognize Satan's lies and hold fast to our loving heavenly Father and the wonderful new identity we have in Christ, we will be truly free. Remember the promise found in Scripture, "Resist the Devil, and he will flee from you" (James 4:7). When we resist Satan with the power of God's truth, he will flee from us.

Liberating freedom comes from being clothed in Christ and His truth. This enables us to triumph over adversity, which we will explore in our next chapter.

Life Application

Renew Your Mind—Memorize and meditate on the following verses and acrostic:

- "You will know the truth, and the truth will set you free" (John 8:32).

- "You have been called to live in freedom—not freedom to satisfy your sinful nature, but freedom to serve one another in love" (Galatians 5:13).

- The FREEDOM acrostic will help you remember that God has set you free from…
  Fear and worry
  Rejection and inferiority
  Ego and self-centeredness
  Envy and bitterness
  Dependencies and lusts
  Oppressive guilt
  Meaninglessness and despair

Take Up Your Cross—Prayerfully reflect upon the five principles of the CROSS acrostic as they apply to your victorious life in Christ: "Holy Father, I praise You that I am a new creation and that You have freed me from the slavery of fear, rejection, and despair. Thank You that I am dead to sin, so I am no longer bound by guilt, envy, bitterness, dependencies, and lust. I offer my body as an instrument of righteousness. I surrender my will and ego to You, for only as a slave of Christ can I experience true freedom. I am dependent upon You. In Jesus' name, amen."

Act by Faith—Do you feel trapped by a bad habit, by the consequences of an unwise decision, or by worry and despair? God is more powerful than any obstacle, and He wants you to experience His supernatural freedom no matter what your circumstances. Give your concerns to Him and ask Him to make His freedom real to you each day. By faith, claim His freedom and live each day, not as a slave to sin, but as an obedient child of the King!

CHAPTER 14

Achieving Triumph Over Adversity

*W*ithout warning, something can happen to you that changes your life forever: A loved one is disabled by an accident or illness. A child dies. A marriage crumbles. A fire, flood, or earthquake destroys your home.

How do you react? Do you fall apart? Do you become bitter? Do you question God?

In the first section of this book, we discovered that we are children of God, heirs of God, saints with a new nature, members of the body of Christ, and citizens of Christ's kingdom. How should this new understanding of who we are in Christ influence the way we respond to the hard times of life? Does allowing Christ to live in and through us make a difference in the face of tragedy? In other words, why do Christians suffer?

About twenty years ago, a young woman entered into a lifetime of severe suffering. Joni Eareckson Tada dove into a lake and broke her neck. When she resurfaced, she had to be pulled from the water. Since then Joni has had no feeling or movement in her arms or legs. The suffering she faced and continues to experience is undoubtedly more than most of us will ever understand.

In her sorrow, Joni asked a question that I am sure all of us have pondered when going through great difficulty or tragedy: "What possible good can come out of what I am now going through?" She also asked, "Why me?"

How many times have you had something happen to you and then asked that same question—a question that seems to be the universal cry of those who suffer?

"The suffering and pain," Joni says, "have helped me mature emotionally, mentally, and spiritually. Pain and suffering have purpose. I believe God was working in my life to create grace and wisdom out of the chaos of pain and depression."[1]

MORE THAN CONQUERORS

Thousands of years earlier, a Hebrew youth named Daniel had his life changed forever by tragedy. His people were conquered by the great pagan ruler, King Nebuchadnezzar of Babylon. Daniel was taken from his homeland of Judah to a foreign country to be trained for service to this pagan despot.

Although his life was turned upside down, Daniel knew one thing had not changed. God is the same yesterday, today, and forever. Daniel put his faith in the Lord, and he conquered his conqueror. He won the king's favor and respect. Nebuchadnezzar came to rely on Daniel's wisdom and admire his faith. Some think this pagan ruler eventually became a believer.

Although Nebuchadnezzar was a conqueror, Daniel was more than a conqueror. Scripture triumphantly proclaims that this same victory belongs to all who are in Christ. God assures us, "Who shall separate us from the love of Christ? Shall trouble or hardship or persecution or famine or nakedness or danger or sword?... No, in all these things we are more than conquerors through Him who loved us" (Romans 8:35,37, NIV).

Let us look at four compelling biblical reasons that we are more than conquerors:

- Jesus Christ was more than a conqueror.
- We are in Christ.
- Nothing can separate us from Christ's love.
- God makes sure we cannot lose.

First, *we are more than conquerors because Jesus Christ was more than a conqueror.* Our Savior suffered overwhelming adversity and through it transformed the world. Listen to this prophetic description of the Messiah from the Old Testament book of Isaiah:

> He was despised and rejected—a man of sorrows, acquainted with bitterest grief. We turned our backs on Him and looked the other way when He went by. He was despised, and we did not care. Yet it was our weaknesses He carried; it was our sorrows that weighed Him down. And we thought His troubles were a punishment from God for His own sins! But He was wounded and crushed for our sins. He was beaten that we might have peace. He was whipped, and we were healed! (Isaiah 53:3–5).

Jesus endured temptation without sinning so He could be the perfect sacrifice for our sins (Hebrews 4:15). He endured rejection and persecution to make us acceptable to God. He defeated death through His resurrection so we could live with Him forever. He loved us while we were still His enemies so we could become His friends.

In the physical world, tremendous heat and pressure can be forces of destruction, but they are also the means by which carbon is transformed into diamonds. In a similar way, Jesus withstood tremendous pressure and difficulties so we could be transformed into spiritual diamonds and share in His glory. God sovereignly used Satan's tools of destruction—death, temptation, persecution, and rejection—as instruments of our redemption.

Secondly, *we are more than conquerors because we are in Christ.* Jesus conquered sin and death, and we are now in Him. We share in His marvelous victory! Paul writes, "How we thank God, who gives us victory over sin and death through Jesus Christ our Lord!" (1 Corinthians 15:57). Elsewhere, Scripture promises, "Everyone born of God overcomes the world. This is the victory that has overcome the world, even our faith" (1 John 5:4, NIV). Christ's power working in us ensures victory over anything this life may bring us.

As we daily place our faith in Christ and allow Him to live His life in and through us, we can experience a life of victory now and for eternity.

Third, *we are more than conquerors because nothing can separate us from Christ's love.* Just listen to this magnificent promise from Romans:

I am convinced that nothing can ever separate us from His love. Death can't, and life can't. The angels can't, and the demons can't. Our fears for today, our worries about tomorrow, and even the powers of hell can't keep God's love away. Whether we are high above the sky or in the deepest ocean, nothing in all creation will ever be able to separate us from the love of God that is revealed in Christ Jesus our Lord" (Romans 8:38,39).

The *Amplified Bible* illuminates the wonderful promise of Hebrews 13:5: "He [God] Himself has said, I will not in any way fail you nor give you up nor leave you without support. [I will] not, [I will] not, [I will] not in any degree leave you helpless nor forsake nor let [you] down (relax My hold on you)! [Assuredly not!]." Whether we are alive or have stepped over into the next life, God is with us. No spiritual force or being can separate us from His amazing love. No future tragedy or difficult circumstance can ever remove us from the presence of Christ's love. It does not matter where we go on earth or even in space, we can never go beyond the boundary of His all-encompassing love. God has even removed the barrier of sin between us and Him, because while we were in the midst of our sin, Christ died for us. What a wonderful promise!

Finally, *we are more than conquerors because God makes sure we cannot lose.* God gives us this magnificent assurance in Romans 8:28: "We know that God causes everything to work together for the good of those who love God and are called according to His purpose for them."

God does not promise that only good things will happen to His children. But He does promise that whatever happens He will use for our eternal benefit. We may not always understand the reason for difficulties in our life, but God can and will use bad things to make us better (James 1:2–4).

Pearls are formed when a tiny foreign particle, such as a grain of sand, finds its way into an oyster shell, causing irritation. This aggravation triggers secretions that form a magnificent gem.

The adversity we face in this world is like a grain of sand rubbing us the wrong way. It gets our attention. And if we are walking with Christ, it makes us rethink our priorities and triggers character growth. Our problems—although sometimes overwhelming in this life—are insignificant compared to the marvelous future glory that awaits us in our Lord and Savior, Jesus Christ.

The Bible promises, "Our present troubles are quite small and won't last very long. Yet they produce for us an immeasurably great glory that will last forever! So we don't look at the troubles we can see right now; rather, we look forward to what we have not yet seen. For the troubles we see will soon be over, but the joys to come will last forever" (2 Corinthians 4:17,18). When we remember the glorious destiny that is ours in Christ, our problems today become easier to endure.

We can live a life of triumph over trials because our amazing Savior was more than a conqueror, because we are in Him, because nothing can separate us from His unfailing love, and because God uses bad situations for our ultimate good.

Let us now look at seven benefits God brings out of adversity. With the acrostic TRIUMPH, you can remember that God uses adversity to produce...

T *Training* in obedience

R *Refinement* of your character

I *Intimacy* with your compassionate God and Savior

U *Understanding* of the hurts of others

M *Maturity* for ministering to others

P *Perseverance* in difficult times

H *Hope* for the future

ADVERSITY PRODUCES TRAINING IN OBEDIENCE

Scripture declares, "Even though Jesus was God's Son, He learned obedience from the things He suffered" (Hebrews 5:8).

We often learn the most in the midst of adversity.

A dear friend of mine whom I had the privilege of introducing to our Savior became one of the most prominent business leaders in his state. In time, this successful, influential man became ill with cancer. As his body was ravaged with disease, he and his wife drew closer and closer to Christ. They read the Scriptures and sang hymns of praise throughout the day. On several occasions he said to me, "I'm so glad I have cancer because it was only when I discovered I was seriously ill that my relationship with Christ really became intimate. I had known about Christ and had received Him. I went through the ritual of being a Christian, but somehow it was not until I became ill and faced my eternal destiny that I looked up and saw the loving, forgiving grace of God."

I had the privilege of taking part in my friend's memorial service. It was a time of celebration because this great man, who had known the best the world could offer, came to know the best God has to offer—through adversity.

ADVERSITY BRINGS US TO THE END OF OURSELVES AND DRIVES US TO GOD.

Toward the end of his life, British broadcaster and Christian apologist Malcolm Muggeridge explained, "Contrary to what might be expected, I look back on experiences that at the time seemed especially desolating and painful with particular satisfaction. Indeed, I can say with complete truthfulness that everything I have learned in my 75 years in this world, everything that has truly enhanced and enlightened my experience, has been through affliction and not through happiness."[2]

Adversity brings us to the end of ourselves and drives us to God. It teaches us about ourselves and about our Lord. As the Puritan Thomas Watson wrote, "A sick-bed often teaches more than a sermon."[3]

ADVERSITY PRODUCES REFINEMENT OF YOUR CHARACTER

In that marvelous passage of Scripture, Psalm 119, we read, "The suffering You sent was good for me, for it taught me to pay attention to Your principles" (v. 71).

The triumph of adversity is often expressed in a renewed walk with God and a refinement of our character.

The Bible compares God's work of maturing us to the process of refining precious metal. Ore is subjected to tremendous heat and liquefied so impurities can be removed. In a similar way, the heat of adversity softens us so God can do His work of refinement and sanctification. Adversity is the touchstone of character. Hardship reveals our strengths and weaknesses. If we have been out of fellowship with God, He may use hard times to restore us. If we are weak, He may use difficulties to strengthen us.

Consider the following true story from *Leadership* magazine:

> When he was seven years old, his family was forced out of their home on a legal technicality, and he had to work to help support them. At age nine, his mother died. At 22, he lost his job as a store clerk. He wanted to go to law school, but his education was not good enough. At 23, he went into debt to become a partner in a small store. At 26, his business partner died, leaving him a huge debt that took years to repay. At 28, after courting a girl for four years, he asked her to marry him. She said no. At 37, on his third try, he was elected to Congress, but two years later, he failed to be re-elected. At 41, his four-year-old son died. At 45, he ran for the Senate and lost. At 47, he failed as the vice-presidential candidate. At 49, he ran for the Senate again, and lost.[4]

Who was this man? He was a person whom many hail as the greatest leader America has ever had—Abraham Lincoln. Consider all the hardships Lincoln faced before becoming president of the United States at the age of 51. These difficulties were not merely footnotes on the way to his election to presidential office. No, they are what built his character. God allowed trials to prepare him to lead America during a time of great national adversity.

ADVERSITY PRODUCES INTIMACY WITH YOUR COMPASSIONATE GOD AND SAVIOR

The biblical character of Job has become synonymous with suffering. After enduring tremendous adversity, Job told God, "I had heard about You before, but now I have seen You with my own eyes" (Job 42:5).

Through adversity, God can deepen our relationship with Him.

In the 1940s, I owned a specialty-foods firm in Los Angeles. One of my partners in the business was a member of my church, and while I was studying at Princeton, I hired his son to oversee the company's day-to-day operations. When I returned from my studies, I found the business greatly changed and discovered that several members of my partner's family were drawing upon our investment! The family became defensive and accused me of being dishonest and not fulfilling my financial commitments to them.

Finally, the situation came to the attention of the pastor of our church. I was cleared of all their accusations, but still I was haunted by the thought that members in my church may have been influenced by this family's gossip and that they now saw me as phony or dishonest. I moved out of my apartment and lived in the company's plant to save money so I could buy out this partner. There I spent many evenings grieving about the situation.

Several years later, I was nominated to be a deacon at my church. As soon as my name was mentioned, my former business partner stood up and accused me of being dishonest. Another family member said that I was "not worthy of such a responsible trust."

You can imagine the pain I felt as a congregation of more than a thousand people heard those accusations. My pastor quickly ushered the nominating committee into another room to discuss the situation. I hurried to the room and begged them to withdraw my name. But my pastor assured the committee that he knew about the situation and that the accusations against me were not true. He insisted that my name remain on the list of deacons.

At that moment, a woman entered the room and announced, "I don't know what the issues are, but I know this: I wouldn't be a Christian today if it weren't for Bill Bright."

The committee returned to the sanctuary, and when it was announced that my nomination would remain on the list, the congregation burst into applause. Those around me rose to their feet, and the many days and nights of doubt and discouragement faded away.

God was humbling me, polishing me, and preparing me for a vision He was soon to give me, which became Campus Crusade for Christ. Had I not gone through that experience, I doubt seriously if God could ever have used me for any holy purpose.

The Bible promises, "The LORD hears His people when they call to Him for help. He rescues them from all their troubles. The LORD is close to the brokenhearted; He rescues those who are crushed in spirit. The righteous face many troubles, but the LORD rescues them from each and every one" (Psalm 34:17–19).

The more adversity we go through with God, the more we learn how faithful He is to help us in our time of need.

ADVERSITY PRODUCES UNDERSTANDING
OF THE HURTS OF OTHERS

Referring to Jesus, Scripture says, "This High Priest of ours understands our weaknesses, for He faced all of the same temptations we do, yet He did not sin" (Hebrews 4:15).

Experiencing adversity allows us to understand and empathize with those who are hurting.

A store owner placed a sign in his window announcing "Puppies for Sale." Soon a small boy came with $2.37 to buy a puppy. The store owner chuckled at the boy's enthusiasm and agreed to let the boy take a look at the litter. When the mother and her pups bounded out of the kennel, one of the puppies lagged behind. The store owner explained that the puppy had a malformed hip socket and would always limp.

The boy excitedly announced that he wanted to buy the limping puppy. He gave the owner the $2.37 and told him he would pay on the balance every month until he had paid for the dog.

The owner tried to discourage the child, warning him that the puppy would never run, jump, and play with him like the other puppies. To that, the boy pulled up his pant leg and revealed a left leg supported by a metal brace. He said, "I know how he feels. He'll need someone who understands."[5]

When we experience hardships, we are better able to empathize with others who are hurting. The Bible explains this "chain of comfort":

> All praise to the God and Father of our Lord Jesus Christ. He is the source of every mercy and the God who comforts us. He comforts us in all our troubles so that we can comfort others. When others are troubled, we will be able to give them the same comfort God has given us (2 Corinthians 1:3,4).

Adversity humbles us and softens our hearts so we are more compassionate and understanding of others.

ADVERSITY PRODUCES MATURITY FOR
MINISTERING TO OTHERS

The Word of God gives this challenge: "So take a new grip with your tired hands and stand firm on your shaky legs. Mark out a straight path for your feet. Then those who follow you, though they are weak and lame, will not stumble and fall but will become strong" (Hebrews 12:12,13).

Adversity prods us to grow and prepares us to minister to others.

When a mother eagle builds her nest, she begins with unlikely materials: rocks, thorns, and bits of broken branches. Before she lays her eggs, she blankets the nest with feathers and fur from animals she has killed. This soft, downy nest makes a perfect home for her eggs. Her growing young are so comfortable that when they are old enough to fly, they are reluctant to leave. That is when the mother eagle begins to "stir up the nest." She uses her iron talons to rip up the lining of feathers and fur, revealing the broken branches and sharp rocks underneath. The nest becomes uncomfortable for her young, prompting them to fly away and pursue the life of mature eagles.[6]

Sometimes God "stirs up the nest" to encourage us to step out of our comfort zone and to mature us in areas we have not encountered before. Hardships make us grow in our understanding of ourselves, others, and our wonderful God. When we emerge victorious on the other side of our "valley of adversity," we are better able to live as we should and to encourage others in the often bumpy journey of life.

The Bible proclaims, "Thanks be to God, who always leads us in triumphal procession in Christ and through us spreads everywhere the fragrance of the knowledge of Him" (2 Corinthians 2:14, NIV).

As we mature in Christ through trials and adversity, the aroma of our lives will attract others to our Lord and Savior.

ADVERSITY PRODUCES PERSEVERANCE IN DIFFICULT TIMES

Scripture tells us, "When your faith is tested, your endurance has a chance to grow" (James 1:3).

God often uses adversity to strengthen our resolve and solidify our commitment to Him.

One of the greatest examples of perseverance took place in England during World War II. At the beginning of the war, Neville Chamberlain was prime minister. As the Nazis swarmed Austria, Poland, Czechoslovakia, and even threatened the shores of Great Britain, Chamberlain tried to appease them.

But when Winston Churchill took the helm, he inaugurated his term as prime minister with these words:

> I have nothing to offer but blood, toil, tears, and sweat. We have before us an ordeal of the most grievous kind. We have before us many, many months of struggle and suffering. You ask, what is our policy? I say it is to wage war by land, sea and air. War with all our might and with all the strength God has given us, and to wage war against a monstrous tyranny never surpassed in the dark and lamentable catalogue of human crime. That is our policy. You ask, what is our aim? I can answer in one word. It is victory. Victory at all costs—victory in spite of all terrors—victory, however long and hard the road may be, for without victory there is no survival.[7]

Churchill's words ring of perseverance. As sirens sounded and bombs pounded Great Britain, he told his people to "never give up."

Are you in the midst of a divorce? Do you have cancer or another deadly disease? Are you worried about your financial situation? No matter how "long and hard the road may be," God will give you the strength necessary to persevere.

Muscles are strengthened by encountering and overcoming resistance. Some weightlifters are able to lift many times their own weight because they have built up their muscles. But the process is painful. They must repeatedly lift heavy weights, causing their muscle fibers to tear, heal, and eventually thicken. This thickening of the fibers is what makes the muscles stronger.

All of us who have experienced sore muscles know that the process of becoming physically stronger is painful. The same is true of developing an unwavering faith. Only when our faith is stretched and tested does it become strong.

As our faith in God grows, our perseverance increases. And as we experience His provision in our trials, something else happens. God brings a seventh benefit out of adversity.

ADVERSITY PRODUCES HOPE FOR THE FUTURE

The Bible promises, "We also rejoice in our sufferings, because we know that suffering produces perseverance; perseverance, character; and character, hope. And hope does not disappoint us, because God has poured out His love into our hearts by the Holy Spirit, whom He has given us" (Romans 5:3,4, NIV).

The marvelous truth of Scripture is that for Christians, suffering leads to hope.

Irena Dragas grew up in the Croatian region of Yugoslavia. When she was 16 years old, her only brother died in a tragic car accident on his way home from a mission trip. When she was 17, war broke out and her town was attacked by militant Serbians. After days of hiding in her basement, she and her family escaped only to find themselves refugees. They traveled from place to place, living in other people's homes, hiding from bombs, and dodging grenades. As she viewed the destruction of cities turned into ghost towns and heard heartbreaking stories of shattered lives, she often wondered how she could find hope in the midst of war and death. Because she was a Christian, she often tried to force herself to feel hopeful, but only met with disappointment.

Then one night she lay in bed in a sparsely furnished apartment temporarily provided to her family by a refugee agency. Although it was a few days before Christmas, there was no Christmas tree, no decorations, and no mementos of cherished memories from the past. Yet suddenly joy and hope washed over her. It was not a joy in her circumstances. War is horrible, and the hardships she had experienced were tragic. But she realized that she could find hope in the One who exists beyond the circumstances. Though her life was turned upside down, God's character had not changed. His love and integrity were still the same. Even in a strange apartment in an unfamiliar city in the middle of a war, she could experience hope because she was in the palm of God's hand.

Author Halford E. Luccock penned these words: "Where there is no faith in the future, there is no power in the present."[8] No matter what our circumstances may be, as Christians we have every reason to have faith in the future because God has promised His beloved children a glorious inheritance and a future of intimate fellowship with Him. Because we can look forward to the future without fear, we can live victoriously today. We know who holds our future, and He is faithful.

Throughout the centuries, believers have suffered great adversity. One of the reasons Christianity conquered the Roman Empire was because of the testimony of the countless Christians who were persecuted and died for their faith in Christ. These Christians sacrificed all they had in this life. But through it, they experienced God's faithfulness in a mighty way. As a result, history was transformed, lives were dramatically changed, and many of those who witnessed their sacrifice found hope in Christ.

We, too, can experience supernatural victory in the midst of adversity. Christ has given us the victory, but we can only share in His triumph by placing our faith in God and His promises and then inviting Christ to live in and through us. As we do, we will experience everlasting peace, which we will discuss in the next chapter.

Life Application

Thank Your Heavenly Father—Thank God that He can bring good out of the darkest situation and turn tragedy into triumph. Praise Him that through adversity He refines your character and draws you closer to Him. Express your appreciation that He produces growth out of difficult times so you can minister to others. Be grateful that adversity teaches perseverance and produces hope for your glorious future with Him.

Renew Your Mind—Memorize the following verse and acrostic:

- "Our present troubles are quite small and won't last very long. Yet they produce for us an immeasurably great glory that will last forever! So we don't look at the troubles we can see right now; rather, we look forward to what we have not yet seen. For the troubles we see will soon be over, but the joys to come will last forever" (2 Corinthians 4:17,18).

- The TRIUMPH acrostic will help you remember that God uses adversity to produce...
  Training in obedience
  Refinement of your character
  Intimacy with your compassionate God and Savior
  Understanding of the hurts of others
  Maturity for ministering to others
  Perseverance in difficult times
  Hope for the future

Reflect on Your New Life in Christ—Recall a difficult or painful situation in your life. How did God use this circumstance to teach you obedience, refine your character, develop intimacy with Him, or help you understand the hurts of others? Reflect on how that situation has made you stronger. How did supernatural hope come from this hardship?

Share the Blessings—Is someone you know going through a difficult time? Encourage them with what you have learned from this chapter.

CHAPTER 15

Knowing Everlasting Peace

ll I want is a little peace."

How often have you heard someone make that statement? And how true it is. We long for peace from the clamor and hassles of life, whether it be hectic schedules, screaming children, or obstinate co-workers. We crave peace from our haunting worries. We want relief from the gnawing pain we feel because of a death, relational crisis, or some other tragedy.

Rock icon Jimi Hendrix had money, talent, and the applause of millions. He indulged in all types of worldly pleasures, including drugs. One night, at the end of a concert, he smashed his guitar. The crowd went wild, then fell silent as Hendrix knelt on the stage, motionless. "If you know real peace," he said, "I want to visit with you backstage."

Evidently, no one responded to his remarkable request. Days later, he was dead of a drug overdose.[1]

Lasting peace eludes individuals and nations. A group of historians calculated that in all recorded history, our world has experienced peace less than 6 percent of the time. Since 3600 B.C., more than 5,300 years have been marred by war. The attempts at peace by world leaders have proven feeble. In that time, more than 8,000 peace treaties have been signed—and broken.[2]

Yet on the night of Christ's birth, angels announced, "Glory to God in the highest, and on earth peace, good will toward men" (Luke 2:14,

NKJ). What is this peace? And can we truly experience God's peace on this earth and in this life?

Consider a contest held to select the perfect picture of peace. Artists from around the world sent paintings of tranquil meadows and lazy summer afternoons. But one painting depicted quite a different setting. A raging waterfall plunged over a cliff beneath a gray and threatening sky. Atop the waterfall, a lone tree perched on the rocks. One branch hung out over the crashing waters. In the crook of that branch was a nest where a small bird sat warming her eggs. This painting won the prize because the bird was a picture of calm, a portrait of peace amid turmoil.[3]

This is the peace each of us can experience in Christ. It is a supernatural peace in the midst of the clamor and unpredictability of life.

THE PRINCE OF PEACE

In the Gospel of John, Jesus told His disciples, "Peace I leave with you; My peace I give you. I do not give to you as the world gives. Do not let your hearts be troubled and do not be afraid" (John 14:27, NIV).

Jesus is the "Prince of Peace" (Isaiah 9:6). Zechariah, the father of John the Baptist, made this prophesy about Christ: "Because of God's tender mercy, the light from heaven is about to break upon us, to give light to those who sit in darkness and in the shadow of death, and to guide us to the path of peace" (Luke 1:78,79).

The Son of God came to earth to make peace possible. Our amazing Savior has made a way for us to experience peace with God for all eternity, the peace of God in every circumstance, and peace with others in the body of Christ.

First, Christ paved the way for us to be at *peace with God* for all eternity. The marvelous prophecy in Isaiah declares, "He was wounded and crushed for our sins. He was beaten that we might have peace. He was whipped, and we were healed!" (Isaiah 53:5).

Christ's death and resurrection on the cross reconciled us to almighty God. Therefore, those who know intimacy with God experience peace. Before Jesus' selfless sacrifice, our sins made peace with God impossible. But now our sins are forgiven and we can enjoy an everlasting, harmonious relationship with our heavenly Father.

Jesus also made it possible for us to experience the *peace of God* in every circumstance. Shalom, the word for peace used in the Old Testament, means "completeness," "soundness," or "well-being."[4] It is this same peace Jesus promised His disciples when He said, "I have told you all this so that you may have peace in Me. Here on earth you will have many trials and sorrows. But take heart, because I have overcome the world" (John 16:33).

Because of Christ, we can experience a sense of well-being, for we are complete in Him. When we surrender our lives to Christ's control, we can be at peace—regardless of our circumstances. We can be at peace with the past because He has freed us from guilt and condemnation. We can be at peace in the present because our God is sovereignly at work in every circumstance and relationship. And we can be at peace with the future because He will fulfill all His promises and purposes.

Third, it is Jesus' command that we be at *peace with others* in the body of Christ.

Because we as Christians are all members of Christ's body, we are to live at peace with each other. Although we have different personalities, various spiritual gifts, distinctive ethnicities, and diverse life experiences, Christ wants His church to work and live in harmony.

In the early church, there were differences as well. Jewish and Gentile believers practiced different customs, which sometimes created conflict. Both slaves and free men held positions of leadership in the church, which often led to complicated relationships outside the church. And both men and women wished to contribute their diverse gifts and perspectives, which produced tension in an age of rigid gender roles and prejudices.

So how can the church maintain peace in the midst of diversity? Paul answers this question by emphasizing our equality before the Lord: "There is no longer Jew or Gentile, slave or free, male or female. For you are all Christians—you are one in Christ Jesus" (Galatians 3:28).

This oneness—this wholeness—is the essence of peace. Paul writes: "[Jesus] Himself is our peace...He came and preached peace to you who were far away and peace to those who were near. For through Him we both have access to the Father by one Spirit" (Ephesians 2:14,17,18, NIV).

What a humbling, yet glorious, thought. Each believer—regardless of ethnicity, age, gender, or social status—has equal access to God through His Holy Spirit. When we recognize the importance of each brother and sister in Christ and focus on seeking the Lord, our differences diminish and we can begin to experience a peace possible only in the family of God.

Tragically, the church is often perceived as a place of discord and conflict. Denominations argue about doctrinal differences even though they may embrace the same basic truths. Similarly, church members tend to highlight areas of disagreement rather than focus on preserving unity. We should rejoice in the common beliefs we share instead of splitting hairs over the points on which we do not agree. What an incredible testimony it is to the world when the community of believers exhibits God's peace—a harmony that is possible only because of the love of Christ working through us.

Because of who Jesus is and who we are in Him, we can enjoy a supernatural peace others only dream about. We can be at peace with God, with others, and with ourselves. And we can enjoy this peace regardless of our circumstances. This peace has five essential elements. The acrostic PEACE will help you remember that peace comes through...

P   *Pardon* for sin
E   *Enlightenment* of God's Word
A   *Acceptance* by God
C   *Confidence* in God
E   *Effort* to pursue unity with others

PEACE COMES THROUGH PARDON FOR SIN

The Scriptures assure us, "Since we have been made right in God's sight by faith, we have peace with God because of what Jesus Christ our Lord has done for us" (Romans 5:1).

Jesus bought our pardon with His death on the cross so we could have peace with God. Since we could not make peace with God on our own, Christ made peace for us. He took our sins upon Himself when He was crucified on the cross. Then He conquered the power of sin and death by rising again.

Martin Luther once had a dream that Satan was attacking him. The devil unrolled first one scroll, then the next, listing Luther's numerous sins. When Satan had finished confronting him, Luther exclaimed, "You've forgotten something."

Satan hesitated as Luther smiled triumphantly. "Quickly write on each of them 'The blood of Jesus Christ God's Son cleanses us from all sins.'"[5]

Knowing that our many sins have been forgiven brings great peace. Famed psychiatrist Karl Menninger once concluded that if he could persuade his patients that they were forgiven, 75 percent of them could walk out of the psychiatric hospital the next day![6]

Thanks to Jesus Christ, our sins have been forgiven. Let us claim this wonderful blessing and enjoy Christ's everlasting peace.

PEACE COMES THROUGH ENLIGHTENMENT OF GOD'S WORD

God's holy Word tells us, "If the Holy Spirit controls your mind, there is life and peace" (Romans 8:6).

Peace comes from having God's point of view on our circumstances. We can experience peace when we claim the marvelous promises of God's Word. The Bible tells us that our loving Father is in control. He cares about us and wants what is best for us. And He is working everything together to accomplish His glorious purposes.

The story of Joseph illustrates this well. When he was a young man, his brothers became extremely jealous of him and sold him into slavery. As a slave in Egypt and as a prisoner for many years, Joseph suffered great hardship, but he remained faithful to God. He believed that God was working out His divine purposes even in the midst of what was extremely unjust. In time, Joseph found favor with Pharaoh and, as a result, attained a position of great wealth and influence in Egypt.

Later when his brothers came to Egypt to find food during a famine, Joseph was able to help them. He made peace with them despite the horrible way they had mistreated him, because he realized that all of his afflictions were part of God's plan to preserve his family. By continuing to look at his circumstances through the lens of God's love and sovereignty, Joseph remained at peace with God, and he made peace with others.

As Joseph forgave his brothers, he proclaimed, "You intended to harm me, but God intended it for good to accomplish what is now being done, the saving of many lives" (Genesis 50:20, NIV).

PEACE COMES THROUGH ACCEPTANCE BY GOD

The Bible proclaims, "So now there is no condemnation for those who belong to Christ Jesus" (Romans 8:1). Later in the Book of Romans, Paul urges, "Accept one another, then, just as Christ accepted you, in order to bring praise to God" (Romans 15:7, NIV).

Peace comes from knowing we are completely accepted by God.

We see an example of how Christ's acceptance brings peace in the story of Zacchaeus. Zacchaeus was a chief tax collector for the Romans. Because he worked for the oppressive Roman government and often charged inflated taxes, he was despised and rejected by his fellow Jews.

GOD'S ACCEPTANCE FREES US FROM FRANTICALLY TRYING TO EARN THE APPROVAL OF OTHERS.

But Jesus knew Zacchaeus was seeking Him, so He ignored popular opinion and enjoyed a meal at this tax collector's home. As a result, Zacchaeus trusted Christ. He found peace with God and promptly sought to make peace with others. He gave half of what he had to the poor and promised fourfold restitution to anyone he had cheated.

God's acceptance frees us from frantically trying to earn the approval of others and from letting the opinions of others determine how we feel about ourselves. When we comprehend the profound privilege of being fully accepted by God, we can be at peace, even when we face rejection. Nonbelievers at work, school, or in our neighborhood may ridicule us for refusing to take part in certain speech or behavior. They may pressure us to participate in questionable social activities, compromise our faith, or engage in premarital sex or gang activities. They may judge us for our conservative social beliefs or our insistence that Jesus is the only way to God. They may exclude us from certain activities because our convictions make them feel uncomfortable. But remember, even though we may not always enjoy the acceptance of this world, we are loved and accepted by the Creator of the world!

PEACE COMES THROUGH CONFIDENCE IN GOD

Consider this marvelous promise in Scripture: "Don't worry about anything; instead, pray about everything. Tell God what you need, and thank Him for all He has done. If you do this, you will experience God's peace, which is far more wonderful than the human mind can understand. His peace will guard your hearts and minds as you live in Christ Jesus" (Philippians 4:6,7).

Peace comes from having confidence in our ever-present, sovereign God and knowing that He always cares for us.

A hurricane is a fierce storm that can cause terrible destruction. But in the center of the storm, known as the "eye" of the hurricane, is an area of relative calm. Here the clouds lift and the high winds stop blowing.

Placing our confidence in God is like entering the eye of a hurricane. No matter what kind of destructive storm of circumstances surrounds us, He is in control. Isaiah declared to the Lord, "You will keep in perfect peace all who trust in You, whose thoughts are fixed on You" (Isaiah 26:3). Even when the storm does not lift, God's peace calms our hearts.

A boy in Pennsylvania often visited his grandparents who lived nine miles away. One night a thick fog covered the hilly countryside as he and his family started for home. He was greatly frightened and asked if his father should drive slower.

His mother replied gently, "Don't worry. Your father knows the way."

As it turns out, his father had walked that road during the war when there was a shortage of gasoline. He had ridden his bicycle along that road to court his mother. And for many years his father had traveled that road on weekly trips to visit his parents.[7]

This is how our heavenly Father takes care of us. When a fog of difficulty clouds the road of life for us, we need not panic. Instead we must remember the wise words: "Don't worry. Your Father knows the way."

PEACE COMES THROUGH EFFORT TO PURSUE UNITY WITH OTHERS

God commands, "Always keep yourselves united in the Holy Spirit, and bind yourselves together with peace" (Ephesians 4:3).

God invested supernatural effort to make peace with us; therefore, He asks us also to be peacemakers.

When Leonardo Da Vinci was working on his masterpiece, *The Last Supper,* he lashed out at a man and threatened him. Then he picked up his brush and attempted to paint the face of Jesus. But he could not. There was too much anger surging inside of him. Finally, he left his fresco, sought out the man he had offended, and asked him for forgiveness. Only when he had received pardon did inner peace return and he was able to paint the face of his Redeemer.

Our holy God has given us so much. In turn, we should be eager to make peace with others. However, such effort requires obedience to Christ and reliance on the power of the Holy Spirit. Only through Christ's power living in and through us can we experience super-natural peace, which is impossible but for God's divine grace and intervention.

In 1956, five missionaries, including Jim Elliot and Nate Saint, were speared and killed by natives in the jungles of northern Ecuador. Jim Elliot's wife, Elisabeth, and Nate Saint's sister, Rachel, returned to bring the gospel of peace to the tribe that had killed their loved ones.

The women sought no prosecution of the killers. Through the power of the Holy Spirit, their supernatural effort to live at peace with all men reaped divine dividends. Many souls were won to Christ.

Years later, one of those in the spear-wielding party, now a pastor, baptized Nate Saint's son.[8] What a wonderful testimony of the grace and peace found in our Lord Jesus Christ!

Because our gracious Father has pardoned us, we are to forgive each other. Since God lovingly accepts us, we are to accept one anoth-er. As we place our confidence in our almighty God, we do not need to control others. And as we allow God to enlighten us, we will see ourselves and others from God's wonderful perspective.

Supernatural peace comes from the Prince of Peace. It is Christ's gracious sacrifice that enables us to experience the peace of being totally accepted by our almighty Creator. It is Christ's life and promises that give us the assurance and security of our eternal future with Him. And it is Christ's power that sanctions us as ambassadors to share His supernatural peace with others.

The Bible declares, "How beautiful on the mountains are the feet of those who bring good news of peace and salvation, the news that the God of Israel reigns!" (Isaiah 52:7). In this world of wars, racial tensions, cutthroat politics, drug and alcohol addiction, teen violence, abortion, abusive relationships, and divorce, people are crying out for peace. We have the answer—a peace that heals hearts and mends relationships. We must tell our friends, families, and acquaintances the wonderful secret we have discovered.

Our God is a God of peace. He promises great blessings to those who seek peace. Scripture proclaims, "A wonderful future lies before those who love peace" (Psalm 37:37).

It is a future filled with joy!

In the next chapter, we will discover the infinite joy that is ours as we live supernaturally in Christ.

Life Application

Renew Your Mind—Memorize the following verses and acrostic:

- "I am leaving you with a gift—peace of mind and heart. And the peace I give isn't like the peace the world gives. So don't be troubled or afraid" (John 14:27).

- "I have told you all this so that you may have peace in Me. Here on earth you will have many trials and sorrows. But take heart, because I have overcome the world" (John 16:33).

- The PEACE acrostic will help you remember that peace comes through...
  Pardon for sin
  Enlightenment of God's Word
  Acceptance by God
  Confidence in God
  Effort to pursue unity with others

Take Up Your Cross—Prayerfully recall the five principles of the CROSS acrostic: "Glorious Father, I praise You that I am a new creation, dead to sin and alive in Christ. Thank You that I am at peace with You because of the death and resurrection of Your Son. I praise You that I can be confident in Your love and commitment to me, for Your Word assures me that You accept me just as I am. I offer my body as an instrument of righteousness and peace. I surrender my will to You and resolve to be a peacemaker. May Your Holy Spirit fill me and may I be enlightened by meditating on Your precious Word. Amen."

Act by Faith—On a piece of paper, write all the situations in your life that rob you of God's peace. Then pray over them, claim God's promises, and surrender them to Him in faith. Next, reflect upon your life. Are you an instrument of peace or do you gossip, complain, and tear down? Ask God to help you promote peace in the lives of others, especially in the body of Christ. Think of constructive ways you can help heal personal relationships and create harmony among others. Make a list and begin to act now.

CHAPTER 16

Possessing Infinite Joy

When you hear the word "joy," what comes to mind? A giggling child cuddling with her father? A young couple, their eyes filled with love, standing at the marriage altar? A beaming athlete holding up a glistening trophy? An elated woman winning the lottery?

Many people believe joy can be acquired through the treasures and perks of this world—a thrilling adventure, a satisfying achievement, or some pleasing acquisition. However, they will be sorely disappointed by their false hopes.

One of America's leading financiers, Jay Gould, failed to find joy in his money. With his own death approaching, he said, "I suppose I am the most miserable man on earth."

The famous poet Lord Byron failed to find joy in a life of pleasure. He wrote, "The worm, the canker, and grief are mine alone."

French philosopher and author Voltaire failed to find joy in intellectual pursuits. He wrote: "I wish I had never been born."

Lord Beaconsfield, 19th century British politician and prime minister, failed to find joy in his fame and position. He wrote, "Youth is a mistake; manhood a struggle; old age a regret."

Alexander the Great failed to find joy in military glory. After he had subdued all his enemies, he wept and said, "There are no more worlds to conquer."[1]

Many of the most wealthy, famous, intelligent, and influential people have failed to experience true joy. Undoubtedly, they have enjoyed periods of happiness, but happiness depends upon circumstances, and once hardships arise, happiness gives way to worry and discontent. However, true joy abides even when life is difficult and unsure.

WHAT IS JOY?

Paul wrote the Book of Philippians—an epistle filled with the message of joy and hope—from a prison cell. How could he be joyful even when he was in chains? It is because joy is not found in our circumstances. Deep, abiding joy is found only in an intimate relationship with the source of all joy—Jesus Christ.

The *Life Application Bible Commentary* defines joy this way: "Joy is the gladdening of the heart that comes from knowing Christ as Lord, the feeling of relief because we are released from sin; it is the inner peace and tranquility we have because we know the final outcome of our lives; and it is the assurance that God is in us and in every circumstance."[2]

Joy flows out of our relationship with Christ.

At the birth of Christ, an angel triumphantly proclaimed: "I bring you good news of great joy for everyone! The Savior—yes, the Messiah, the Lord—has been born tonight in Bethlehem, the city of David!" (Luke 2:10,11).

God became man and died to pay the penalty for our sins. What a reason for rejoicing! Because of Christ's great sacrifice, we have been made right with our all-powerful Creator. We have a new identity. We are God's dearly loved children, heirs of His incredible blessings, saints with a new nature, members of the body of Christ, and citizens of Christ's kingdom. Because of Jesus Christ, we can live in friendship with our magnificent God and be filled with His Holy Spirit. When we grasp the magnitude of this marvelous truth, we, too, will rejoice with the shepherds!

Once we understand our new identity and invite Christ to live His life in and through us, joy will abound. For joy is a fruit produced by Christ's Spirit working in us (Galatians 5:22). An apple tree—if it is healthy and receives a sufficient amount of sunshine, water, and nutrients—will bear apples. It was created and designed for that purpose. In the same way, if we, as children of God, depend on the Holy Spirit to feed and nourish us, we will experience the fruit of joy in our lives.

Joy is the natural result of living a Christlike life. As we think with the mind of Christ, we will dwell on noble, uplifting thoughts that nurture joy. As we speak with the words of Christ, we will cultivate joy in our heart and the hearts of others. And as we behave with the character of Christ, we will reap joy as a benefit of leading a godly life.

British scholar and writer C. S. Lewis expresses it well: "Our Lord finds our desires not too strong, but too weak. We are half-hearted creatures, fooling about with drink and sex and ambition, when infinite joy is offered to us, like an ignorant child who wants to go on making mud pies in the slum because he cannot imagine what is meant by the offer of a holiday at the sea. We are far too easily pleased."[3]

Because of who Christ is and who you are in Him, you have a threefold source of joy. The acrostic JOY can help you remember to experience joy in...

J	*Jesus*
O	*Others*
Y	*Yourself*

JOY IN JESUS

The Bible tells us, "Since we were restored to friendship with God by the death of His Son while we were still His enemies, we will certainly be delivered from eternal punishment by His life. So now we can rejoice in our wonderful new relationship with God—all because of what our Lord Jesus Christ has done for us in making us friends of God" (Romans 5:10,11).

We can experience joy in Jesus because He is our Savior, not our slayer.

We were enemies of God worthy only of death and eternal punishment. But instead of condemning us, Christ gave Himself to be crucified for our sins. Now instead of everlasting damnation, we enjoy eternal blessings in Christ. Because of Jesus, we can know constant joy in our salvation and have fellowship with God.

The well-known conductor Reichel was leading his choir and orchestra through a rehearsal of Handel's glorious masterpiece, *The Messiah*. The soprano soloist sang the inspiring aria, "I Know That My Redeemer Liveth," with flawless technique, effortless breathing, and clear diction. When she finished, everyone turned to Reichel expecting a pleased response. Instead, he motioned for silence and walked over to the soloist. Sorrowfully, he said, "My daughter, you do not really know that your Redeemer lives, do you?"

Embarrassed, she replied, "Why, yes, I think I do."

"Then sing it!" he cried. "Tell it to me so that I'll know you have experienced the joy and power of it."

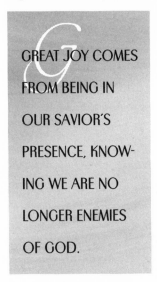

GREAT JOY COMES FROM BEING IN OUR SAVIOR'S PRESENCE, KNOWING WE ARE NO LONGER ENEMIES OF GOD.

He raised his baton for the orchestra to begin, and the soloist sang the truth with a passion that revealed her personal knowledge of the risen Lord. Many who were listening wept, and Reichel, his eyes moist with tears, said to her, "You do know, for this time you have told me."[4]

God has given us a wonderful gift in His Son, Jesus. How we should thank, praise, and worship Him, for only because of Jesus can we experience God's presence both now and for eternity! King David foretold this great promise in Psalm 16: "You will show me the way of life, granting me the joy of Your presence and the pleasures of living with You forever" (Psalm 16:11). Great joy comes from being in our Savior's presence, knowing that we are no longer enemies of God.

JOY IN OTHERS

Many passages of Scripture record the great joy Paul took in those to whom he ministered. In 1 Thessalonians, we read, "After all, what gives us hope and joy, and what is our proud reward and crown? It is you! Yes, you will bring us much joy as we stand together before our Lord Jesus when He comes back again. For you are our pride and joy" (1 Thessalonians 2:19,20).

In Christ, we can experience joy in others because they are *opportunities* for ministry, not *obstacles* in our way.

More than two hundred years ago, a young Oxford man mounted the stairs of a monument called the "Market Cross" in the center of Liverpool, England. He leaned against the cross and gazed out at the industrial ghetto before him. The streets teamed with dirty miners and sea-hardened sailors cursing, drinking, and even fighting in drunken brawls. After whispering a prayer, the young man opened his mouth and sang:

> O, for a thousand tongues to sing,
> My great Redeemer's praise.
> The glories of my God and King,
> The triumphs of His grace.

The heads of the masses turned toward him because the melody was a popular tune. They listened to the words that fell easily from his lips—words he had authored in honor of the first anniversary of his conversion to Jesus Christ.

As the young man continued singing, the bickering stopped. The brawling was silenced. Never before had the masses heard such a note of joy in anything religious. To them, church was a boring ritual reserved for the pious and the old. To them, religion was for the saved, not for the damned like themselves. To them, God was a distant watchmaker who wound His creation and left it running without caring what happened to the world.

The man was the well-known songwriter, Charles Wesley. No wonder he captivated their attention. His joyful hymn spoke of a God of love who offered forgiveness and grace for all through His Son Jesus Christ. Because of Charles Wesley, the teaming masses in Liverpool felt the power of Christ's joy![5]

When we see people through the loving eyes of our Father, we, too, will experience the power of joy. We will see nonbelievers as wonderful opportunities to share Christ's love. Rather than merely condemning them, we will rejoice in the forgiveness and life-changing possibilities they can experience if they will only invite God to work in their lives.

When we fellowship with our Christian brothers and sisters, we will see them as opportunities for ministry, for only together can we build up the body of Christ and reach out to a despairing world. Rather than becoming jealous or competitive, we will take joy in what Christ is doing in their lives. We will not despair because another believer has more power, spiritual fruit, or money than we do. Instead, we will rejoice that our sovereign and loving Father is working in and through them to further the kingdom of Christ.

JOY IN YOURSELF

Jesus said, "I have loved you even as the Father has loved Me. Remain in My love. When you obey Me, you remain in My love, just as I obey My Father and remain in His love. I have told you this so that you will be filled with My joy. Yes, your joy will overflow!" (John 15:9–11).

We can experience joy because, through the Holy Spirit, we are yearning for God with our new nature, not yoked to sin by our old nature.

Many years ago, I met with the heads of several Christian organizations—InterVarsity, Young Life, Youth for Christ, Navigators, and others. We had a marvelous time of rejoicing in the Lord. Soon it was my time to give a devotion. As I was reading from one of my favorite passages, John 17, which is our Lord's high priestly prayer, I was suddenly gripped with something I had read on numerous occasions, but had never really seen before. Jesus prays to the Father, "I have given them the glory You gave Me, so that they may be one, as We are—I in them and You in Me, all being perfected into one. Then the world will know that You sent Me and will understand that *You love them as much as You love Me*" (John 17:22,23).

I was so ecstatic that I wanted to jump up and shout. To think that the great Creator God and Father of the universe loves a little old nobody, a sinful person conceived in sin, as much as He loves Jesus! This was more than my finite mind could comprehend. Yet our Savior, who loved us so much that He died for us, says it is so. Oh, how God loves us!

Yes, we still stumble and fall short of the expectations we have for ourselves, but God loves us! He has adopted us and endowed us with immeasurable blessings. Once we grasp our amazing identity in Christ, we have ample reason to rejoice in who we are and to praise our wonderful Savior who has made this all possible.

Joy is ours! In the third century, a dying man wrote these words to a friend: "It's a bad world, an incredibly bad world. But I have discovered in the midst of it a quiet and holy people who have learned a great secret. They have found a joy which is a thousand times better than any pleasure of our sinful life. They are despised and persecuted, but they care not...They have overcome the world. These people are Christians—and I am one of them."[6]

THE JOY-BREAKERS

How wonderful to experience a joy that need not be limited by favorable circumstances. Yet many of us do not consistently enjoy this blessing. Why is that?

There are several "joy-breakers" that inhibit the flow of joy in our lives. These attitudes or habits can short-circuit our joy and cause us to wallow in despair and frustration.

One joy-breaker is worry. An old man was once asked what had most robbed him of joy in his life. He answered, "Things that never happened!" How true it is that worry about the future steals our joy today. That is why Jesus said, "Therefore do not worry about tomorrow, for tomorrow will worry about itself. Each day has enough trouble of its own" (Matthew 6:34, NIV).

Another joy-breaker is disobedience to God. It steals our joy by harming the relationship that is the source of all joy—our relationship with God. Joy is a fruit of the Spirit, and we can only bear fruit as we abide in Christ. Jesus said, "A branch cannot produce fruit if it is severed from the vine, and you cannot be fruitful apart from Me" (John 15:4).

Our sin severs us from the vine. No, we are not removed from God's love, nor is our salvation in doubt; however, until we repent of the sin, the sweet nourishment of the Holy Spirit cannot fill us as He desires. We cannot deliberately disobey God and continue to abide in Christ. Just as a disobedient child cannot be happy knowing he has disappointed his parents, so we cannot be joyful until we have repented and renewed our relationship with our merciful heavenly Father.

A third joy-breaker is guilt. After King David sinned by committing adultery with Bathsheba, he wrote these words, "When I refused to confess my sin, I was weak and miserable, and I groaned all day long. Day and night Your hand of discipline was heavy on me. My strength evaporated like water in the summer heat. Finally, I confessed all my sins to You and stopped trying to hide them. I said to myself, 'I will confess my rebellion to the LORD.' And You forgave me! All my guilt is gone. Therefore, let all the godly confess their rebellion to You while there is time, that they may not drown in the floodwaters of judgment" (Psalm 32:3–6).

A fourth joy-breaker is the failure to seek God wholeheartedly.

Seeking God wholeheartedly refers to the quality of our love, desire, and devotion to God. When we seek God with our whole heart, our desire for closeness and intimacy with God becomes increasingly consuming. Our joy increases as our love for our Lord becomes more intimate.

Our relationship with our Creator will only grow as far as our desire permits. Hebrews 11:6 states, "[God] rewards those who sincerely seek Him." There are great rewards in seeking our glorious Creator. The Word of God promises in Psalm 34:10, "Those who trust in the LORD will never lack any good thing." We are to seek God wholeheartedly so that we can experience the intimacy with Him that He desires and develop a passion for Him and His purposes. When we strive to

OUR RELATIONSHIP WITH OUR CREATOR WILL ONLY GROW AS FAR AS OUR DESIRE PERMITS.

love the Lord our God with all of our heart, soul, and mind (Matthew 22:36,37), we will reap the abundant joy that comes from a deep, contented relationship with almighty God.

When the Jews returned from exile, they wept because of Israel's great sin. Nehemiah encouraged them, "The joy of the LORD is your strength" (Nehemiah 8:10). We, too, can be comforted by the strength of God's supernatural joy. We can take joy in our amazing Savior whose sacrifice allows us to experience grace, forgiveness, and an eternal life of intimate fellowship with our Creator. We can enjoy others because they are precious souls with whom we can share His joy. And we can rejoice in the work that God has done in our lives because we have a new identity in Christ.

One day we will enter into the heavenlies and stand before Jesus. How wonderful it will be to hear the words, "Well done, my good and faithful servant. You have been faithful in handling this small amount; so now I will give you many more responsibilities. Let's celebrate together!" (Matthew 25:21). What eternal happiness and joy will be ours if we faithfully serve our Lord and Savior!

Praise God for the unspeakable joy of His abundant blessings! May we delight in what we have in Him: an eternal Father and Savior; an eternal inheritance; an eternal holiness; an eternal family; and an eternal kingdom.

What a marvelous identity we have in Christ. In His power we can think, speak, and behave in a way that reaps a life of power, freedom, triumph, peace, and joy. What wonderful blessings! And what a supernatural life we should be living.

Yet, there is one whose deepest desire is to keep us from experiencing the glorious life Christ offers. We will talk about him and how to overcome his evil schemes in our final chapter.

Life Application

Thank Your Heavenly Father—Thank God that He is a God of joy! Express your appreciation for the wonderful gift of His Son, Jesus Christ. Praise God that you can have an intimate relationship with Him and that you can enjoy Him for eternity. Gratefully acknowledge His blessing of friends, family, co-workers, neighbors, and church and the joy they bring to your life. Thank Him for yourself and the unique creation He made in you. Praise Him that He has specially chosen you as His dearly loved child. And rejoice!

Renew Your Mind—Commit the following verses and acrostic to memory:

■ "Always be full of joy in the Lord. I say it again—rejoice!" (Philippians 4:4).

■ "I have told you this so that you will be filled with My joy. Yes, your joy will overflow!" (John 15:11).

■ The JOY acrostic will help you remember to experience joy in . . .
   Jesus
   Others
   Yourself

Reflect on Your New Life in Christ—Close your eyes and picture God loving and enjoying you like a parent taking pleasure in his child. Then, imagine yourself with your friends, family, and acquaintances. See yourself sharing this same love and joy with them. Praise God that because you are His dearly loved child, you can rejoice in who you are in Christ and share this joy with others.

Share the Blessings—Commit yourself to truly enjoy one person this week. Focus on all the positive aspects of this individual. Find ways to display your love and appreciation to him or her. Be sure to tell this person the good news that God takes great joy and delight in him or her.

CHAPTER 17

Standing Victoriously in Christ

*A*s the chapters of this book have unfolded, we have explored the abundant, supernatural life we can enjoy as followers of Christ. Because we have placed our trust in Jesus, the risen Son of God, and have accepted by faith the facts and power of His death and resurrection, we have an amazing new identity. We are God's dearly loved children in whom He delights, heirs of His incredible blessings, saints with a new nature, members of the body of Christ, and citizens of Christ's kingdom. The Holy Spirit empowers us to live extraordinary, supernatural lives, which reflect our new identity in Christ. Now we can demonstrate His marvelous, boundless love as we think with the mind of Christ, speak with the words of Christ, and behave with the character of Christ.

As we claim our new identity and allow Christ to live in and through us, we will experience a life of supernatural power, liberating freedom, triumph over adversity, everlasting peace, and infinite joy. What an incredible adventure we can have in Christ! This world can offer nothing that compares to our supernatural life in Him.

OUR GREAT ENEMY

Yet, as mentioned at the beginning of this book, there is one who longs to steal the knowledge we have of our glorious new identity in Christ and replace it with doubt, fear, confusion, and insecurity. He desires to kill the righteous thoughts, words, and deeds that come from a Christlike character and replace them with what is hateful, bitter, divisive, hurtful, and degrading. He seeks to destroy the divine and supernatural life we can have in Christ and replace it with mediocrity, defeat, and insignificance. His name is Satan; he is the architect of the world system, the great deceiver, and the enemy of God and His people.

Satan is determined to destroy us and every vestige of Christ's kingdom. Peter writes, "Be careful! Watch out for attacks from the Devil, your great enemy. He prowls around like a roaring lion, looking for some victim to devour" (1 Peter 5:8). But Satan is a defeated foe. Scripture proclaims, "The reason the Son of God appeared was to destroy the devil's work" (1 John 3:8, NIV). When Christ died and rose from the dead, Satan's power over us was completely destroyed.

Consider the following analogy:

The bite of a cobra is deadly, but science has developed an antidote. First, venom is drawn from the snake and injected into the bloodstream of a Belgian stallion. This mighty horse becomes deathly ill, but does not die because the antibodies in its blood are stronger than the cobra's poison. Then the horse's blood is used to make an antitoxin serum, which, when injected into the bloodstream of a cobra's victim, can save the person's life. In this way, the blood of the mighty stallion overcomes the power of the venom and preserves numerous lives.[1]

Jesus Christ spilled His precious blood to defeat the "ancient serpent" and his poison of sin and death. The writer of Hebrews explains, "[Jesus] too shared in their humanity so that by His death He might destroy him who holds the power of death—that is, the devil" (Hebrews 2:14, NIV).

Satan appears to be so powerful. He controls the world system. He is the author of pornography, abortion, and all evils contrary to the Word of God. Often, we gape in awe and tremble at his power. But he is a roaring lion who has been defanged. Thanks to Christ, he is a defeated enemy, doomed to eternal destruction.

Satan knows he has been defeated, and that is why, like a cornered animal, he lashes out at those who are devoted to Christ. Since he cannot attack God directly, he hopes to hurt the One who defeated him by harming those Christ saved and loves.

Satan frantically plots to undermine our relationship with God. He devises schemes to make us doubt our new identity and sabotage our supernatural life in Christ. He ensnares us in the daily worries and distractions of life, enticing us to neglect the study of God's Word, to forgo Spiritual Breathing, and to forsake fellowship with other believers. He fills us with pride until we are deaf and blind to the sin in our lives. He stirs up bitterness between us and fellow Christians to rob us of the wonderful peace intended for God's family. And he whispers lies into our minds so we distrust our heavenly Father's flawless character.

We have been given a free will to choose the way of God or the way of Satan, so Satan works hard to deceive us. In the Garden of Eden, Eve heard the deceptive words of Satan, then chose to believe them and eat the forbidden fruit. Satan will tempt us, but God has equipped us to resist any temptation (1 Corinthians 10:13).

We are not defenseless. Paul admonishes Christians, "Be strong with the Lord's mighty power. Put on all of God's armor so that you will be able to stand firm against all strategies and tricks of the Devil" (Ephesians 6:10,11).

OUR SPIRITUAL WAR

We are at war, and this war is far more serious than all the wars that have ever been fought. This war has eternal consequences. But regardless of Satan's strategies, we can stand firm. We can do this not because of our own goodness or might, but by relying on the supernatural strength of our supreme Savior. Christ frees us through His Word by revealing to us our identity in Him. He equips us for spiritual battle by clothing us in Himself and becoming our spiritual armor.

A unique member of God's amazing creation illustrates this point well. The "Moses sole" is a small, innocent-looking flatfish that thrives around the Red Sea. Named by Israelis, this fish resembles an ordinary flounder or sole, but actually contains a life-preserving secret. Its secret is a defense against one of the deadliest life forms on earth—the great white shark. This fierce predator evokes terror in humans and inhabitants of the sea because of its ability to rip any foe to pieces. Any foe, that is, except the Moses sole.

A National Geographic team of researchers discovered that the giant of the sea was powerless against this small flounder. The shark stealthily slices through the water toward the helpless fish, his mighty jaws wide open and his razor-sharp teeth glistening, but his jaws never close. Instead, the stunned predator hurries away, his jaws frozen open, while the delicate Moses sole contentedly continues swimming around as though nothing had happened. The researchers learned that the Moses sole secretes a poison from glands along its dorsal and anal fins. This milky poison is lethally toxic and envelops the gentle fish with a halo of protection.[2]

What a beautiful picture of the protection we can have against our deadly predator Satan, thanks to the power of Christ. Because we are covered with the blood of Jesus, Satan cannot devour us. The Bible proclaims, "The One who is in you is greater than the one who is in the world" (1 John 4:4, NIV).

OUR EFFECTIVE ARMOR

Our glorious Savior wants us to live a supernatural life of victory over Satan and his schemes. Scripture explains the protection Christ offers by comparing it to a Roman soldier's armor. Paul explains:

> Use every piece of God's armor to resist the enemy in the time of evil, so that after the battle you will still be standing firm. Stand your ground, putting on the sturdy belt of truth and the body armor of God's righteousness. For shoes, put on the peace that comes from the Good News, so that you will be fully prepared. In every battle you will need faith as your shield to stop the fiery arrows aimed at you by Satan. Put on salvation as your helmet, and take the sword of the Spirit, which is the word of God (Ephesians 6:13–17).

Let us more closely explore this profound analogy of our spiritual armor.

A Roman soldier's belt was essential. The soldier tucked all the loose parts of his tunic under his belt so he could move freely without getting tangled in his clothes. The belt also held his breastplate in place and the scabbard for his sword.

Similarly, the belt of truth keeps our perception of reality securely bound to God's absolute truth. Satan's tactic is to deceive us with lies and distortions. But if we hold firmly to God's truth, we will have an accurate understanding of our spiritual identity and the magnificent character of our wonderful God. The belt of truth will keep us from getting tripped up by Satan's deceptions.

The Roman breastplate or body armor covered the torso from the neck to the thighs. It was intended to protect the heart and other vital organs. The Hebrews believed emotions originated in this part of the body.

In a similar way, the breastplate of righteousness protects our spiritual self-image. Satan's scheme is to berate us with accusations and condemnation. But Christ has imparted His righteousness to us so we can enjoy an open and guilt-free relationship with our heavenly Father. And righteous living guards our deepest emotions and protects us from the mortal wounds caused by disobeying God.

A Roman soldier's boots gave him necessary traction and protection from the rugged terrain, therefore enabling the soldier's freedom of movement.

Likewise, the shoes of peace promote freedom of movement and unity in the body of Christ. Satan wants to alienate us from God through disobedience, bitterness, and unforgiveness, for we are vulnerable when we are isolated from God and fellow believers. But when we allow peace to reign in our hearts and lives, we move closer to God and others. The shoes of peace equip us to dodge Satan's arrows of dissension and bitterness so we can stand in unity.

The Roman shield was almost as big as a refrigerator door. A line of soldiers bearing such shields formed a wall of protection against the flaming arrows of the enemy.

Similarly, the shield of faith protects us against Satan's assaults. Satan bombards us with troubles and temptations. He entices us with worldly pleasures so we will distrust God's Word, doubt God's character, and dispute God's motives. Satan knows that the more we question God's commitment to us, the more we will depend upon ourselves. As we do, our shield is lowered, and we expose ourselves to Satan's wrath. But when we hold fast to our faith in God and join forces with our fellow believers, we are safe. For the shields Christ has provided for the church form a wall of protection against Satan's fury.

The Roman helmet protected soldiers from enemy cavalrymen taking aim at their heads with a three- to four-foot-long double-edged sword. The head is a strategic target because it gives direction to the rest of the body.

The helmet of salvation protects us against Satan's efforts to attack our mind with poisonous thoughts. Standing firm in the knowledge of our salvation gives us the hope, confidence, and assurance we need to withstand Satan's propaganda. It wards off his efforts to provoke worry, fear, and discouragement within us, which can paralyze our Christian walk.

The helmet of salvation also deflects any thoughts of despair with the hope that comes from God's promise of future glory. That is one reason Paul writes:

> Always be full of joy in the Lord. I say it again—rejoice!...Remember, the Lord is coming soon.
>
> Don't worry about anything; instead, pray about everything. Tell God what you need, and thank Him for all He has done. If you do this, you will experience God's peace, which is far more wonderful than the human mind can understand. His peace will guard your hearts and minds as you live in Christ Jesus (Philippians 4:4–7).

Paul closes his letter with this admonition, "Fix your thoughts on what is true and honorable and right. Think about things that are pure and lovely and admirable. Think about things that are excellent and worthy of praise" (Philippians 4:8).

Spiritual battles often begin in our minds. That is why it is essential for us to "put on salvation as our helmet."

OUR MIGHTY SWORD

The only offensive weapon Paul lists as part of our spiritual armor is the sword of the Spirit, which is the Word of God. The emphasis in this passage is on its use as a precision instrument like the Roman sword, a weapon that required skill and precision. The soldier used his sword to defend himself and attack his opponent. If we know and understand God's Word, the Holy Spirit can guide us to use specific passages against Satan in each situation. Empowered by the Spirit, we can use God's powerful, inspired Word to attack strongholds of deception and drive Satan away.

King David wrote, "I have hidden your word in my heart, that I might not sin against you" (Psalm 119:11). When Jesus was tempted by Satan in the wilderness, He defended Himself by quoting the Word of God. If we meditate on and memorize Scripture, we, too, can hurl the truth of God's Word at Satan in times of temptation and hardship.

The following are promises you may want to commit to memory:

If you make the LORD your refuge, if you make the Most High your shelter, no evil will conquer you; no plague will come near your dwelling (Psalm 91:9,10).

Remember that the temptations that come into your life are no different from what others experience. And God is faithful. He will keep the temptation from becoming so strong that you can't stand up against it. When you are tempted, He will show you a way out so that you will not give in to it (1 Corinthians 10:13).

God blesses the people who patiently endure testing. Afterward they will receive the crown of life that God has promised to those who love Him (James 1:12).

As you read God's Word, identify strategic passages to memorize that you can add to your arsenal of ammunition against Satan.

GOD'S MIGHTY POWER

Satan is an intimidating foe so we should take him and his schemes very seriously. However, our awesome God is infinitely more powerful. When we rely on His mighty power, we can be assured of victory. Scripture promises in James, "Humble yourselves before God. Resist the Devil, and he will flee from you" (James 4:7). Satan has strongholds in this world, but miraculous things happen when Christians band together in the power of the Holy Spirit.

In Cali, Columbia, the lucrative business of illegal drugs was destroying the town. The entire community was filled with terror because of the seven drug cartels that controlled the city. Hit men would kill anyone standing in the way of the drug kingpins.

A local pastor, Julio Ruibal, a beloved personal friend of mine, wanted to mobilize churches to pray against this stronghold of Satan. But there was dissension among the pastors in Cali because they were intimidated by their enemies.

After much fasting and prayer over the situation, Pastor Ruibal spoke openly and powerfully against the drug cartels. As a result, he received many death threats.

Shortly after making his stand for what was right, Pastor Ruibal was shot and killed. At his memorial service, his wife described how her husband had lived under constant threat and how the enemy had tried to intimidate him in many ways. She then explained his great desire for the churches in Cali to be unified in the battle between Christ's kingdom and Satan's.

Hearing of Pastor Ruibal's example, the pastors were convicted of their failure to speak out and formed a covenant of unity with each other. God led them to hold an all-night prayer rally in the city's stadium attended by tens of thousands of people.

God began to do incredible things in Cali. Government officials were so impressed with the positive results of the prayer movement that they allowed the churches to continue using the stadium free of charge. Within nine months, six out of the seven drug lords were arrested and the power of the drug cartels was broken.[3]

Our Lord and Savior is more powerful than any stronghold of Satan. To put on the armor of God is to put on Christ. Jesus is the Truth. Scripture identifies Him as the Prince of Peace. We are clothed in His righteousness. He is the author of our faith. He bought our salvation with His blood. He is the Word made flesh who has set us free. And He is our Deliverer from the evil one. To experience the reality of our deliverance, we must understand God's character and attributes and who we are in Him.[4] Then, by faith, we can live in accordance with who we are in Christ.

PAUL'S SUPERNATURAL RACE

Paul knew all about living a supernatural life in the midst of spiritual battle. He understood that the only way to be victorious is to first be crucified with Christ. He lived the words of Galatians 2:20, "I have been crucified with Christ and I no longer live, but Christ lives in me. The life I live in the body, I live by faith in the Son of God, who loved me and gave Himself for me" (NIV).

Not only did Paul surrender himself and everything he had to God, he even gave his life for the cause of Christ. After Paul had faithfully served his Lord and Savior for more than three decades, the Roman Emperor Nero ordered his execution by beheading. Some may question why God allowed this valiant, devoted servant to die such a tragic death. But the blood of the martyrs is precious to the Lord (Psalm 116:15). We have only once to live and once to die, and what better way to die than for the sake of our wonderful Savior and His eternal kingdom? Truly, Paul understood the truth of Jesus' words, "Whoever finds his life will lose it, and whoever loses his life for My sake will find it" (Matthew 10:39, NIV).

Years ago when I knelt in the dungeon in Rome where Paul await-ed his execution, I wondered what it would be like to have seen him and listened in on his thoughts in those last hours before his death.

Can you picture Paul as he sits in that dreary dungeon? His face is weathered from the harsh winds of sea voyages and the intense sun of his many missionary journeys. Lines and furrows underscore the great strength of character mirrored in his expres-sion. His gaze is unwavering and direct. His eyes blaze with purpose, yet reveal an eter-nal depth of peace. They reflect a clear con-science and shine with the joy of his fellow-ship with Christ.

OUR LORD AND SAVIOR IS MORE POWERFUL THAN ANY STRONG-HOLD OF SATAN.

As he stands, we see that his body is bat-tered, scarred from lashings, beatings, ship-wrecks, and even a stoning. His back is bent from years of hard labor and from giv-ing himself wholeheartedly for the church to the glory of Christ. But the spiritual mus-cles rippling beneath the wrinkled skin are stronger than ever. For him, to live has been Christ and to die will be gain. He runs all the faster in his race to live wholeheartedly for God now that he sees the finish line before him.

And what of his armor? It has stood the test of time and every assault of the evil one. His helmet of salvation has been dented, but not pierced. His belt of truth, which is stained with perspiration and blood, fits him more securely than ever. His breastplate of righteous-ness, battered by enemy fire, has remained intact. His boots of peace are well worn from the many miles he has traveled since he first met Christ those long years ago on the road to Damascus. Yet in this last lap of his dedicated journey with his mighty, sovereign Savior, their traction and protection make his steps sure. His shield of faith has not failed him these many years. The myriad of burn marks and embed-ded broken shafts in the shield bear witness to its steadfast service in countless battles.

But it is Paul's sword of the Spirit that stuns his foes. Sharpened to a razor edge, it glistens like the sun and slices like a laser. Paul is skilled in wielding it. In these last hours, that sword is never out of

Paul's hand. Even while chained between two centurion guards from Caesar's palace, he continues to preach the gospel. And though the guards are rotated every two hours to avoid being converted to Christ, many believe and take the life-transforming message of God's love and forgiveness back to Caesar's household.[5]

Now the soldiers come for him. He walks with them to his execution. He looks back—not at the great city of Rome, but at his life. He has no regrets—only joy at the countless people he has introduced to his wonderful Savior. His life has been an unimaginable adventure. Despite untold hardships, he would not trade one moment as a follower of Christ for years of wealth, notoriety, or ease. He rejoices that he has shared Christ's suffering, for he knows that he will now share Christ's glory. He has learned to be content in all things—even death.

A soldier raises a sword above him. Paul does not see it. He sees the finish line. He has run the good race. He has fought the good fight.

As his head falls from his body, his soul crosses the finish line into eternity. His race is finished. In that instant, one of God's heavenly masterpieces named Paul hears those glorious words, "Well done, good and faithful servant."

God's intricate embroidery, which appeared during Paul's lifetime as tangled threads of adversity, supernatural victory, and unceasing labor, can now be viewed as God intended. Angels marvel at the indescribable beauty of the tapestry—Paul conformed to the image of Christ!

WE ARE GOD'S PRICELESS MASTERPIECES

Paul writes, "We are God's masterpiece. He has created us anew in Christ Jesus, so that we can do the good things He planned for us long ago" (Ephesians 2:10). Like Paul, we, too, are God's priceless masterpiece, which He is carefully weaving into the image of Christ.

Each of us is a new creation in Christ with a wonderful new identity. We have the power of the Holy Spirit within us to think, speak, and behave as we should. And we have a marvelous destiny both now and for eternity. Our Lord said, "I have come that they may have life, and have it to the full" (John 10:10, NIV). God assures us, "I know the plans I have for you...They are plans for good and not for disaster, to give you a future and a hope" (Jeremiah 29:11).

Before you were even born, before you placed your life into the hands of your wonderful Savior, God carefully designed a supernatural plan for you. He equipped you with a unique personality and special abilities to accomplish His purpose for your life and to further His eternal kingdom. Wherever you go and whatever you do, you are Christ's ambassador. God wants you to introduce many others to your Savior and King.

Christ came to this world for one purpose—to seek and to save the lost (Luke 19:10). He said, "Come, follow me...and I will make you fishers of men" (Matthew 4:19, NIV). Everything else pales in importance by comparison. Your supernatural walk with Christ involves faithfully sharing the message of our wonderful Lord and Savior with others as a way of life. Invite Christ to live His fruitful life in and through you. Then you will experience a rich, full, and abundant life filled with divine purpose, deep meaning, eternal significance, and supernatural fruitfulness.

What spiritual legacy will you leave to your loved ones? Will they see your walk as worthy? Your feet standing firm on God's truth? Will your battered body reflect the beauty of God's character? Will you, like Paul, be an inspiring masterpiece in the gallery of people's hearts, attracting others to the One who died for you?

You have embarked on an incredible adventure. You do not know what awaits you around the next bend in life's journey. You cannot anticipate what dangers, hardships, or trials you may face. But you do know the One who walks with you. He is all-powerful, He is faithful, and He is worthy of your praise, your trust, and your total devotion. And He is always with you (Hebrews 13:5).

The 19th century minister and hymnwriter Phillip Brooks inspired countless believers with this admonition: "Do not pray for easy lives; pray to be stronger men and women. Do not pray for tasks equal to your powers, but pray for powers equal to your tasks. Then the doing of your work shall be no miracle, but you shall be a miracle. Every day you shall wonder at yourself—at the richness of life which has come to you by the grace of God."[6]

Put your hand in the hand of Jesus and, like the apostle Paul, walk with Him down that glorious and eternal road called *living supernaturally in Christ.*

Life Application

Renew Your Mind—Memorize the following:

- "Humble yourselves before God. Resist the Devil, and he will flee from you" (James 4:7).

- "I have hidden Your word in my heart, that I might not sin against You" (Psalm 119:11, NIV).

- Put on the armor of God to stand against Satan's schemes:
  - The belt of truth
  - The shoes of peace
  - The helmet of salvation
  - The breastplate of righteousness
  - The shield of faith
  - The sword of the Spirit

Take Up Your Cross—Living supernaturally is impossible without first acknowledging, by faith, that you have been crucified and raised with Christ. Pray through the five principles of the CROSS acrostic: "Almighty Father, I praise You for the truth that I am a new creation. Thank You that I have been set free from the power of Satan, that I am dead to sin, and alive in Christ. I offer my body as an instrument of righteousness and thank You for the protection of Christ's armor. I surrender my will to You. I praise You for Your Word that is more powerful than any scheme of Satan. Through the enabling of Your Holy Spirit, help me to meditate on these glorious truths daily. I ask this in the powerful and victorious name of Your only begotten Son, Jesus Christ. Amen."

Act by Faith—In this book, you have discovered the amazing identity you have in Christ. You have explored how through the power of the Holy Spirit you can think, speak, and behave like Christ. You have glimpsed the wonderful promise of supernatural power, liberating freedom, triumph over adversity, everlasting peace, and infinite joy. Ask the Holy Spirit to make these revolutionary truths a daily reality in your life. Invite Christ to live in and through you. Let nothing hinder the work of His Spirit in your life. As a result, you will experience the awesome adventure of living supernaturally in Christ!

APPENDIX A

Who Is This Jesus?

ho, in your opinion, is the most outstanding personality of all time? The greatest leader? The greatest teacher? Who has done the most good for mankind and lived the most holy life of anyone who has ever lived?

Visit any part of the world today, and talk to men of any religion. No matter how committed to their particular religion they may be, if they know anything of the facts, they will have to acknowledge that there has never been a man like Jesus of Nazareth. He is the unique personality of all time.

Jesus changed the course of history. Even the date on your morning newspaper gives witness to the fact that Jesus of Nazareth lived on earth nearly 2,000 years ago.

HIS COMING FORETOLD

Hundreds of years before Jesus' birth, Scripture recorded the words of the great prophets of Israel foretelling His coming. The Old Testament, written by many individuals over a period of 1,500 years, contains more than 300 prophecies detailing His coming, all of which came true exactly as predicted during Jesus' life, death, and resurrection.

The life Jesus led, the miracles He performed, the words He spoke, His death on the cross, His resurrection, His ascent to heaven—these all point to the fact that He was more than a man. Jesus claimed: "The

Father and I are One" (John 10:30); "Anyone who has seen Me has seen the Father" (John 14:9); and "No one can come to the Father except through Me" (John 14:6).

HIS MESSAGE EFFECTS CHANGE

Trace the life and influence of Jesus Christ, and you will observe that His message always effects great change in the lives of people and nations. Wherever His message has gone, the sacredness of marriage, women's rights, and suffrage have been acknowledged; institutions of higher learning have been established; child labor laws have been enacted; slavery has been abolished; and a multitude of other changes have been made for the good of mankind.

ATHEIST'S LIFE TRANSFORMED

Lew Wallace, a famous general and literary genius, was an avowed atheist. For two years, Mr. Wallace studied in the leading libraries of Europe and America, seeking information to write a book that would forever destroy Christianity. While writing the second chapter of his book, he suddenly found himself on his knees crying out to Jesus, "My Lord and my God."

Because of solid, irrefutable evidence, he could no longer deny that Jesus Christ was the Son of God. Later Lew Wallace wrote *Ben Hur*, one of the greatest novels ever written concerning the time of Christ.

Similarly, the late C. S. Lewis, professor at Oxford University, was an agnostic who denied the deity of Christ for years. But he, too, in intellectual honesty, submitted to Jesus as his God and Savior after studying the overwhelming evidence for His deity.

LORD, LIAR, OR LUNATIC?

In his famous book *Mere Christianity*, Lewis makes this statement:

> A man who was merely a man and said the sort of things Jesus said would not be a great moral teacher. He would either be a lunatic—on the level with the man who says he is a poached egg—or else he would be the devil of hell. You must take your choice. Either this was, and is, the Son of God; or else a madman or something worse. You can shut Him up for a fool…or you can fall at His feet and call Him Lord and God. But let us not come

with any patronizing nonsense about His being a great human teacher. He has not left that open to us.

Who is Jesus of Nazareth to you? Your life on this earth and for all eternity is affected by your answer to this question.

Take Buddha out of Buddhism, Mohammed out of Islam, and the founder of various other religions out of their religions, and little would change. But take Jesus Christ out of Christianity, and there would be nothing left, for Christianity is not a philosophy or ethic, but a personal relationship with a living, risen Savior.

A RISEN FOUNDER

No other religion claims that its founder has been raised from the dead; Christianity is unique in this regard. Any argument for its validity stands or falls on the proof of the resurrection of Jesus of Nazareth.

Many great scholars have believed, and do believe, in His resurrection. After examining the evidence for the resurrection given by Gospel writers, the late Simon Greenleaf, an authority in jurisprudence at Harvard Law School, concluded, "It was therefore impossible that they could have persisted in affirming the truths they have narrated, had not Jesus actually risen from the dead; and had they not known this fact as certainly as they knew any other fact."

John Singleton Copley, recognized as one of the greatest legal minds in British history, comments: "I know pretty well what evidence is; and I tell you, such evidence as that for the resurrection has never broken down yet."

I have yet to meet a man who has honestly considered the overwhelming evidence concerning Jesus of Nazareth, who does not admit that He is the Son of God. While some do not believe, they are honest in confessing, "I have not taken the time to read the Bible or consider the historical facts concerning Jesus."

THE VISIBLE EXPRESSION OF THE INVISIBLE GOD

Consider these passages concerning Jesus, taken from the Bible: "Christ is the exact likeness of the unseen God. He existed before God made anything at all, and, in fact, Christ Himself is the Creator who made everything in heaven and earth..." (Colossians 1:15,16, TLB).

"God has told us His secret reason for sending Christ, a plan He decided on in mercy long ago; And this was His purpose: that when the time is ripe He will gather us all together from wherever we are—in heaven or on earth—to be with Him in Christ forever" (Ephesians 1:9,10, TLB).

A LIVING WORD

Because of Jesus' resurrection, His followers do not merely comply with the ethical code of a dead founder, but rather can have vital contact with a living Lord. Jesus Christ lives today and anxiously waits to work in the lives of those who will trust and obey Him. Blaise Pascal, a French physicist and philosopher, spoke of man's need for Jesus when he said, "There is a God-shaped vacuum in the heart of every man, which only God can fill through His Son, Jesus Christ."

Would you like to know Jesus Christ personally? You can! As presumptuous as it may sound, Jesus is so eager to establish a loving relationship with you that He has already made all the arrangements. The major barrier that prevents us from enjoying this relationship is ignorance of who Jesus is and what he has done for us.

The following appendix, "The Four Spiritual Laws," contains four principles that will help you discover how to know God personally and experience the abundant life He promised. Read on and discover for yourself the joyful reality of knowing Jesus personally.

APPENDIX B

The Four Spiritual Laws

Just as there are physical laws that govern the physical universe, so are there spiritual laws that govern your relationship with God.

LAW 1: *God loves you and offers a wonderful plan for your life.*

God's Love
"God so loved the world that He gave His one and only Son, that whoever believes in Him shall not perish but have eternal life" (John 3:16, NIV).

God's Plan
[Christ speaking] "I came that they might have life, and might have it abundantly" [that it might be full and meaningful] (John 10:10).

Why is it that most people are not experiencing the abundant life? Because...

LAW 2: *Man is sinful and separated from God. Therefore, he cannot know and experience God's love and plan for his life.*

Man Is Sinful
"All have sinned and fall short of the glory of God" (Romans 3:23).

Man was created to have fellowship with God; but, because of his own stubborn self-will, he chose to go his own independent way and fellowship with God was broken. This self-will, characterized by an attitude of active rebellion or passive indifference, is an evidence of what the Bible calls sin.

Man Is Separated

"The wages of sin is death" [spiritual separation from God] (Romans 6:23).

This diagram illustrates that God is holy and man is sinful. A great gulf separates the two. The arrows illustrate that man is continually trying to reach God and the abundant life through his own efforts, such as a good life, philosophy, or religion—but he inevitably fails.

The third law explains the only way to bridge this gulf...

LAW 3: *Jesus Christ is God's **only** provision for man's sin. Through Him you can know and experience God's love and plan for your life.*

He Died In Our Place

"God demonstrates His own love toward us, in that while we were yet sinners, Christ died for us" (Romans 5:8).

He Is the Only Way to God

"Jesus said to him, 'I am the way, and the truth, and the life; no one comes to the Father but through Me'" (John 14:6).

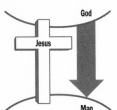

This diagram illustrates that God has bridged the gulf that separates us from Him by sending His Son, Jesus Christ, to die on the cross in our place to pay the penalty for our sins.

It is not enough just to know these three laws...

LAW 4: *We must individually **receive** Jesus Christ as Savior and Lord; then we can know and experience God's love and plan for our lives.*

We Must Receive Christ

"As many as received Him, to them He gave the right to become children of God, even to those who believe in His name" (John 1:12).

We Receive Christ Through Faith

"By grace you have been saved through faith; and that not of yourselves, it is the gift of God; not as a result of works that no one should boast" (Ephesians 2:8,9).

When We Receive Christ, We Experience a New Birth

(Read John 3:1–8.)

We Receive Christ Through Personal Invitation

[Christ speaking] "Behold, I stand at the door and knock; if any one hears My voice and opens the door, I will come in to him" (Revelation 3:20).

Receiving Christ involves turning to God from self (repentance) and trusting Christ to come into our lives to forgive our sins and to make us what He wants us to be. Just to agree intellectually that Jesus Christ is the Son of God and that He died on the cross for our sins is not enough. Nor is it enough to have an emotional experience. We receive Jesus Christ by faith, as an act of the will.

These two circles represent two kinds of lives:

Self-Directed Life
S – Self is on the throne
† – Christ is outside the life
● – Interests are directed by self, often
    resulting in discord and frustration

Christ-Directed Life
† – Christ is in the life and on the throne
S – Self is yielding to Christ
● – Interests are directed by Christ,
    resulting in harmony with God's plan

Which circle best represents your life?
Which circle would you like to have represent your life?

The following explains how you can receive Christ:

You Can Receive Christ Right Now by Faith Through Prayer
(Prayer is talking with God)
God knows your heart and is not so concerned with your words as He is with the attitude of your heart. The following is a suggested prayer:

> *Lord Jesus, I need You. Thank You for dying on the cross for my sins. I open the door of my life and receive You as my Savior and Lord. Thank You for forgiving my sins and giving me eternal life. Take control of the throne of my life. Make me the kind of person You want me to be.*

Does this prayer express the desire of your heart?

If it does, I invite you to pray this prayer right now, and Christ will come into your life, as He promised.

How to Know That Christ Is in Your Life
Did you receive Christ into your life? According to His promise in Revelation 3:20, where is Christ right now in relation to you? Christ said that He would come into your life. Would He mislead you? On what authority do you know that God has answered your prayer? (The trustworthiness of God Himself and His Word.)

The Bible Promises Eternal Life to All Who Receive Christ
"God has given us eternal life, and this life is in His Son. He who has the Son has the life; he who does not have the Son of God does not have the life" (1 John 5:11–13).

Thank God often that Christ is in your life and that He will never leave you (Hebrews 13:5). You can know on the basis of His promise that Christ lives in you and that you have eternal life from the very moment you invite Him in. He will not deceive you.

An important reminder…

Do Not Depend on Feelings

The promise of God's Word, the Bible—not our feelings—is our authority. The Christian lives by faith (trust) in the trustworthiness of God Himself and His Word. This train diagram illustrates the relationship among fact (God and His Word), faith (our trust in God and His Word), and feeling (the result of our faith and obedience). (Read John 14:21.)

The train will run with or without the caboose. However, it would be useless to attempt to pull the train by the caboose. In the same way, as Christians we do not depend on feelings or emotions, but we place our faith (trust) in the trustworthiness of God and the promises of His Word.

Now That You Have Received Christ

The moment you received Christ by faith, as an act of the will, many things happened, including the following:

- Christ came into your life (Revelation 3:20; Colossians 1:27).
- Your sins were forgiven (Colossians 1:14).
- You became a child of God (John 1:12).
- You received eternal life (John 5:24).
- You began the great adventure for which God created you (John 10:10).

Can you think of anything more wonderful that could happen to you than receiving Christ? Would you like to thank God in prayer right now for what He has done for you? By thanking God, you demonstrate your faith.

To enjoy your new life to the fullest...

Suggestions for Christian Growth

Spiritual growth results from trusting Jesus Christ. A life of faith will enable you to trust God increasingly with every detail of your life, and to practice the following:

G   *Go* to God in prayer daily (John 15:7).

R   *Read* God's Word daily (Acts 17:11); begin with the Gospel of John.

O   *Obey* God moment by moment (John 14:21).

W   *Witness* for Christ by your life and words (Matthew 4:19; John 15:8).

T   *Trust* God for every detail of your life (1 Peter 5:7).

H   *Holy Spirit*—allow Him to control and empower your daily life and witness (Galatians 5:16,17; Acts 1:8; Ephesians 5:18).

Fellowship in a Good Church

God's Word instructs us not to forsake "the assembling of ourselves together" (Hebrews 10:25). If you do not belong to a church, do not wait to be invited. Take the initiative; call the pastor of a nearby church where Christ is honored and His Word is preached. Start this week, and make plans to attend regularly.

Jesus: An Investigative Bible Study

The Bible gives us an in-depth picture of who Jesus is and why He came to this earth. If you are still unsure of who Jesus is or if you want to become better acquainted with His life, death, and resurrection, this Bible study will help. The study goes through the Gospel of Luke, one of four writers who walked and talked with Jesus and gave us an accurate account of the life of Jesus.

Use your Bible to answer the questions. To help you understand how the scriptural principles you learn apply to today's problems, reflect on the "To Think About" sections. Also, carefully respond to the personal application sections to experience the adventure God has planned for you.

JESUS: HIS BEGINNINGS

In this study we will see:

- How Luke's Gospel fits into history
- That Jesus is "the Son of God"
- What Jesus said He came to do

Background to the New Testament

The New Testament is made up of several short books and letters. Our English Bibles are translations of what the early Christians actually wrote. The experts tell us that we can be sure that the text on which these translations are based has very few mistakes in it. How can we be sure?

In the days of the first Christians, there were many writings about the life of Jesus. But some had special quality—they had been written by Jesus' followers or their close friends. These gospels and letters were carefully copied by hand. Over the years, archaeologists have found thousands of manuscripts containing portions of the New Testament and even some complete copies. By comparing these, we can get very close to what the New Testament writers originally wrote. Some of these copies are dated less than 100 years after the original gospel or letter was written.

For an idea of how good this evidence is, compare the New Testament with other writings that are about the same age. For example, Julius Caesar wrote a book called *The Gallic War* about 50 years before Christ was born. We obviously do not have the original copy. Yet, we do have nine or ten copies, and the earliest of these was made about 900 years after the original. This is a normal gap for ancient writings.

In examining the historical evidence relating to the Bible, we find that the great number of early manuscripts gives us good reason to believe that we know almost exactly what Luke, Paul, and the others wrote.

About the Author

The author of this Gospel, Luke, also wrote another book in the New Testament, the Acts of the Apostles. Luke was a doctor, and was the only New Testament writer who was not Jewish. Independent evidence confirms that he was a very careful and accurate historian.

Luke's Gospel: Fact or Fiction?

Read Luke 1:1–4.

1. Where did Luke get his information? (v. 2)

2. How did he write it? (v. 3)

3. Why do you think Luke wrote this introduction?

Where Did Jesus Come From?

Luke gives details of the unique origin of Jesus, and the following passage explains how Jesus' birth was foretold.

Read Luke 1:26–38.

1. What would the future hold for Mary's child? (vv. 32,33)

2. How would Jesus be conceived? (vv. 35–37)

3. Jesus is said to be the Son of God. What do these verses say about Jesus' dual origin?

Jesus Explains His Purpose

Jesus was born in Bethlehem in Judea, in the south of Palestine. He grew up in Nazareth, a very ordinary town in Galilee, in the north of Palestine. Jesus was a carpenter, but at the age of 30 He became a religious teacher, moving from town to town.

In Luke 4:14–22, we read what happened when Jesus began teaching. He went to the synagogue, which was the local place of worship. Although He probably had no more religious education than the average Jewish man, people wanted to hear Him. He was asked to speak at the synagogue in Nazareth.

Read Luke 4:14–22.

1. What kinds of people had Jesus come to help? (v. 18)

   Who do you think this means?

2. What was He going to announce? (v. 19)

   What does this mean?

3. What do you think the people in the synagogue understood when He said the words in verse 21?

To Think About

Jesus came to help the "poor," the "captive," the "blind," and the "oppressed." Are there ways in which people today are poor, captive, blind, or oppressed?

JESUS: THE HEALER

In the first part of this study, we saw that Jesus was not just an unusual person; He was God's Son. He came into the world in order to meet the deepest needs of men and women.

Now we will look at how Jesus met the needs of two particular people. Everywhere Jesus went, He came across needy people. Often, the people He met had incurable diseases, but He was able to change their lives completely by healing them.

Those He healed include: Simon's mother-in-law, a Roman officer's servant, a man with a shriveled hand, a crippled woman, a paralyzed man, people suffering from spiritual and mental disorders, lepers, blind people, and He even raised the dead. "People throughout the village brought sick family members to Jesus. No matter what their diseases were, the touch of His hand healed every one" (Luke 4:40).

A Blind Beggar is Healed
Read Luke 18:35–43.

1. What do you think life was like for this blind man?

2. Why do you think he kept calling for Jesus?

3. What did Jesus do and say once He had heard the man? (vv. 40–42)

4. In what way did the man show he believed in Jesus?

5. If you had seen this miracle, what would you have thought of Jesus?

This was a blind man to whom Jesus gave "recovery of sight" (Luke 4:18, NIV). He healed many people of different physical illnesses. But He also healed people in other ways.

Jesus and Zacchaeus
The Romans gave the job of collecting taxes to the highest bidder. Tax collectors did not get any wages for their work. They collected as much money as they could so there would be plenty left over for themselves after paying the government. Zacchaeus was one of these tax collectors—a greedy and unpopular man.

Read Luke 19:1–10.

1. What was Zacchaeus' attitude toward Jesus? (vv. 3,4,6)

2. Many people grumbled about Jesus talking to such a man. What was Jesus' attitude toward Zacchaeus? (vv. 5,9,10)

3. How did Zacchaeus change after meeting Jesus? (v. 8)

4. What do you think Jesus meant by "the lost"? (v. 10)

5. What does this incident show about Jesus?

To Think About

Zacchaeus was "captive" to his own greed. Jesus gave him freedom.

Jesus said that he had come "to seek and to save the lost." People changed when they met Jesus. How do you think meeting Jesus would affect your life?

JESUS: THE TEACHER

People didn't come to Jesus just to be healed by Him; they also wanted to listen to Him. Large crowds from all over the country would come to hear what He had to say. He talked about God's Kingdom, prayer, wise and foolish lifestyles, love and forgiveness, and also Himself.

Not everyone liked Jesus' teaching. He was outspoken against the religious leaders who were hypocrites. He had enemies who tried to trick Him with questions, but He always managed to give wise answers. Even when the religious leaders wanted to kill Jesus, they found it difficult because the crowds wanted to listen to His teaching, "and they hung on every word He said" (Luke 19:48).

Let us look at two of the best-known parables that Jesus told. (Parables are stories that teach biblical truth.)

The Good Samaritan

1. What would you say are the most important things in life?

Many people went to Jesus with their important questions. For one man, his concern focused on what would happen to him after his death. He asked Jesus how he could "receive eternal life." Jesus got the man to answer it himself, from the Scriptures (Luke 10:27).

Read Luke 10:25–28.

2. What did the man say were the two most important things in life? (v. 27)

   What do you think of these answers?

   Jesus was then asked, "Who is my neighbor?" He answered by telling the story of the good Samaritan.

Read Luke 10:29–37.

3. What did the priest and Levite do that was wrong? (vv. 31,32)

   Did they break the Law?

   Did they disobey the principle to treat others the way they would like to be treated?

4. Due to their religious and cultural upbringings, Jews looked upon the Samaritans (Gentiles) with contempt. How did the Samaritan in this parable show love?

5. How would you answer the question, "Who is my neighbor?"

   Jesus acts as a good Samaritan toward us. He sees our needs and failures, and instead of passing by, He reaches out to help.

The Lost Son

This is a simple story, yet one of the greatest in the world of literature. Using the problems that often arise between people, this story illustrates how men and women react toward God.

Read Luke 15:11–32.

1. What do you think the younger son was thinking as he left home? (vv. 12,13)

   Where did he go? (v. 13)

   How do you think the father felt when his son had gone?

2. Things went fine for a while. What happened when things got bad? (vv. 14–16)

3. The son changed his mind. Why? (v. 17)

   How did he show that his attitude had changed? (vv. 18–20)

4. What was the father's attitude? (vv. 20,22–24)

5. In what ways do you think this story is a picture of our relationship with God?

This story shows us that God still offers His love in spite of our willful selfishness. It also shows us that we can come back to God, no matter how far we have wandered from Him.

To Think About

What do you identify with more: the attitude of the son as he left home or his attitude when he decided to return?

Can you believe that God would accept you as completely as the father accepted his son?

You may be at a point in your life where you know that you need God and want to return to Him. Perhaps you would like to pray:

> Dear Father, I have wandered away from You, and I have sinned against You. I have not loved You or other people as I should. I want to come back to You now, just as the lost son came back to his father. Please forgive me, and come into my life, so that I can be the person You want me to be. Amen.

The next section will explain what Jesus did to make our return to God possible.

JESUS: THE REDEEMER

At the trial of Jesus it seemed that both the weak-willed Roman governor, Pilate, and the shouts of the crowd sent Jesus to death. In fact, the Bible tells us that these events amazingly formed part of God's purpose.

Jesus took the twelve disciples aside and said to them, "As you know, we are going to Jerusalem. And when we get there, all the predictions of the ancient prophets concerning the Son of Man will come true. He will be handed over to the Romans to be mocked, treated shamefully, and spit upon. They will whip him and kill Him, but on the third day He will rise again." But they didn't understand a thing He said (Luke 18:31–34).

(See the sidebar on page 238 for background notes on unfamiliar terms.)

BACKGROUND NOTES

Passover (Luke 22:7–19). The Passover is an annual religious festival when the Jews recall how God rescued their nation from slavery in Egypt. They remember particularly how the angel of death killed the first-born of all Egyptians, yet "passed over" all the Jewish families. God told them that they would be protected by sprinkling lamb's blood on their doorposts. It was after this event that the Egyptians finally allowed the Jews to leave Egypt. An important part of the Passover festival was the killing and eating of the Passover lamb.

New Covenant (Luke 22:20). God had promised in the Old Testament (Jeremiah 31:31–34) that He would bring in a new era. This promise is known as the new covenant. In the New Testament, Jesus says that this era is now beginning and that His death would confirm it. This is how God guarantees that He will forgive us and that we will have a special relationship with Him.

Messiah (Luke 22:67). The Hebrew word "Messiah" means "anointed one." (To anoint someone with olive oil was to honor him or to appoint him to do some special work.) In Greek, the language of the New Testament, "Messiah" is translated "Christ." The Jews hoped that the promised Messiah would come as a king, to deliver the nation from foreign rule and to set up a righteous, divine kingdom in Israel. There are many verses in the Old Testament that speak of this anointed One who was to come. Although Jesus claimed to be the Messiah, He did not do what the Jews expected. Instead He came as a servant and as One who would suffer. His Kingdom was established, not in a palace, but in the hearts of men and women. Yet in the end, all things will be brought under His rule.

Son of Man (Luke 22:69). Jesus most often describes Himself as "Son of Man." In Luke 22:69, He refers to an Old Testament passage (Daniel 7:13,14) about a son of man (human being) who was given an everlasting kingdom. The Jews have understood Daniel to be referring to the promised Messiah.

The Passover Meal and "The Last Supper"

On the last night of His life, Jesus ate a meal with His disciples.

Read Luke 22:7–20.

1. What do you think the atmosphere was like during that meal?

2. What did Jesus say about the bread and cup of wine? (vv. 19,20)

3. What did you think Jesus meant when He said His body was "given for you" and His blood was "poured out for you"?

The Trial

After the Passover meal, Jesus was arrested in the Garden of Gethsemane. He was taken before the Jewish ruling council.

Read Luke 22:66–71.

1. What did the Jewish leaders want to find out from Jesus?

2. What did Jesus tell them?

3. How did the Jewish leaders respond? (v. 71)

The Cross

Jesus was not condemned to death for anything He had done. He was condemned for who He claimed to be.

Read Luke 23:32–49.

1. What did the following groups say about Jesus:

   Jewish leaders (v. 35)

   Soldiers (v. 36)

   The criminal (v. 39)

2. How was the second criminal's reply different from that of the first? (vv. 39–42)

   What did he recognize about Jesus?

3. What did the army officer say when Jesus died? (v. 47)

4. What do you think Jesus' attitude was while He was being crucified? (vv. 34,43,46)

This part of the study is called "Jesus the Redeemer." To redeem something means to buy it back, to recover it by payment. Jesus' death was for the sake of other people, to pay the death penalty for their sins and bring them back to God.

To Think About

As the criminal faced his own death, he asked Jesus to remember him in His future Kingdom. Jesus promised that the robber would be with Him that day in Paradise. In what ways can we have the same hope as the criminal did after hearing Jesus' words?

JESUS: THE LIFE-GIVER

The last chapter of Luke gives a clear account of the fantastic miracle of the resurrection. After Jesus' crucifixion, His disciples were afraid of the Jews. While they continued to meet, they did so in secret. Suddenly, Jesus came to them.

C. S. Lewis, a famous writer and Christian, wrote: "The New Testament writers speak as if Christ's achievement in rising from the dead was the first event of its kind in the whole history of the universe. He has forced open a door that has been locked since the death of the first man. He has met, fought, and beaten the king of death."

The Resurrection
Read Luke 24:1–53.

1. How do you think the disciples felt after seeing Jesus crucified?

News began to reach them that Jesus was alive again. The disciples' reaction shows that they did not expect this. They thought the story was nonsense (v. 11). The two on the road said that they were surprised by the news (v. 22), and Jesus Himself confirmed that they had doubts in their minds (v. 38). Nevertheless, various people became convinced that Jesus had risen from the dead.

2. What convinced the women? (vv. 5–8)

3. What convinced the two people on the road? (vv. 25–32)

4. What convinced the group of disciples? (vv. 36–46)

5. How did the disciples' attitude toward Jesus change? (vv. 52,53)

The resurrection of Jesus Christ was the climax of His life's work. Jesus rose from the dead as He said He would. This challenges us to believe that the other things He said about Himself are also true. The resurrection demands a response from us, one way or another.

Responding to Jesus

Let's look at one particular woman about whom Luke wrote, and see how she responded to Jesus.

Read Luke 7:36–50.

This woman had a bad past. Her behavior toward Jesus was very different from the stiff and starchy response of Simon the Pharisee.

1. Why do you think the woman acted as she did? (vv. 37,38)

2. Jesus told Simon a story to explain the woman's actions (vv. 40–43). Why do you think He did that?

3. How were the woman's debts cleared before God? (vv. 48,50)

4. What does "faith" mean? (v. 50)

5. What did "go in peace" mean to this woman? (v. 50)

She could be sure that she was at peace with God. Jesus had welcomed, accepted, and forgiven her because of His love and mercy. Nothing she had done could have earned His response. But she was now free to live as a new person.

We can be sure in this same way. We can never pay God the debt we owe Him for our sinful behavior. But, if we come to Jesus as this woman did, we can know that He forgives and accepts us completely. In the previous section, we discussed how this happens through Jesus' death on our behalf.

Becoming a Christian

The sinful woman came to Jesus and recognized her sin. She trusted Jesus to forgive her and, by her actions, thanked Him for the new life He offered her. We must do the same if we want to be at peace with God, both now and eternally.

You could pray something like this:

Jesus, I realize that I have been running my own life and have rebelled against You. Thank You for dying for my sins. I open my life to You and ask You to be my Savior and Lord. Make me the kind of person You want me to be. Amen.

Growing as a Christian

This study has shown us who Jesus is and why He came.

Luke 6:46–49 teaches that we must not only hear what Jesus said, but put it into practice.

Read Luke 6:46–49.

A decision to become a Christian is just the beginning of a lifetime of getting to know God better.

APPENDIX D
The Spirit-Filled Life

Every day can be an exciting adventure for the Christian who knows the reality of being filled with the Holy Spirit and who lives constantly, moment by moment, under His gracious direction.

The Bible tells us that there are three kinds of people:

1. **Natural Man:** One who has not received Christ.

Self-Directed Life
S – Self is on the throne
† – Christ is outside the life
● – Interests are directed by self, often resulting in discord and frustration

"A natural man does not accept the things of the Spirit of God; for they are foolishness to him, and he cannot understand them, because they are spiritually appraised" (1 Corinthians 2:14, NASB).

2. **Spiritual Man:** One who is directed and empowered by the Holy Spirit.

"He who is spiritual appraises all things" (1 Corinthians 2:15, NASB).

Christ-Directed Life
S – Christ is in the life and on the throne
† – Self is yielding to Christ
● – Interests are directed by Christ, resulting in harmony with God's plan

3. **Carnal Man:** One who has received Christ, but who lives in defeat because he trusts in his own efforts to live the Christian life.

Self-Directed Life

S – Self is on the throne

† – Christ is outside the life

● – Interests are directed by self, often resulting in discord and frustration

"I, brethren, could not speak to you as to spiritual people but as to carnal, as to babes in Christ. I fed you with milk and not with solid food; for until now you were not able to receive it, and even now you are still not able; for you are still carnal. For when there are envy, strife, and divisions among you, are you not carnal and behaving like mere men?" (1 Corinthians 3:1–3).

The following are four principles for living the Spirit-filled life:

1 GOD HAS PROVIDED FOR US AN ABUNDANT AND FRUITFUL CHRISTIAN LIFE.

"Jesus said, 'I have come that they may have life, and that they may have it more abundantly'" (John 10:10, NKJ).

"The fruit of the Spirit is love, joy, peace, patience, kindness, goodness, faithfulness, gentleness, self-control; against such things there is no law" (Galatians 5:22,23).

Read John 15:5 and Acts 1:8.

The following are some personal traits of the spiritual man that result from trusting God:

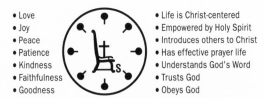

● Love
● Joy
● Peace
● Patience
● Kindness
● Faithfulness
● Goodness

● Life is Christ-centered
● Empowered by Holy Spirit
● Introduces others to Christ
● Has effective prayer life
● Understands God's Word
● Trusts God
● Obeys God

The degree to which these traits are manifested in the life depends on the extent to which the Christian trusts the Lord with every detail of his life, and on his maturity in Christ. One who is only beginning to understand the ministry of the Holy Spirit should not be discouraged if he is not as fruitful as more mature Christians who have known and experienced this truth for a longer period.

Why is it that most Christians are not experiencing the abundant life?

2 CARNAL CHRISTIANS CANNOT EXPERIENCE THE ABUNDANT AND FRUITFUL CHRISTIAN LIFE.

The carnal man trusts in his own efforts to live the Christian life:

- He is either uninformed about, or has forgotten, God's love, forgiveness, and power (Romans 5:8–10; Hebrews 10:1–25; 1 John 1; 2:1–3; 2 Peter 1:9).
- He has an up-and-down spiritual experience.
- He wants to do what is right, but cannot.
- He fails to draw on the power of the Holy Spirit to live the Christian life (1 Corinthians 3:1–3; Romans 7:15–24; 8:7; Galatians 5:16–18).

Some or all of the following traits may characterize the carnal man—the Christian who does not fully trust God:

- Legalistic attitude
- Impure thoughts
- Jealousy
- Guilt
- Worry
- Discouragement
- Critical spirit
- Frustration
- Aimlessness
- Fear
- Ignorance of his spiritual heritage
- Unbelief
- Disobedience
- Loss of love for God and for others
- Poor prayer life
- No desire for Bible study

(The individual who professes to be a Christian but who continues to practice sin should realize that he may not be a Christian at all, according to 1 John 2:3; 3:6–9; and Ephesians 5:5.)

The third truth gives us the only solution to this problem...

3 JESUS PROMISED THE ABUNDANT AND FRUITFUL LIFE AS THE RESULT OF BEING FILLED (DIRECTED AND EMPOWERED) BY THE HOLY SPIRIT.

The Spirit-filled life is the Christ-directed life by which Christ lives His life in and through us in the power of the Holy Spirit (John 15).

- One becomes a Christian through the ministry of the Holy Spirit (John 3:1–8.) From the moment of spiritual birth, the Christian is indwelt by the Holy Spirit at all times (John 1:12; Colossians 2:9,10; John 14:16,17).

  All Christians are indwelt by the Holy Spirit, but not all Christians are filled (directed, controlled, and empowered) by the Holy Spirit on an ongoing basis.

- The Holy Spirit is the source of the overflowing life (John 7:37–39).
- In His last command before His ascension, Christ promised the power of the Holy Spirit to enable us to be witnesses for Him (Acts 1:1–9).

How, then, can one be filled with the Holy Spirit?

4 WE ARE FILLED (DIRECTED AND EMPOWERED) BY THE HOLY SPIRIT BY FAITH; THEN WE CAN EXPERIENCE THE ABUNDANT AND FRUITFUL LIFE THAT CHRIST PROMISED TO EACH CHRISTIAN.

You can appropriate the filling of the Holy Spirit right now if you:

- Sincerely desire to be directed and empowered by the Holy Spirit (Matthew 5:6; John 7:37–39).

- Confess your sins. By faith, thank God that He has forgiven all of your sins—past, present, and future—because Christ died for you (Colossians 2:13–15).

- Present every area of your life to God (Romans 12:1,2).

- By faith claim the fullness of the Holy Spirit, according to:

    His command: Be filled with the Spirit. "Do not get drunk on wine, which leads to debauchery. Instead, be filled with the Spirit" (Ephesians 5:18).

    His promise: He will always answer when we pray according to His will. "This is the confidence we have in approaching God: that if we ask anything according to his will, he hears us. And if we know that He hears us—whatever we ask—we know that we have what we asked of Him" (1 John 5:14,15).

How to Pray in Faith to be Filled With the Holy Spirit

We are filled with the Holy Spirit by faith alone. However, true prayer is one way of expressing your faith. The following is a suggested prayer:

Dear Father, I need You. I acknowledge that I have been directing my own life and that, as a result, I have sinned against You. I thank You that You have forgiven my sins through Christ's death on the cross for me. I now invite Christ to again take His place on the throne of my life. Fill me with the Holy Spirit as You commanded me to be filled, and as You promised in Your Word that You would do if I asked in faith. I pray this in the name of Jesus. As an expression of my faith, I now thank You for directing my life and for filling me with the Holy Spirit.

Does this prayer express the desire of your heart? If so, bow in prayer and trust God to fill you with the Holy Spirit right now.

Resources

OTHER "LIVING IN CHRIST" RESOURCES

Why Do Christians Suffer?
Bill Bright
Why do Christians suffer? It's a valid question that many believers—even some nonbelievers—wrestle with from time to time. As a stand-alone booklet or a companion piece to Dr. Bright's book *Living Supernaturally in Christ*, this informative purse or pocket guide will direct you to the Bible's illuminating answers. By remembering the acrostic TRIUMPH, you can experience God's peace even in the midst of adversity, pain, and heartache. Ideal for personal reference or to share with friends in need.
Booklet / 40p / ISBN 1-56399-149-7 / $.99

Are You Prepared for Battle?
Bill Bright
For Christians, battling the awesome powers of darkness is inevitable. But victory is attainable—in fact, assured—for those who are properly prepared. This excellent, conveniently-sized booklet explores the secrets of standing firm against the devil's schemes, defusing the power of his attacks and sending him fleeing in retreat. Learn to dress for spiritual success by wearing God's protective armor. *Are You Prepared for Battle?* is an ideal companion booklet to *Living Supernaturally in Christ*, *Why Do Christians Suffer?* and *The Supernatural You*.
Booklet / 40p / ISBN 1-56399-148-9 / $.99

The Supernatural You
Bill Bright
Written in a convenient, take-along format, this booklet helps you discover and live according to your new, supernatural identity in Christ. The booklet outlines five essential steps to living supernaturally in

Christ, made easily memorable by the acrostic CROSS. As you apply these biblical truths, you'll discover a life of incomparable power, liberating freedom, triumph over adversity, everlasting peace, and infinite joy. *The Supernatural You* is an ideal companion booklet to *Living Supernaturally in Christ*, *Why Do Christians Suffer?* and *Are You Prepared for Battle?*

Booklet / 40 p / ISBN 1-56399-147-0 / $.99

A Child of the King
Bill Bright with Marion Wells
"When the nights grow dark and the stars grow bright and families tell stories by the fire, a few of the old ones recall an ancient legend. Long ago, it is said, an orphan lad had a chance to be adopted by a mighty king…"

A Child of the King is an exciting, fictional tale based on the truths of Dr. Bright's book *Living Supernaturally in Christ*. Written in the tradition of C. S. Lewis's *Chronicles of Narnia* and J. R. R. Tolkien's *The Lord of the Rings*, this thrilling allegory will teach adult and teen readers alike the invaluable truths of supernatural living, even in the midst of spiritual darkness and warfare. Follow the adventures of Jotham, the People of the Book, and others in the Kingdom of Withershins…and realize your own high calling as a child of the King.

Trade Paperback / 192p / ISBN 1-56399-150-0 / $11.99

"DISCOVER GOD" RESOURCES

GOD: Discover His Character
In this thorough, easy-to-grasp book, Dr. Bright helps make God knowable as few books (save the Bible itself) have done. Based on more than five decades of intense, personal study, Dr. Bright's penetrating insights into God's character—and its significance to mankind—are certain to energize your walk with God.

Paperback / 336p / ISBN 1-56399-125-X / $14.99

GOD: Discover His Character Video Series
Bill Bright
Thirteen 30-minute video segments, complete in three volumes, help you (and those to whom you minister) discover God's awesome char-

acter. All are presented with powerful teaching, dramatizations, and graphics to help adult and teenage audiences appreciate God as our Great Creator, our Perfect Judge, and our Gracious Savior. Your life, worship, and ministry will never be the same.

Vol. 1: Our Great Creator will teach you about God's attributes of ability—His power, knowledge, presence, and sovereignty.

Video (with Viewer's Guide) / 150 minutes / (Five 30-minute sessions) / ISBN 1-56399-122-5 / $19.99

Vol. 2: Our Perfect Judge explores God's attributes of integrity—the fact that God is holy, truthful, righteous, and just.

Video (with Viewer's Guide) / 120 minutes / (Four 30-minute sessions) / ISBN 1-56399-123-3 / $19.99

Vol. 3: Our Gracious Savior contains four compelling lessons about God's attributes of relationship—how God is loving, merciful, faithful, and never-changing.

Video (with Viewer's Guide) / 120 minutes / (Four 30-minute sessions) / ISBN 1-56399-124-1 / $19.99

GOD: Discover His Character Audio Edition
"Everything about our lives is determined and influenced by our view of God," says Bill Bright in this awe-inspiring audio edition. Based on more than five decades of intense study and close, personal fellowship, Dr. Bright's insights into God's wondrous character are certain to attract many non-Christians to faith, and to energize the walks of many believers. In each of 15 dynamic messages, Bill Freeman, familiar voice of Campus Crusade's WorldChangers Radio, enhances the learning experience with practical life application questions.

Two audio cassettes / 240 min. / ISBN 1-56399-139-X / $14.99

GOD: Knowing Him by His Names
El-Elyon, Adonai, Jehovah-Sabaoth. To most Christians, the Hebrew names of God are unknown and unpronounceable. But much can be gained from understanding the meaning and significance of the names by which the Israelites knew their Creator and Protector. In this compact overview of God's names, today's Christians will not only learn more about our heavenly Father, but also become more worshipful of

His nature. The booklet includes 16 character-revealing names of God, and concludes with the "Names of Christ" and "Applying God's Names."

Booklet / 40p / ISBN 1-56399-140-3 / $.99

GOD: Seeking Him Wholeheartedly

Based on the greatest commandment, recorded in Matthew 22:36,37 ("Love the Lord your God with all your heart..."), this booklet explains seven steps for seeking God with a whole heart. Bill Bright deals with the sincerity of our love for God, the priority of our relationship with Him, and the evidence of our wholehearted devotion— obedience. His insights enable any follower of Christ to grow closer to our heavenly Father and to enjoy the fullness of His blessings.

Booklet / 40p / ISBN 1-56399-141-1 / $.99

GOD: 13 Steps to Discovering His Attributes

In this abbreviated guide to discovering God's attributes, Dr. Bill Bright shares the fruit of his lifelong study of God. These wonderful truths are certain to enrich your life and energize your walk with God. Keep this booklet handy in your pocket or purse to read during quiet moments, or to share with friends and loved ones.

Booklet / 40p / ISBN 1-56399-126-8 / $.99

GOD: Discover the Benefits of His Attributes

As an individual resource, or as a companion to *GOD: Discover His Character* or *GOD: 13 Steps to Discovering His Attributes*, this sturdy, four-color laminated card will energize your Christian life as you're frequently reminded of God's amazing character. Just 3" × 5", it makes a great bookmark, slips easily into a purse or pocket, and is conveniently sized to share with friends.

Pocket card (pkg. of 10) / ISBN 1-56399-130-6 / $3.99

End Notes

Chapter 1: Our Supernatural Identity in Christ

1. Billy Rose, *Pitching Horse Shoes*, 1948.
2. Robert Strand, "The Final Bid," *More Stories for the Heart*, compiled by Alice Gray (Portland, OR: Multnomah Press, 1997), pp. 126,127.
3. *Sermons Illustrated*, (Holland, OH: 1987).
4. Gerald F. Hawthorne and Ralph P. Martin, eds., *Dictionary of Paul and His Letters*, (Downers Grove, IL: InterVarsity Press, 1993), p. 251.

Chapter 2: Faith: The Key to Supernatural Living

1. Jack Canfield, et al., *Chicken Soup for the Christian Soul*, (Deerfield Beach, FL: Health Communications, Inc., 1997), pp. 198,199.
2. George Mueller, *Leadership*, Vol. 12, No. 4.
3. "Illustrations for Preaching and Teaching," *Leadership Journal*, Craig Brian Larson, ed., (Grand Rapids, MI: Baker Book House, 1993), p. 78.
4. Richard W. De Haan, "Pattern and Power," *Our Daily Bread*, May 16, 2000, (Grand Rapids MI: RBC Ministries, 1999).

Chapter 3: Christ Living In and Through Us

1. Alice Gray, "Dime Store Pearls," *Pulpit Helps*, Volume 24, Number 6, June 1999, p. 6.
2. Elisabeth Elliot, *Shadow of the Almighty*, (San Francisco: Harper & Row, 1956), p. 247.
3. This dungeon has become far more presentable in recent years because it has become a tourist attraction.
4. *Sermons Illustrated*, (Holland, OH: 1987).
5. Ian L. Wilson, "New Creation." www.sermonillustrations.com/new%20creation.htm.
6. Dr. Ralph Sockman, *Today in the Word*, (Chicago, IL: Moody Bible Institute), October 1990, p. 14.
7. Lynn Jost, "Sacrifice," www.sermonillustrations.com/s/sacrifice.htm.
8. Donald Grey Barnhouse, *The Invisible War*, (Grand Rapids, MI: Zondervan, 1965), p. 41.
9. Bruce Larson, *Believe and Belong*, (Old Tappan, NJ: Power Books, 1982).

Chapter 4: Living as a Child of God

1. Leslie Flynn, *Sermons Illustrated*, (Holland, OH: November/December 1988).
2. "Theology News and Notes, October 1976," *Multnomah Message*, Spring 1993, p. 1.
3. David Judge and Helmut Teichert, *Discovering God's Best: Right Thinking for Supernatural Living*, (Sun River, MT: Turning Point Productions, 1994), Unit 6, Lesson 10.
4. Linda Seger, *The Art of Adaptation*, (New York: Holt, 1992), p. 2.
5. "Entry," *Parables, Etc.*, (Platteville, CO: Saratoga Press), Dec. 1986.
6. "The One Who Would Die," *The Pastor's Story File*, (Platteville, CO: Saratoga Press), Mar. 1992.

Chapter 5: Living as an Heir of God

1. Watchman Nee, "We Are Christ's Heirs," www.bible.org/illus/s/s-152.htm.

2. Millard J. Erickson, *Christian Theology*, (Grand Rapids, MI: Baker Book House, 1985), p. 1234.

3. Morning star is defined as "possession of Jesus Christ and the blessed hope of life everlasting" in *The International Standard Bible Encyclopedia*, Vol. 3, (Grand Rapids, MI: W. B. Eerdmans Pub. Co., 1986), p. 413.

Chapter 6: Living as a Saint with a New Nature

1. George Vandeman, *Planet in Rebellion*, (Nashville, TN: Southern Publishers Association, 1960).

2. David Judge and Helmut Teichert, *Discovering God's Best: Right Thinking for Supernatural Living*, (Sun River, MT: Turning Point Productions, 1994), Unit 6, Lesson 12.

3. H. A. Ironside, *Illustrations of Bible Truth*, (Chicago, IL: Moody Press, 1945), pp. 33,34.

Chapter 7: Living as a Member of the Body of Christ

1. Charles Colson and Ellen Santilli Vaughn, *Against the Night: Living in the New Dark Ages*, (Ann Arbor, MI: Servant Publications, 1999), p. 98.

2. Lewis Timberlake, "Interdependence," www.sermonillustrations.com/interdependence.htm.

3. *Today in the Word*, (Chicago, IL: Moody Bible Institute), June 22, 1992.

4. David Judge and Helmut Teichert, *Discovering God's Best: Right Thinking for Supernatural Living*, (Sun River, MT: Turning Point Productions, 1994), Unit 6, Lesson 14.

5. Paul Brand, M.D. and Philip Yancy, *Fearfully & Wonderfully Made*, (Grand Rapids, MI: Zondervan, 1980), pp. 175–177.

6. *Bits & Pieces*, June 25, 1992. www.bible.org.

7. Jack Kyrtle, "Ford Encouraged by Edison," *Encyclopedia of 7,700 Illustrations, Signs of the Times*, Ed. Paul Lee Tan, ThD., (Hong Kong: Nordica International, Ltd., 1996), pp. 338,339.

8. G. Franklin Allee, ed., "Co-operation in Attaining the Goal," *Evangelistic Illustrations for Pulpit and Platform*, (Chicago, IL: Moody Press, 1961), p. 103.

9. Calvin Hunt, February 1998 interview by John Barber, *WorldChangers* radio, (Orlando, FL: Campus Crusade for Christ).

10. "Bringing in the New," *The Pastor's Story File*, (Platteville, CO: Saratoga Press), June 1992.

Chapter 8: Living as a Citizen of Christ's Kingdom

1. David Judge and Helmut Teichert, *Discovering God's Best: Right Thinking for Supernatural Living*, (Sun River, MT: Turning Point Productions, 1994), Unit 6, Lesson 15.

2. Donald Grey Barnhouse, *Let Me Illustrate*, (Westwood, NJ: Fleming H. Revell Company, 1967), p. 176.

Chapter 9: Thinking with the Mind of Christ

1. Ted Bundy interview by Dr. James Dobson, from the video *Fatal Addiction: Journey Into the Mind of a Madman* (Colorado Springs, CO: Focus on the Family, 1989).

2. Samuel Smiles, *Bartlett's Familiar Quotations*, (Boston: Little, Brown and Company, 1992), p. 781:6.

3. Kate B. Wilkinson, "May the Mind of Christ, My Savior," *Great Hymns of the Faith*, John W. Peterson, ed., (Grand Rapids, MI: Zondervan, 1968), #333.

Chapter 10: Speaking with the Words of Christ

1. F. J. Gould, "The Tongue and How to Use It," *The Moral Compass*, William J. Bennett, ed., (New York: Simon and Schuster, 1995), pp. 149,150.

2. *God's Little Devotional Book for Women*, (Tulsa, OK: Honor Books, Inc., 1996), p. 57.
3. "Coarse Jokes and Foul Language," www.bible.org/illus/s/s-160.htm.
4. "The Wise Old Owl," *The Moral Compass*, William J. Bennett, ed., (New York: Simon and Schuster, 1995), p. 152.

Chapter 11: Behaving with the Character of Christ
1. Dwight L. Moody, as quoted in Alice Gray, *More Stories for the Heart,* (Sisters, OR: Multnomah Publishers, 1997), p. 117.
2. *Our Daily Bread*, (Grand Rapids, MI: RBC Ministries), January 6, 1993.
3. John W. Schlatter, "A Simple Gesture," *Chicken Soup for the Soul*, Jack Canfield and Mark Victor Hansen, eds., (Deerfield Beach, FL: Health Communications, Inc., 1993), pp. 35,36.
4. Corrie ten Boom, *The Hiding Place*, (Old Tappan, NJ: Fleming H. Revell, 1971).
5. *God's Little Devotional Book for Women*, (Tulsa, OK: Honor Books, Inc., 1996), p. 277.
6. Myra B. Welch, "The Touch of the Master's Hand," *Chicken Soup for the Soul*, Jack Canfield and Mark Victor Hansen, eds., (Deerfield Beach, FL: Health Communications, 1993), pp. 293,294.
7. Lloyd M. Perry and Charles Sell, *Speaking to Life's Problems,* (Chicago, IL: Moody Press: 1983), p. 198.
8. Fred Craddock, "Consecration," www.bible.org/illus/f/f-07.htm.
9. F. B. Meyer, "Quotes," www.bible.org/illus/f/f-07.htm.

Chapter 12: Experiencing Supernatural Power
1. Steve Blankenship, "Power," www.bible.org/p-q/p-q-77.htm.
2. Lyle W. Dorsett, "Ministry Maverick," *Moody Magazine Online*, (Chicago, IL: Moody Bible Institute, 2000), www.moodypress.org/MOODYMAG/maverick.htm.
3. Robert A. Morey, *Battle of the Gods: The Gathering Storm in Modern Evangelicalism*, (Southbridge, MA: Crown Publications, 1989), p. 36.
4. Donald G. Barnhouse, *Let Me Illustrate*, (Westwood, NJ: Fleming H. Revell, 1994), p. 317.
5. Benjamin Browne, *Illustrations for Preaching*, (Nashville: Broadman Press, 1977), p. 154.

Chapter 13: Enjoying Liberating Freedom
1. Colin Chapman, *An Eerdman's Handbook: The Case for Christianity*, (Grand Rapids, MI: W. B. Eerdman's Pub. Co., 1981).
2. E. Bartlett Kerr, *Surrender and Survival: The Experience of American POWs in the Pacific, 1941–1945*, (New York: W. Morrow, 1985), pp. 271,292.
3. J. Alistair Brown, www.sermonillustrations.com/victory.htm.
4. "Give Everything to God," www.bible.org/illus/w/w-54.htm.
5. "They Heard the Bells," www.bible.org/illus/w/w-54.htm.
6. Shirley MacLaine, "Yourself," www.bible.org/illus/s/s-40.htm.
7. Since the invention of the Hubble telescope, astronomers now believe the universe contains 100 to 200 billion galaxies.
8. "Now We Are Small Enough," www.bible.org/illus/s/s-53.htm.
9. "D. L. Moody," www.bible.org/illus/e/e-33.htm.
10. "Freedom," *Parables, Etc.,* (Platteville, CO: Saratoga Press), February 1982.

Chapter 14: Achieving Triumph Over Adversity
1. Joni Eareckson Tada, *Her Story*, (New York: Inspirational Press, 1994).
2. Malcolm Muggeridge, "Learning Through Afflictions," www.bible.org/illus/a/a-30.htm.
3. Thomas Watson, *All Things for Good*, reprint of 1663 original, (Edinburgh, UK: The

Banner of Truth Trust).

4. *Leadership Magazine*, Vol. 4, No. 1, p. 83.

5. Jack Canfield and Mark Victor Hansen, eds., *Chicken Soup for the Soul*, (Deerfield Beach, FL: Health Communications, Inc., 1993), 65.

6. *Today in the Word*, (Chicago, IL: Moody Bible Institute), June 11, 1989.

7. Winston Churchill, first speech as Prime Minister to House of Commons, May 13, 1940, London, England, www.winstonchurchill.org/blood.htm (The Churchill Center, Washington, D.C.).

8. Halford E. Luccock, *Unfinished Business: Short Diversions on Religious Themes*, (New York: Harper, 1956).

Chapter 15: Knowing Everlasting Peace

1. Vernon C. Grounds, *Our Daily Bread*, (Grand Rapids, MI: RBC Ministries), May 21, 1999.

2. *Today in the Word*, (Chicago, IL: Moody Bible Institute), June 1988, p. 33.

3. Berit Kjos, *A Wardrobe from the King*, (Wheaton, IL: Victor Books, 1988), pp. 45,46.

4. J. D. Douglas, ed., *New Bible Dictionary*, (Wheaton, IL: Tyndale House Pub., 1962), pp. 901,902.

5. Kurt E. Koch, *Occult Bondage and Deliverance*, (Grand Rapids, MI: Kregel Pub., 1971), p. 10.

6. *Today in the Word*, (Chicago, IL: Moody Bible Institute), March 1989, p. 8.

7. "Your Father Knows the Way," *Parables, Etc.*, (Platteville, CO: Saratoga Press), June 1984.

8. Russell G. Shubin, "Strength in the Face of Adversity," *Mission Frontiers*, (Pasadena, CA: U.S. Center for World Missions, August 1999), Vol. 21 No. 5-8, pp. 20–22.

Chapter 16: Possessing Infinite Joy

1. "The Bible Friend," *Turning Point Magazine*, (San Diego: Turning Point), May 1993.

2. Philip Comfort, PhD., ed., *Life Application Bible Commentary: Philippians, Colossians, Philemon*, (Wheaton, IL: Tyndale House, 1995), p. 25.

3. C. S. Lewis, *The Weight of Glory*, (New York: Collier Books, 1980), p. 4.

4. C. Neil Strait, "Do You Know," *Parables, Etc.*, (Platteville, CO: Saratoga Press), August 1990.

5. David L. McKenna, *MegaTruth: The Church in the Age of Information*, (San Bernardino, CA: Here's Life Publishers, 1986).

6. *Today in the Word*, (Chicago, IL: Moody Bible Institute), June 1988, p. 18.

Chapter 17: Standing Victoriously in Christ

1. Ralph W. Harris, *Enrichment Magazine: Journal for Pentecostal Ministry*, (Springfield, MO: Gospel Publishing House), Summer 1996.

2. "God Is Greater," *The Pastor's Story File*, (Platteville, CO: Saratoga Press), April 1995.

3. *Transformations: A Documentary*, produced by Global Net Productions, (The Sentinel Group, 1999).

4. For further study on the attributes of God, see the *God: Discover His Character* products in the Resources.

5. Adapted from R. Kent Hughes, *Ephesians: The Mystery of the Body of Christ* (Wheaton, IL: Crossway Books, 1990), pp. 254, 256.

6. Philip Brooks, "What to Pray For," *The Pastor's Story File*, (Platteville, CO: Saratoga Press), October 1987.

Response Form

☐ I have received Jesus Christ as my Savior and Lord as a result of reading this book.

☐ As a new Christian I want to know Christ better and experience the abundant Christian life.

☐ I want to be one of the two million people who will join Dr. Bright in forty days of prayer and fasting for revival for America, the world, and the fulfillment of the Great Commission.

☐ Please send me *free* information on staff and ministry opportunities with Campus Crusade for Christ International.

☐ Please send me *free* information about the more than 50 other books, booklets, audio cassettes, and videos by Bill and Vonette Bright.

NAME (please print)

ADDRESS

CITY   STATE   ZIP

COUNTRY   E-MAIL

Please check the appropriate box(es), clip, and mail this form in an envelope to:

> Dr. Bill Bright
> Campus Crusade for Christ
> P.O. Box 620877
> Orlando, FL 32862-0877 U.S.A.

You may also fax your response to (407) 826-2149, or send E-mail to newlifepubs@ccci.org. Visit our website at www.newlifepubs.com.

This and other fine products from *NewLife* Publications are available from your favorite bookseller or by calling **(800) 235-7255** (within U.S.) or **(407) 826-2145** (outside U.S.).